WHAT THE STONES REMEMBER

WHAT THE STONES REMEMBER

A Life Rediscovered

PATRICK LANE

TRUMPETER

Boston · 2005

Trumpeter Books
An imprint of Shambhala Publications, Inc.
Horticultural Hall
300 Massachusetts Avenue
Boston, Massachusetts 02115
www.shambhala.com

9 8 7 6 5 4 3 2 1

First Trumpeter Edition
Printed in the United States of America

⊚ This edition is printed on acid-free paper that meets the
American National Standards Institute z39.48 Standard.
Distributed in the United States by Random House, Inc.

Library of Congress Cataloging-in-Publication Data
Lane, Patrick
[There is a season]
What the stones remember: a life rediscovered / Patrick Lane—1st
Trumpeter ed.
p.   cm.
Originally published as: There is a season. Toronto: McClelland &
Stewart, ©2004
ISBN 1-59030-254-0 (hardcover: acid-free paper)
1. Lane, Patrick. 2. Lane, Patrick—Homes and haunts—British
Columbia. 3. Recovering alcoholics—Canada—Biography. 4. Poets,
Canadian—20th century—Biography. 5. Natural history—British
Columbia. 6. Naturalists—Canada—Biography. 7. Gardeners—
Canada—Poetry. 8. Gardening—British Columbia. I. Title.
PR9199.3.L32Z476 2005
811'.54—DC22
2005009421

For my brothers, Dick, Johnny,
and Mike, and my sister, Linda

"If you listen you can hear me.
My mouth is open and I am singing."

—"Fathers & Sons,"
from *Mortal Remains*
by Patrick Lane

ACKNOWLEDGMENTS

I WOULD LIKE to acknowledge *Geist* and *The Globe and Mail,* in which short excerpts of this book previously appeared. I want to thank my friend Brian Brett, who traveled this year with me; Ellen Seligman for her encouragement; Dinah Forbes, my Canadian editor, for her wise suggestions; Emily Bower, my American editor, for her sharp eye and ear; Kathryn Mulders, my agent; my children; my friends; and the myriad writers who contributed through their art to this book. Finally, this would not have been written without the endurance, love, and support of my wife, the poet Lorna Crozier: "There are no stories but that which held me in the night."

WHAT THE STONES REMEMBER

If what we know is what resembles us,
what we know is a garden.

I STOOD ALONE among yellow glacier lilies and the wind-flowers of spring, the western anemone, their petals frail disks of trembling clotted cream. I was a boy and the mountain ridge I'd climbed was only a half-hour hike from the back door of my home. In the east the blue peaks of the Monashee Range rose up against the Selkirks and beyond them the far Rockies and the plains. I had wandered that morning among sheltered coulees and rocky hills and, finally resting, stared out at the paling distance.

The high hills and mountains were my solitary land and I hiked the trails year-round. The days were all one to me back then, and the scuffed pad of a cougar's track in the wet clay of Six Mile Creek in summer was no less wondrous than the spread toes of a coyote's paw print in a fringe of thin January snow on the BX Ranch where he had braced to leap upon a vole or scurrying mouse who had come lucklessly into the thin winter sun.

There were black bears and the occasional cougar or bobcat in those hills, but when I saw one I felt awe, not fear. Even then I knew what a blessing an animal was. Any creature's appearance was a gift the wilderness gave me. The animals of the backcountry were unused to humans in those days and they stepped around me as much as I did them. Sometimes a cougar would take a lamb or two in spring from some flock and then the game warden would walk his dogs into the hills to track the big cat down. He hated killing cougars.

Often he would take me along on those trips; why, I don't know. Perhaps he felt sorry for me or perhaps my father asked him to in the hope it would make me a man. Gazing at a cougar lolling on a high limb of a ponderosa pine above Lumby while the cougar dogs slung their howls from the foot of the tree at the flick of its black-tipped tail was to look at a god. I watched from the back of an old white horse as Mr. Frisbee pulled his Winchester from beside his saddle and brought the cougar down with a single shot. The cougar falling from the sky was my first huge death.

I remember touching the rough blond hair of a dead cat's nape, the curve of its long yellow incisors, and the dead ball of its eye as it stared sightless through me to the fading sun. These deaths drew me toward a compassion I didn't fully understand. All I knew was that such sentiments were not spoken of among men or boys. Feeling deeply about something was never shown.

But it is not the cougars or bobcats, the bears or rattlesnakes of that early wilderness I think of now. It is another early memory that stays in my mind. I was up in the Bluebush hills west of Kalamalka and Okanagan Lake. I had hiked back into the hills with a peanut butter and jam sandwich, two apples, and a water bottle in the army satchel my father had brought back from the Second World War. I took it with me whenever I hiked out for a day. I stood on a crest in a frothing meadow of glacier lilies and anemones, and their fragile beauty remains with me. It lives in the blood and muscle of me and I can still call it up and bring it into spirit.

Grasses, their stalks flattened and flung by the winter snow, lay like fallen hair upon the earth, and their new green spears caught the wind with frail hands. A mountain meadow and a boy in the long-ago of the last century. Did I know then it was a garden I looked out upon? Had I been asked I would not have understood the question. Garden? Wilderness? I gave the meadow no thought. Had someone asked me if what I saw was beautiful I would not have known what he meant. A boy is a boy and he is the place he inhabits. He is what surrounds him and the boy I was remains with me in the image of yellow lilies and creamy anemones among the grasses and scattered stones.

What was I, ten years old? A child, a stripling boy, but those mountains and deserts live in me still and when I go back into that country my heart surges with sudden blood. The past hurls itself at me at times. My bones remember the water and the stones. I grew my body from that mountain earth, and my cells remember the cactus and pines, the lilies and grasses. I am as much blessed as burdened by this.

It is such beauty that made me into a gardener. Perhaps by planting flowers and shrubs and trees I am trying to return to that earlier paradise. Yet finally, not. My garden today is another kind of paradise, and I am not the boy wandering in what another might call loneliness but to me was solitude.

What I do remember is squatting and building a small cairn of stones in the middle of the meadow. There was no death to cover over, no occasion to ritualize other than the day itself and the curious busyness of a boy. But, like all animals, I wanted to leave some mark that I had been there so others who followed would know of my passing. Perhaps the mound of stones is still there or perhaps it's been kicked over by a deer or coyote or some other boy who pillaged the cairn to make his own curious mark. Perhaps the snow, ice, and wind have spilled it. Whether or not the cairn is gone, the stones remain like ghosts in my hands and that is enough.

Today, fifty-two years later, I am not in a mountain meadow in southern British Columbia. I am in my garden on Vancouver Island and it is early in January in the first year of the new century. The sky is gray and the small drops of rainwater gathered on moss and fallen leaves glimmer like opals in the winter sun. In the declivities of grass, apples lie where they fell three months ago. Under the scrabbled branches of the apple tree a red-shafted flicker carves white flesh from a fallen fruit. He feeds on the slim bounty of the season and doesn't fully trust the grass and moss I still call a lawn though each year I starve it, encouraging the mosses to flourish. The flicker's claws are better suited to the bark of trees where he spends the day climbing patiently up the trunks in search of insects who have buried themselves in slits to sleep out the gloomy winter months.

A little apple for a bird to round out the insect flesh of morning. The red shafts on the flicker's cheeks gleam like the skin of the fruit he eats. Above him, chestnut-backed chickadees and nuthatches slide and jerk in the air as they argue over this black sunflower seed or that. The flicker ignores their bickering.

The chickadees' arguing is mostly play. The fledglings of last spring, some bigger than their parents, flit among the bare branches of the apple and plum. Their backs echo the rich brown of the redwood where they go to play hide-and-seek. A black-capped chickadee, one without the chestnut coat of the others, lights upon the lawn and sips a single drop of water from the frayed edge of a brown maple leaf. The water, a tiny bit of moon, disappears into his body, just as my memory of the meadow and the lilies slips inside me, images lost in clouds and rain.

❧

I am withdrawing from the scourge of forty-five years of drinking. Two months ago I stumbled into a treatment center for alcohol and drug addiction. Now, I am barely detoxed. Standing here among the sword ferns my senses seem to be thin glass, so acute at their edges I am afraid I will cut myself simply by touching the silicon edge of a bamboo leaf. The flicker's blade of beak as it slices into the apple makes me wince. My hands are pale animals. The smallest sounds, a junco flitting between viburnum leaves, a drop of water falling on the cedar deck, make me cringe. I can smell the bitter iron in the mosses on the apple tree's branches. My flesh at times is in agony, and I feel as if I have come out from some shadowed place into light for the first time. I feel, for the first time in years, alive.

The opal drop of water the chickadee drank is no different than the droplet at the tip of a bare apple tree bud that I lift my hand to. I extend my trembling finger and the water slides onto my fingernail. I lift it to my lips and take a sip of what was once fog. It is a single cold on the tip of my tongue. I feel I am some delicate creature come newly to this place for, though I know it well, I must learn again this small half-acre of land with its intricate beauties, its many arrangements of earth, air, water, and stone.

The garden begins with my body. I am this place, though I feel it at the most attenuated level imaginable. Once dead, I am come alive again. Forty-five years of addiction and I am a strangeling in this simple world. To be sober, to be without alcohol and drugs in my cells, is new to me and every thing near me is both familiar and strange.

The chickadee is back on the bird feeder staring at me with cocky delight. *Welcome,* he seems to say. *Where have you been?*

I could tell him I've been ill for a long time and I could also tell him I've been in a ten-year-old's body in the high mountains, but I don't. The tiny bird is in the now and so should I be. He dips his bright beak and takes a black sunflower seed from the feeder. With the seed wedged securely under an obsidian claw, he strips away the shell and lifts out the kernel. *Welcome back,* he seems to say, and flicks up into the plum tree to eat his first seed of the morning.

The chickadees are friendly little birds, quite brazen. I call them with the sound of a kiss on my lips, the breath inward, and they cock their heads and fly over to see what I am talking about. Sometimes they get quite angry, and I wonder if the sound I make is a long, complicated avian curse. I kiss a lisp with my tongue and lips and the chickadee chitters back at me, his head cocked sideways, irritated by my song. *For God's sake, get it right,* he says.

The red-shafted flicker lifts his head from the apple. Whatever he has heard or seen has made him suddenly aware he is grounded. Basho, our young cat, named for the Japanese poet, makes a golden rush from under the viburnum by the deck. He is still quite young and a hapless hunter. The flicker rises above the lawn on his sharp wings. His flight is an undulating sway, a rise and fall like a sleeping breath. He crests the fence and is gone.

Basho stops by the partly eaten apple and grooms his ruff. Once more the yard is his but for the chickadees and pine siskins who scold him from the branches above. On the deck Roxy, our other cat, colored like a Guernsey cow, rises and arches her back. She has watched Basho's run and is slightly weary with it all. She reminds me of a chubby Audrey Hepburn, slightly rotund, yet graceful on her slender, delicate legs. The garden is her purview and she seems to reign over it, benign and bored, though, truth be told, she has been banished to the deck by Basho.

A northwest crow passes over and gives a hoarse cry at nothing and everything. The songbirds ignore his black silhouette, sharp as a blade. They know he is not the Cooper's hawk who hunts this garden every four or five days. He is only a crow carrying a potato chip robbed from some garbage bag down the street. He passes over in the way of crows, with a destination in mind I do not know just as I do not know where the flicker went when he lifted over the fence.

Theirs are the way of birds. Their paths are known only to themselves, though if you watch them closely you can see them following invisible pathways in the air. Only when they are frightened do they break their patterns of travel, and that shattering of habit is more about survival than chaos. As it is in the bird world, so in ours. We break our path when fear tells us to live.

The appearance of the Cooper's hawk or his more common relative the sharp-shinned hawk sends all the birds into a panic and they rush wildly into the thickets of branches near them. Usually the hawks make a kill one out of three tries, a rare chickadee but usually a siskin or junco. All of them come and go from this winter garden.

"Gardens, like the wild places of nature, are the premises of transcendence." Des Kennedy said that and I agree. I touch upon the beauty of mine every day. I sit by the pond on a block of raw jade from the Coquihalla River and look at the slate path as it lifts over a fir root and descends behind the two bronze cranes that stand at the edge of the water. Above the path a tight solar system of tiny male flies circles and circles around a nonexistent sun. The insects are waiting for a female to be drawn into their frenzied dance so one of them can mate with her.

I always think these flies appear too early, yet I trust their nature and know they are here because it is the right time for them, just as it is the right time for me to be in the garden. The flies are beautiful and their dance is not much different than my own human dance. The transcendent is always there at my fingertips. I touch upon it all the time, but I've learned not to grasp it for when I do it slips away. Right now an unseen god takes the shape of a breeze among sword ferns. There is no wind, only a slight and visible parting of the fronds as the god moves toward the pebble path I cannot see, the one just beyond the ferns beside the forsythia and the birdbath. There and gone. I turn back and the flies are gone as well.

These first weeks back from the treatment center are a blessing. I am not thinking of what I will do, I am just trying to feel where I am. Perhaps because of this new body I have, these cells that no longer stare through the cold mask of vodka and cocaine, I am feeling the garden in the way a child feels things. I imagine myself touching sand for the first time, or a pebble from the Kootenay Mountains I must have touched when I was a baby on a blanket below the mine where my father worked. What must it have felt like to feel something cold for the first time? What was mountain water from Sheep Creek like when my mother dripped it on my skin? My presence here is that new.

❦

Sheep Creek, a village tucked into the Purcell Range down in the southeast corner of British Columbia, is where I was born six months before the beginning of the Second World War. I was the third of three boys, Dick, John, and Pat, all of us born within three years of each other. I was born only because my mother wanted to replace my brother John. When she was eight months' pregnant with him she was told her father was dying in Nelson. It was deep winter and the roads were clogged with heavy snow. They were too dangerous for her to risk. She blamed the child in her womb when she could not go. She said to me once, *I cursed the child in my womb.* My father had to hire a woman to care for Johnny. My mother would neither nurse nor touch him. A few months after he was born she was pregnant with me.

Back then Sheep Creek was a mining village high in the mountains above the town of Salmo. Lead, zinc, and silver ore were dragged from those mountains. Today nothing is left but a shaft that leads deep into the mountain and a few weathered and beaten logs and boards. The shacks that once were the homes of the miners and their families are gone.

My mother and father moved to Sheep Creek in the 1930s after the Depression jobs on the Kootenay River dams ended. My father was a hard-rock miner for six years until the war when he joined the army and left my mother and the three of us boys to go to Europe.

I can still feel those dark mountains. They rose like mourning clothes from Kootenay Lake. I can remember being three years old, small and hard as a fist. It was high summer and I watched the mountains to the north burning. There was a pall of smoke and the sun was a dark orb, a deep red ball with a corona of yellow in the summer sky. The smoke drifted down Kootenay Lake and wandered among the trees and houses of Nelson like a wraith in search of anything alive. On the porch of our yellow house high on the hill my mother was crying.

She told me years later she was bereft. My father had been back but only for five days. Now he was returning to Vancouver and then to Ontario where he would guard the Welland Canal. A year later he would return again and we would live for a few months in Nanaimo on Vancouver Island before he shipped off to Europe and the war.

I remember her grabbing my father by the shoulders and shaking him. He took her in his arms. She turned, and he walked away. The sky swirled with ribbons of smoke, thick as a yellow shroud.

My father lifted me up from the boardwalk. He was wearing his uniform. I could smell the thick wool on his shoulder and my hand touched the red hairs that curled across the back of his hand. There were brass buttons shining by my lips. Below me my brothers turned in circles with their arms in the air. They were calling out to him to lift them up too, but he had no hands free. He was carrying me in one arm and in the other he was holding a bag of oranges, a gift from the wife he had left behind on the porch. She refused to go down to the station. She believed there had been no need for him to join up.

My father was eight years old at the end of the First World War. All his life he had waited for another one. Now it had come. My mother stood on the porch of our yellow house. She had made herself beautiful for him in her best skirt and blouse. Her long slim legs were sheathed in silk that glistened like burnished copper. This was the image she wanted him to take to Europe. This was what he would remember.

I was the white-haired child in his arms and I pushed my face into my father's neck. I smelled his sweat and felt the roughness of his cheek. It rasped my ear.

At the end of the boardwalk my father stepped to the worn path that led down to the station and the train that would take him away. We were to go with him partway down the hill and then return to the woman on the porch.

I never cried again, she said to me on her deathbed twenty-five years after my father was murdered. And she hadn't. All I heard was silence after my brother's death. It was the death of the first of her blood and the first of mine to die. She retreated behind the locked bedroom door and I crouched outside, my arms around my knees.

I remember the bag of oranges breaking and the bright fruit falling. I can see my brothers running down the path in front of him as the oranges bounded on ahead. They laughed as they followed the golden balls, picking up one and then another from among the fir cones and needles, desiccated ferns, and stones. I wanted to be with them. I squirmed in his arms and he laughed a great laugh and took me in his two huge hands and held me out in front of him. I wriggled, desperate to be put down. My brothers were far ahead of me on the path. They were stuffing oranges into their ragged shirts. My father laughed. He lowered me for a moment as if to put me down. Then he threw me high in the air.

Today it feels as if I never returned from that sky.

My mother never forgave him going away. She scrabbled as best she could on a soldier's pay in Nelson, where this early memory was born. The following winter she sold her sewing machine to buy the three of us coats. That sacrifice became a family myth, an emblem of her struggle. After the war, after my father returned, we moved to the desert country of the Okanagan Valley because of his silicosis, the gift the hard-rock mines gave to him. I can still hear the hiss of his lungs as he breathed.

I remember the years of war. I remember my father gone and the room where I slept with my mother. Her bedroom was light, the pillows high and white, the blanket red with a black stripe. I was perhaps four years old, sitting up in my mother's bed. It was where I slept each night. In the smaller bedroom across the hall my brothers slept together.

I have tried many times to climb inside that child. Everything then was a listening, was smell, touch, and sight. I couldn't write yet, couldn't read. Nothing was translated into the human. I was someone else, someone I have forgotten. I sit here and I wish that child well, though I know his life, know what was to come.

In that moment I was happy. I was wide awake at first light. There was birdsong and I listened into the dawn, the cries of robins and sparrows floating through the open window above my head.

My mother was sleeping. Her dark hair drifted upon the pillow beside me. I lifted one curl in my small hand, felt its many threads among my fingers. I moved with her breathing. Her sleeping rocked me gently, the bed moving delicately around me. Yet there was a heaviness to her, a weight, as if her flesh were tired. Mine wasn't. I knew, if I wanted, I could leave my body, rise into the light and enter my flying dream, the lake and forests far below me, the hawks and gulls quelling under my flight. Flying was like fainting, my spirit leaving my body in the little sickness of petit mal. My body was a weightless shell, the slit carapace of a chrysalis, the discarded catafalque of some vanished thing.

This moment in my mother's bed was the quiet time. I knew I must not wake her. On a morning such as this I would pick up my coloring book and crayons from the low table beside the bed, but this morning the book was not there, only stubs of crayons in a small glass bowl, bits and pieces of colored wax.

There was a newness to the world I inhabited. What I felt was a quickening, like a shard of red jasper in a field when the sun first touches it, so alive it seems to be more than life. To me everything was light. It caressed me as my mother's hands caressed me in the bath, as her hands placed the food in my mouth.

I loved my mother's smell, loved lying close to her and placing my face against her neck, breathing in her body. I loved her flesh touching me, the warmth, the texture of her against my chest and belly. At night, my mother would pull me to her body, holding me against her, singing quietly as she rocked us both to sleep. "Mood Indigo," she sang, so softly her words created night.

The blanket had fallen from her white shoulders and I moved it down gently until her back was bare. She wore only a thin, white slip.

My pajamas were a faint gray. The cloth was thin, worn to a rare fineness, and my skin blazed through to meet the sun. I looked at the clean bones of my mother's back, her spine, the curve of her shoulder blade, her breast gentle on the sheet. I picked up a piece of crayon. It was a deep red, my favorite color. Carefully, so she wouldn't waken, I began to draw upon the skin of her back, the crayon just above her flesh. I moved it slowly in curves and arabesques. After a moment, I put the crayon down and selected another, a blue as dark and deep as the red I had discarded.

I cannot see what I drew, but I knew what I was making. It was a tattoo, something I embedded in her flesh.

I can see it there in all its richness and ferocity.

The bones remember what the flesh forgets. This small place, this half-acre of land on the southern tip of Vancouver Island, is paradise to me. I shake the past from my mind and ask myself the question, What is a garden that I should want one?

Horace, that old Roman poet and philosopher, prayed for a garden. He said, "This was among my prayers: a piece of land not so very large, where a garden should be and a spring of ever-flowing water near the house, and a bit of woodland as well as these." And I might pray for such a place though I know I will never have a stream or spring or a bit of woodland to call my own and even if I had them how could I call them mine? Gardens belong to no one. A garden is a real place imagined and, with time and care, an imagined place made real.

It is the way of gardens to tolerate intrusion. A day lily sighed at my hapless urge a year ago when I moved it from one bed to another, replacing the lily with a white campanula that had done poorly elsewhere. The valerian nearby accepted the campanula but only barely. Neither did well last summer, but I have new hopes for the lily just as I have hopes for myself and this painful sobriety I have brought to the garden.

Gardens are passed on to gardeners. They can live through a generation of neglect only to find someone who values them enough to nurture them a few years more. Some gardens disappear altogether and remain only as words. "A little spot enclosed by grace, / Out of the world's wide wilderness," said Isaac Watts, and who knows now where Watts's garden was back in the eighteenth century? Yet I can imagine it just as I imagine Horace's in the last few decades before the birth of Christ. "A piece of land not so very large," he wrote. That is enough for me or for anyone.

I can see old Horace, long poems poking from the folds of his toga, tottering around among his prized irises, his ordered olive groves, and stopping a moment to stare at the petals of the Cretan ebony he brought three years before from the dry hills south of Knossos. He reaches up and touches a branch of ripening olives in the grove just east of the catacombs where the Via Apia cuts in a cruel line toward the blue hills of his Roma. Testicles of the sun, he thinks, Orphic bags of light.

Some gardens are as small as three containers of red geraniums circled by blue lobelia on a balcony in a high-rise apartment. A garden can be a single petunia in a pot on a windowsill. The smallest I ever saw was a thimble planted with moss. Others are hundreds of acres of woodland, lake, and hill. For most of us who grow our flowers and vegetables, a garden is the bit of land left over after the house is built.

A garden is a place where someone spends a few hours each day in a wild place he tries to shape to his desire. It's a place of harmony, of balance, and it is made from living things. All creatures that fly, swim, burrow, crawl, or run are there.

A polished stone with an aching arc of quartz, plucked from the sea at low tide near Port Renfrew, rests at the base of a young Douglas fir. Bracken, now crisp gold, hangs above its polished surface. Beside it, flat on the earth, lie the damp, heart-shaped leaves of a Frances Williams hosta. I can see through the desiccated leaves to the moss and earth below. The three create a small balance of shapes beside the rough trunk of the fir. Needles, tiny brown spears, cross-hatch the ground. Two cones ripe with pitch touch their tips beside the veins of a single hosta leaf. They are together the accident beauty has made.

I have gathered stones all my life. That little cairn I built on a mountain when I was a boy has become in my life a series of stone markers. I have measured my life with the bones of this good earth. I lived up the North Thompson River back in the early 1960s. I was a petty clerk and Industrial First Aid Man in a sawmill in the tiny village of Avola. In those days, it took four to five hours to drive out to Kamloops on the single-lane dirt road. I moved there with my young wife and our two small sons. My daughter was not yet born. When she was, her crib was the four-foot bathtub. There was nowhere else to put her. I remember lying awake worrying she would somehow turn on the hot-water tap and scald herself to death.

I was twenty-one years old. That first day in the north I had our small trailer home jacked up. Sticking out from the thirty-degree mountainside, it looked like a wrecked ship's prow, beached and pointing at the river far below. The sawmill with its banging chains and whistles spewed out construction lumber by the riverbank. My exhausted wife rested in the trailer as the boys slept and I, wasted from hauling timbers and jacks, stepped into the forest to where a small creek, less than a yard wide, purled down from the mountain on its way to the river.

I sat on a moss-covered stone and watched the clear, clean snowmelt slip among small stones and swirl the fine gravel it had washed for fifteen thousand years. I stared into the ripples, then knelt and scooped the water in my cupped hands and washed my face with last winter's snowmelt. As I blinked through the cold I saw an oval bit of granite near the bank and, reaching into the shallow drift, I moved it so the water, baffled, had to shift to find its way. The water curled and began to cut into the sand and gravel, creating a small eddy behind it. Black spruce needles trapped for years swirled in a growing circle and were swept out and down toward the river and the six hundred miles to the far Pacific.

Over the next few years I moved stones, moss, and a few logs and made of that small place in the wilderness a garden where my small sons played and my wife and I could sit a moment, together or alone, and find some peace in our young lives. A garden? Yes, a garden, and different than the vegetable garden I dug below the trailer for corn and beans, peas and carrots, all of which grew stunted and poor in the glacial drift of gravel I had turned in hopes of a crop to come. The little pool with its moss and carefully placed stones was not my first garden, but was, perhaps, the first where I found solace in those hard years. I was barely a man with a young family among mountains that spent their days cheating the valley of the sun. My wife and I were so young we couldn't see beyond the light and dark of the days.

Stones, water, moss, and wood—the building blocks of seclusion and peace. That garden was vaguely Asian, but I didn't know that then. I built with the materials at hand. A cluster of big laughing Gym mushrooms that appeared by a mossy log I moved that first fall was joy enough for me. A bear's paw print in the damp sand was a gift from the mountains.

I move across the moss to the stepping-stones that lead to the pond. When I stop beside the fallen leaves of the golden bamboo where they rest on a bit of driftwood log I find harmony, but I must step into it to see each bamboo leaf, the way they lie upon each other, crosshatched, a slender filigree upon the gray of driftwood.

Do the living things of this garden perceive the same as I do? Does the chickadee step inside himself or is he always what surrounds him? Is it only me who is separate, a man who wishes himself in the world?

A red-breasted nuthatch works her way headfirst down the trunk of the fir. Her sharp beak probes the crannies in the bark for insect eggs. The white stripe above her eye gives her a jaunty look. She is always in a hurry. She flitters away in jerky flight to the dark skirts of the redwood in front of the house, her nasal call to the chickadees heralding her presence. She is a solitary bird, rarely with anyone but her mate. Sometimes I'll see three or four of them, but they're very territorial and quarrel with interlopers of their own species. My garden contains only one breeding pair. All the others have been driven off by the fierce male. He is the size of my thumb but has a heart bigger than an eagle's.

In the past, solitude was my addiction. Yet even in the depth of withdrawal from the human world I have never been alone. On these early January days I talk to a river stone brought down from Haida Gwaii as a gift from a friend now in prison. I touch the delicate tip of a branch on the red cedar I planted ten years ago, and sing to a siskin my own song of early morning. Lao Tzu said, "True fullness seems empty, yet it is wholly present." The nuthatch knows that and so does the Okame-zasa bamboo.

The sun glints off a flake of mica. For a moment I am blind and in the darkness I am taken away again to my childhood and that faraway war. The present slips into the past and I am once again a child. The troop train is leaving.

The station platform in Nelson was crowded with soldiers, women, and children. Some cried and some laughed and some were silent while they held each other. Then there were the sullen drunks who looked as if they were going nowhere, leaving a place they were losing for somewhere equally lost.

I had come down to the station to watch the soldiers leave. It was the same every week, the men in their clean and pressed uniforms holding on to women who were crying. Crying was something I knew how to do. But I had to find the right soldiers to cry for. The ones who had no women with them, no children.

The two soldiers I followed were like that. The tall one had his arm around the shoulder of the other. They were weaving down the platform to the end of the train, steam screaming from the engine, the billows of black smoke, the noise and confusion I loved. I had no idea of anywhere other than where I was. What was beyond the mountains was nothing, was nowhere, something not even imagined. It was like when my mother read to me from *The Wind in the Willows, Winnie the Pooh,* or *The Water Babies.* The places and things were not real yet, were only words in my mother's mouth where the stories came from.

When I saw the soldiers stop, I walked over slowly, the tears already streaming down my cheeks.

Are you my father? I asked the tall soldier.

What?

I'm looking for my father, I said, the tears still coming.

After a minute, the soldier squatting beside me, I told the same old story, the one about my father lost in the war. The man listened and then, because the soldier didn't know what else to do, put his hand in his pocket and took out a handful of coins. He poured the pennies, nickels, and dimes into my hands. *Go home now,* he said. *Go home to your mother.*

Every time I came to the station it was like that. All I had to say was that my father was killed in the war and then cry. I put the money in the pocket of my torn pants and wiped the tears from my face.

I think now of that boy as he stepped off the back of the platform and headed across the tracks into the trees where the trail led up the long hill to his home. It's hard to imagine him, his wiliness, his ability to act out such a story and make it believable. He was five years old, his white hair glinting like silver in the summer sun. His bare feet were hard and brown.

He was mercurial, a shape-shifter, a charmer, quick and fast. But there was something at the heart of him that was hidden, something he carried inside himself I can't see, can't read now I am sixty years older.

Mine was a dangerous game, the soldiers always drunk. One man gave me money in a corner of the station where the shadows were. The man put his hand in my pants. I let him do it. It had happened before and there was always money afterward. It had felt good, the man touching me there. The first time I had been frightened, but of what I didn't know.

The last I see of that early self is my white hair going into the trees where the path up the mountain began. I was a blink of light and gone. The trees gathered me in, their green skirts pulling me into the shadows that were patience and knowing, a long, slow murmuring that was the song of limbs and branches.

I shake my head and light forms itself into images, a leaf, a stone. Let the dead bury the dead, I say to myself and wonder where the dead begin and where the living end. That boy I was asked for his father, and the stories of disappeared fathers are as old as men.

I keep no photographs, keep no family album. But I can remember my childhood father. He was a stocky, burly man. He had broad shoulders, a heavy chest, strong legs, and arms that I thought back then could lift a mountain and put it down in another valley. He was tough and strong. I can see the pride in him. He was an ignorant kid from the tiny farming town of Pincher Creek, Alberta, who'd made his own way through the plains and into the mountains. Barely literate, he took weeks and months to read a Luke Short western, and until the day he died he signed his name by drawing, not writing, the letters.

Other men liked him, looked up to him. Dick, my oldest brother, inherited that gift. Both my father and he had a way of speaking, a way of holding men to them, a way of trust that made others follow them. Men placed the darkness of their lives in my father's hands, my brother's hands, so they could worry it back into a shape they could live with. It was enough for the men to pick themselves up and return to the misery of their lives for one more terrible try at poverty and loss. My father and my brother.

The only record I have is the story.

I dislike photographs, those stopped glimpses of time, that weasel-steal of shape and form and substance. My father loved the camera. He made an endless record of our lives. My mother stacked the family albums by her chair in those long years after my father's murder. She would pat them with her hand while she watched

Jeopardy on television. The talismanic images she touched are silent for me. In the tension of remembering in these early weeks of sobriety I feel sometimes I have an ax in my eyes. It helps me keep to what I know, that shining blade worn into a delicate glaze so sharp it could cut a mind in half, or a word.

There is too much anger in me.

My mother could shut my father up with a look or a word. It didn't happen often. My father's stories of his past were rare, but my mother never liked sharing storytelling with him. Her family and her history were the important ones. My father's family were violent, lower-class farmers and roustabouts and, in my mother's mind, nothing to brag about. She was from better stock, her father a shopkeeper. Years later, before she died, she burned all the letters and documents that might have told me who my father was. I begged her to pass on to me the cigar box of records my great-uncle had left to me in his will. My mother was executrix of that gentle man's scant estate. When I came for them she told me she'd burned them along with the rest of his things. *What do you want with that old Lane stuff?* she said. I sat by the polluted well behind the house and wept with frustration.

I get up from the stone bench at the foot of the garden and go back to the deck. It is the present I seek. Not to deny the past and not to ignore the future, but to have them live where they must, in memory and imagination.

Wherever I am, I am always here.

Thomas Jefferson in his *Garden Book* said, "But though an old man, I am but a young gardener." That is true for me as I labor in the daily meditations of earth, air, stone, and water. There are only young gardeners. The red-shafted flicker is back eating the winter apple. His bright eyes reflect the clubs of moss upon which he stands.

The gardener is made young by the seasons as they turn. I think of my mother when she was my age and I can see her hands working the soil. Such memories are the happiest I have of her. To her the hands she moved through the earth were as young as they had always been, were made young by the time she spent among the scattered alluvial stones and dense clay. I can see her weeding the rose bed by the driveway. Each rose there was planted for a grandchild.

At the corner of the walk was a peace rose planted for her first grandchild, who died of cancer when she was five.

My mother's years after my father was murdered were filled with working the earth in a slow and sometimes forgetful way, yet her pleasure in the garden was as palpable as the gleam of sweat on her forehead when she removed her red babushka and sat at the kitchen table with the last cup of coffee from the pot. There was no vegetable garden after my father's death in the late 1960s, and the flower gardens slowly faded away. Still, she puttered there. Fifteen years before, when we first moved to that house, she lived for her garden. I know my own love for gardening comes partly from her obsession. Even during her mad years the garden bloomed.

My little space here on the coast is new this year as I am new. A robin gorges on the brilliant red berries of the holly tree at the front corner of the house and then flies to the weathered, gray cedar fence by the apple tree and promptly defecates the berries she ate yesterday. The flesh of the berries has been digested and the hard seeds surrounded by guano drop to the ground where I accidentally step on one of them and push it into the ground. In another year a holly tree will begin, always male and I don't know why. I've pulled a dozen of them up today. If I left them, in a few years I would be surrounded by the shining evergreens with their spiked leaves.

I think I should explain where my garden is. The old Canadian question laid down by Northrop Frye is still a valid one.

Where is here?

My garden is near the southern tip of Vancouver Island on the Saanich Peninsula just north of Victoria. It sits in the middle of a small suburb surrounded by farms and woodland a few miles south of the airport and the terminal at Swartz Bay where you can take a ferry to Vancouver or one of the many Gulf Islands. A little to the north lies the town of Sidney with its many bookstores and to the south Victoria stares across Juan de Fuca Strait at the Olympic Mountains of Washington State.

The Saanich Peninsula is a long, irregular nipple of land stretching north from the city. It is bound on the east by the Georgia Strait and on the west by the Saanich Inlet and above it to the west the Malahat Mountains and beyond them the Pacific. To the east in the Georgia Strait lie the Gulf Islands; Saltspring, North and South

Pender, Galiano, Mayne, Saturna, and a dozen or more smaller ones. Beyond the mountains and ocean to the west are far Russia, Japan, China, and Southeast Asia. To the east is the dormant volcano, Mount Baker. Around and behind that white cone rise the blue mountains of the Coast Range.

This place on the northwest coast of North America is a gardener's dream. The temperatures are mild year-round. It might slip down below freezing but only for a few days. Only the rare winter threatens a minor frost. It rains during the winter months but only half as much as in Vancouver, a city crowded up against the Coast Mountains. Clouds ride over the island to the high ranges above Vancouver and drop their rain on those western flanks of stone, drowning the great city below.

There are islands in the gulf such as Texada that get very little rain and there grow cactus and spare grasses you'd expect to find on the prairie. The late spring through midautumn here is dry and sunny and the winters somewhat cloudy and wet. This is a temperate island with all the benefits of the Japanese ocean current with its steady temperatures. For a gardener there is no better place, for living things flourish here with only a bit of care and a watchful eye.

Right now the crocuses are up, their tips promising purples and mauves and yellows. Snowdrops lie scattered among the flower beds and the Lenten rose is up six inches, almost ready to droop its pale white and mauve flowers under the crested creamy blooms of the viburnum. It's the coastal winter here, and it will last until late March when the rest of the garden begins in concord with gardens everywhere else.

It is a sunny afternoon, a rarity this time of year. The garden seems at rest now, but if I look closely I can find many changes since October when I left to go to the treatment center. Twenty pine siskins and their occasional companions, four house finches, range through the apple trees and peck at the apples I left for them on the branches. Most of the fruit has fallen, but there are always a few that cling stubbornly. They are what remains of autumn. The siskins are a busy, flocking lot and their wheezing babble as they chat endlessly with each other is a scribble of sound.

The birds ignore me as I cut the fallen leaves of the Japanese iris at the edge of the pond. The leaves splayed outward on the water are like the long hair a woman throws forward to dry in the sun. How beautiful the neck of my woman when the sun touches her hidden flesh. The irises have already begun to push up their first green spears. They'll bloom in late spring, a spray of startled blue. They have no beard, just a thin stripe of gold on the curved petals. They are smaller than the fretted yellow of the Siberian iris. It needs cleaning up as well. I love the long yellow petals and the brush of soft brown on the standards. Like the other irises, they delight in the acid soil near the Douglas firs. They are aptly named for Iris, who was the messenger of the gods in Homer's *Iliad*. She was the bright attendant to the needs of Zeus and Hera and her blooms are a pointillist's dream against the background of greens.

Winter is about patience, something I must learn. I lost the autumn. Those months in the treatment center among counselors and addicts were their own strange dream, yet they have left clear images I never wish to lose of a time and place so foreign it could have happened in some strange fiction by Borges, a surrealist poem by Lorca.

Lorna, my lover, companion-gardener, friend, and fellow-poet, and who I call in careful jest my assistant gardener, cleaned up much of the garden last fall, put away the lawn and deck furniture, pruned and clipped most of the plants, raked leaves, and partly filled the compost bin. I call her my assistant gardener with deep affection. Lorna has a remarkable eye for plants, but being from the prairie where most native plants grow low to the ground because of the sparsity of rain and the hard winters, she tends toward plants that are large and showy. When she's in a planting mood, the shy viola or creeping thyme is not for her.

We have lived together twenty-two years. She stands now on the deck by the back door. I stare at her through the bare limbs of the apple tree. She has suffered my addiction for years. Her small arms around me in these new nights are another kind of garden. She waits now and watches, unsure of who I am, who I will be. My sobriety is as strange to her as it is to me. She doesn't fully trust it yet and why should she? There have been disappointments enough in the past.

Lorna steps back into the kitchen and closes the door. I close my eyes.

I've been home for a month and there is work to be done. Tools need to be seen to and plans have to be made. As these first weeks stretch out I have begun to feel a little stronger. My first tentative reaching is now more sure, though there are moments when I stand alone by the bamboo and tremble like its leaves.

Everywhere there are the gentle nuances of plants pushing delicately into the scant warmth of a sun a bare month or so past the solstice. Even on a gray day like this the air has a smell to it, or is it just that my hands are already covered in the wet mulch of earth? I can taste the earth quickening. The irises know. So do the skimmia. Their leaves are a brighter green and the red berries on the female glow in the muted light. They reflect in the pond beside the falling water as it burbles over the pitted sandstone. A second red shimmer in the dark water is a surface reflection of the estivating fish sleeping at the bottom, their tails moving slowly as they wait for the warmer spring to come. They will begin to rise for food in late February, a little thinner than they were in October when they settled into the season of short days and long nights.

Patience, I say, be like the koi in deep water. There is a time for everything. The gardener knows his hours, just as the fish do. All things in this garden wait for the sun to climb higher. I must only remain aware and bring to my daily life the knowledge of sixty-odd years and the thousands more of the generations who taught me. Moving a single stone in my garden is a motion as old as the hands of my great-grandfather lifting a stone from a broken field in Alberta. Earth-knuckles, they rose like fists on the backs of ice.

I move from bed to bed, a bit of weeding, some pruning, a general cleanup of the day lilies and the many other leftovers from autumn. Lorna couldn't get to it all when I was away. This garden is a shared space and one gardener alone cannot keep up to its demands. I hesitate to clean too much in case of a rare snowfall or frost. Last year's leaves protect the sleeping flowers.

Patience, go slowly, stop and watch the squirrel attack the bird feeder by the woodpile. I have given up driving her away and now accept she has her own needs. What am I trying to save, a handful a day of black oil sunflower seeds? I let her have her due. I enjoy her slender busyness, the way she scolds the cats if they get too close, the way she sits in the crotch of a fir branch thirteen feet up and calmly pulls the seeds from her cheeks to shell and eat. She is as much a denizen of this place as the birds. Come late spring she will appear with a consort or even two. The ways of squirrels are fine with me. I delight in her long journey along the top of the fence, the precise path she takes from fence to fir to redwood to cedar and then gone down the block in her pursuit of whatever it is squirrels desire.

I squat on a cedar round by the pond and watch the many birds at their play. The crow of a few hours ago passes over, this time heading west. Is it the same crow? I recognize some of them from season to season because of their peculiar habits. One uses the birdbath to soak bits of meat from roadkills or chicken legs scavenged from garbage bags. She drops the bits of bone and cartilage into the birdbath all spring and summer long. The songbirds don't seem to mind and flail about among small floating islands of pork or chicken grease when she's gone. You'd think they would recognize the smell of another bird who has been deep-fried, but they don't. I gave up long ago dissuading the crow from soaking her food. Who ever convinced a crow to do other than what she wishes?

Her fledglings sometimes learn the trick, but it is her I recognize. She has two small white feathers in the helmet curve above her left eye. It is the eye she stares at me with, as if to say she knows exactly who I am and she does. After all, I'm the gardener who fiddles and diddles about this patch of ground. "A piece of land not so very large," "a little spot enclosed by grace," as Horace and Watts had it. I have it the same way.

I have to spray the fruit trees with dormant oil and lime sulfur. The insects have planted their many eggs in the cracks and crannies. Some pruning needs to be done as well. The suckers are a punk hairdo on the apple trees. The compost needs turning. The detritus of autumn Lorna didn't have time to get to still lies in piles on the other side of the house. It has to be barrowed over to the truck and taken to the recycling depot. If I had been home I would have done this weeks ago and now the piles are a wet mess, a bed for sleeping slugs and sow bugs.

Procrastination is the gardener's worst enemy. The words *I'll do it next week* can stretch time into months. Procrastination was my constant companion in the years of drinking. Every task became secondary to my desperation.

I don't like where the previous years' cuttings are dumped. The east side of the house is narrow and heavily shaded. One task this year is to turn it into a modest shade garden with ferns, stone, and moss. Over the years it seemed there was nowhere else to pile the vegetation as it accumulated.

Time to cut some branches from the back of the forsythia and force them in a vase in the front hall. Their deep lemon-yellow flowers are a wonder in this earliest of months. There are already several flowers on the bush and the other buds strain toward blossoming. I will place a branch in a slender jar by the tub upstairs where Lorna bathes each morning. I try to keep a flower blooming there every day of the year. I love to see her in the bath with the seasonal blossoms beside her.

Color in a garden is not the only thing to look for. Shapes are beautiful as well. The contorted hazel in the large blue pot beside the magnolia is a maze of arabesques against the cedar fence. Catkins hang from the tips of its branches. I want to touch them each time I pass by. The hazel is lovely at all seasons but particularly in winter after the leaves fall. It is then you see the net of branches as they spiral and curve.

Right now two slate juncos perch on its highest branches. Their pale gray backs and breasts are a complement to the shifting blue of the ceramic planter below them. They are as common in my garden as the Oregon juncos and seeing them today is a kind of blessing. Robins, varied thrushes, and rufous-sided towhees are eating the purple berries of the daphne that come ripe in spring, an early feast for the birds. The males storm about in mock fights while the females watch with seeming disregard as they feed. Robins are particularly aggressive and many fights come to blows and beaks as they explode in the branches of some tree or other. No wonder they are sometimes called the American robin. Like our neighbors to the south, they can be very belligerent. The towhees are much quieter. Their battles are mostly song with an occasional rush toward some other male who has wandered by chance onto the lawn. Such slight aggression rarely ends up in a fight, the lesser bird quickly vacating the garden.

The beauty of winter is a wonder and mostly because I have to look past the show of early bulbs to the other, less obvious delights.

The contorted hazel is only one of many beauties here. Behind me water warbles from the tube of timber bamboo under the skimmia. The towhees and juncos love to go up to the falling water and sip from the tiny pools that have gathered in the piece of sandstone I found with my friend and fellow writer, Brian Brett, on a beach near Saltspring Island.

That is beauty, to stop a moment and watch the endless play of light on water and stone and see how the living things of the garden come to drink or just to gaze as I do now at the surface of the pond. The cats have a terrible time seeing past the reflections on the water. Both Basho and Roxy will sit by the pond and stare into it. When a fish rises they are shocked by the sudden presence of a life that exists below. They will extend a paw sometimes and touch the water as if they can't quite believe it.

Grace, patience, beauty, what else has come to mind on these January days? That seems enough for now. Right now I've got to load the truck with the piles of garden cuttings. When the truck is full we'll drive out to the composting facility just east of Saanich Inlet. Lorna loves the drive to the dump, as I do.

In Vernon, the town I grew up in, my brothers and I would drift out to the dump to hunt among the garbage of the postwar years. The huge dump burned high on a western hill above town. At night it was a smoldering smut with flashes of flame as a tire caught fire or a drum with leftover gas or diesel ignited, the thud of the explosion like a distant bomb. The waste of the valley was taken there and dumped over the tip into the flames below. Baby carriages, abandoned couches, broken chairs and tables, dead horses and sheep, the heads and skins of bear and deer, car bodies, anything and everything was there. Crows, gulls, and magpies tore at the garbage as it spilled open. Rats built catacombs and labyrinths there. Whole cities of flies and wasps were born and died there. Bits of pale meat clung to broken cattle bones and mixed with hard crusts of bread and the pulp of rotting potatoes and carrots.

All the waste and wanton wreckage tumbled down the spill until it lodged against a burned-out wagon or a twisted nest of broken boards from some building torn apart and trucked away. Kitchen, sawmill, and farm waste mixed with the soiled paper of the *Vernon News* and the *Vancouver Sun* and the scuffed pages of the *Saturday*

Evening Post, Liberty, and *Reader's Digest.* As the papers reached the flames they ignited and the ashes of stories rose like crows in the whirl of heat. Their thin wings sputtered with red jewels, then turned black and rose higher into the cloud of smoke above them. They fluttered there until the winds drifted them from the center of the dump and then fell crippled into the fields beyond.

Sometimes the wind shifted hard to the southeast and the cloud of yellow smoke fell on the town where it found its way through windows and screen doors. Women, hard at their ironing or washing, looked up for a moment and wiped the sweat from their faces. They went outside and stripped the damp clothes from the lines and carried the still-wet bundles back into the houses. They cursed the wind as their children stumbled around their legs. Small hands clutched at their dresses as the women stepped over and around their needs. There was work to be done. Bread had to be baked, dinner prepared, wood to be brought in, cleaning, cooking, washing, everything that was their daily round, the eighteen hours of work they called a day. A child was cursed or loved, was told to go outside and play and not to come back until dinner. *Get out, get out,* were the bywords of our lives.

After lunch the smoke lifted as the wind lagged. My mother carried the clothes back out and hung them on the sagging line. *Get out, get out,* she said. Up in the hills my brothers and I watched the wind fall away. We squatted among metal hulks of abandoned cars and watched a horse and wagon go by piled high with garbage. The man on the seat flicked his whip over the ears of the geldings and they leaned harder into the traces, their ribs a xylophone for flies. The hill here was steep, the ruts deep. A broken-down army truck blew black exhaust as it grumbled past the horse and wagon. Behind the truck were three more, all piled with apples from the orchards. There was no market for them anywhere in Canada and rather than give the fruit away it was burned. The trucks rumbled onto the flat and then backed up to the tip where they disgorged their loads.

The edge of the dump was a cliff of fruit. At the bottom were women and children. They were Chinks, Ragheads, Injuns, Bohunks, Polacks, or Wops to us. They were at the dump to scavenge apples. They leaned into the charred pile and tried to find fruit that hadn't been burned. When they found a fresh lode they carried armfuls to small wagons and wheelbarrows they had pulled or pushed all the way from town. The man on the tip watched them and when they began to cluster around a spill of fruit he would pick up a can and fling a twist of kerosene and diesel down the slope. When it flowed through the burning air, it exploded and the women and children dragged their wagons back. The man on the tip rolled cigarettes and smoked as he watched them sidle back into the billowing smoke and flame.

Quiet among the rusted car bodies, we watched as the empty army trucks returned to the orchards and packing houses for more apples. Then we made our way to the bottom of the drift away from the slope of burning fruit. There was almost no fire where we were. Here and there a pocket of thin flame flickered among torn clothing and broken chairs, but most of what was there was still intact.

I remember poking a stick into a mottled paper bag. The thin paper tore and a small cotton bundle fell out onto the inverted curve of a rusty fender. The bundle was knotted in the middle and I took the stick and picked at the knot. My brothers were below me, sifting through the discarded effluvium of the town. The knot gave way and I flicked at what looked like a cotton shirt. It slowly unfolded at my prodding and a tiny arm fell out, its fingers clenched, its skin a pale blue.

I stared at the thin arm and prodded until the rest of the cloth gave way. It was a baby, a girl, and I gazed at her infant limbs, her swollen belly, and the bruises that suffused her skin. I pushed the edge of the fender with my bare foot. The metal tipped and the body fell into a crevice, the fender coming down and covering it. I looked at the flaking paint and moved away. The small body both existed and didn't exist in my mind. I walked away from the secret grave and placed the dead baby somewhere deep inside where it could be lost.

There was no one I could tell, not even my brothers and not my mother or father or friends. If I did it would somehow be my fault. We were not supposed to be at the dump. The last time we were caught our father had taken us to the woodshed and beaten us with a strip of boxwood. I didn't want to be beaten again.

From high on the tip the man yelled at us to get away. My brothers turned and looked at me. We glanced up at the man and then continued our search for treasure. I leaned down and picked up two glass doorknobs, stuffed them into my sack along with a sheaf of pure white paper I had found just before the dead baby girl. We knew the man would only yell at us. He wouldn't come down from the tip. We heard a truck labor up the steep track below and we faded across the road and back into the safety of a rusted-out Studebaker.

Behind the truck, at the edge of the apple slope, a boy we did not know had made a whip from copper telephone wire. He was flaying the decaying head of a coyote. Its tail was gone for bounty. Bits of fur and rotting flesh flittered through the air. The boy's face was red with intensity as he cracked the whip across the coyote's empty eyes. We watched him intently as another truck passed. A woman grabbed the boy and tore the whip from his hand. She had made a basket from the skirt of her dress for the apples. On her feet she wore the bottoms of a man's rubber boots tied there with binder twine. On her head was a cracked straw hat. The boy began to cry and the woman slapped his face hard, then grabbed his arm and pulled him back around the edge of the pile where we couldn't see them. Apples by the hundreds of thousands rolled down the slope into the flames. The man threw down more gas and kerosene. It settled in a mist on the smoldering fruit, then exploded in a fury of flame and smoke.

We sorted through our finds and then wound our way around the dump and down toward the south end of Swan Lake and home.

The three of us were wild children. We were sent out to play at seven in the morning and told not to come back until dinnertime when our father returned from work. We would take our sandwiches and disappear, either walking out to Kalamalka Lake three miles from town to swim all day or to plunder the green garbage bins in the alley back of Main Street. We could go to the dump or gather kids from around the neighborhood to play war on Cactus Hill three blocks away.

I had found a dead baby in the catafalque of a wrecked and rusted car fender. The apples and flames would cover her in a day or two. She was not a newborn. I'd seen my sister when she was brought home from the hospital. Why the baby was thrown away or who the mother was, some teenage girl perhaps, too young, and pregnant out of wedlock, a child smothered, an unwanted daughter drowned in a bucket or washtub, or one beaten to death.

Those were hard and brutal years. There was only one policeman in town and he was ineffectual at best. That wives and children were murdered and babies aborted with coat hangers or boots was a thing left to a family. Privacy was the measure of freedom. My friend's father prostituted his Down's-syndrome daughter for twenty-five cents to anyone who had the money. When his father wasn't home, my friend sold her to older boys for half a Popsicle. I learned early to hide such knowledge for whatever I might tell would have repercussions, involve my family in things that were better left alone.

Dead babies, the dump, memories of childhood, swirl around in me. Who should I tell now? What good comes out of the past? To go back over those days brings down on myself the caul of childhood. That a neighbor beat a small friend to death in his woodshed when I was six, that another neighbor locked his idiot daughter away in an attic for years, and that a man my father worked with beat his wife senseless every weekend were what I thought was normal. Secrets and the silences that surrounded them governed my young life. To do or say anything was anathema. Grief and memory are burdens that cannot be lifted by going back.

Yet there were moments of such joy that to remember them makes me reel through the thin air of the past. I think of my brothers and me sitting at the feet of our mother as she read to us in the evening quiet, the war far away, the little mountain town of Nelson falling toward sleep just as we fought not to. The evening reading was a ritual for all of us. It was on my mother's lap or tucked into the folds of her dress as I fingered a seam of thin cotton I listened with my brothers to Huckleberry Finn on a raft on the Mississippi with Jim, the nigger. My mother's voice was a soporific. It insinuated itself into all of our hearts and brought us to a waking sleep. It was a treasure of words, their rhythms and patterns, she was giving me and I have never forgotten it. What I learned then I retain still. The night just before sleep was a happiness that abides in me to this day and while it is lost forever to me I can feel it in my bones and breath and that is enough.

Such joy wasn't a rare thing, for though my young world was paced and measured by violence and loss, I did not trace it solely by them. My childhood laughter as I played with my brothers inhabits me today and though I find that exuberance missing in these first weeks of sobriety I know it is not entirely gone. My laughter will return and my mother's voice, gone forever now, will also come alive in me again, for the art of reading aloud is part of my poetry, my art, and the first learning of reading aloud was given me by her. I will always be grateful for that.

That babies were murdered, and women beaten, does not entirely take from me the other happiness I knew. I think what makes the dark side of my early years so traumatic is how its extreme balances the extremities of joy. Always, for me as for my brothers, life was lived at the highest possible level of intensity. It seems now there was no quiet, reflective side to my life inside the family with the exception of those nighttime readings and the sound I can only imagine now of those three childish voices asking for yet another page to be read and then hearing the book slapping shut and my mother saying to us that it was late and tomorrow was another day. We carried her words with us to our beds and they remained with us as we slept, the only stay we had against the darkness that surrounded us, the terrible shape of the monsters behind our closet door or under our beds. Silence was our only enemy. Today it is even more so.

I lean over the pond and Basho leaps onto my back and clambers to my shoulders. He rides with me across the yard to the deck where he jumps off and fiercely investigates the garbage can for the scent of some truant cat who might have passed through. Satisfied, he walks over and sits on my knee. It is almost time for a snack, he seems to be saying and he is right. A cup of tea for me and one for Lorna and a few tidbits for Basho and for Roxy if I can rouse her from her sleep on the living-room couch. The afternoon wanes and the sun, low to the south, is already casting its pall across the lawn.

❧

Another day, and winter light melts through the tangled plum branches. An early car goes by, windows open, radio too loud, and I listen to the beat of a military tune left over from another time, another place. It brings back a story my mother told me of the summer my father shipped out for Europe from Nanaimo on Vancouver Island. I was three years old.

As I sit in the story I can hear the soldiers marching to the ships. Down the hill to the sea there is an endless line of men marching in step. Each man's eyes are upon the harbor where the docks creak against metal hulls. The Pacific is ahead, the Panama Canal, and then the Atlantic and the U-boats. The men will sit among men and smoke and talk as they wait for the hours to take them to England. What they have left behind has been placed in a metal box behind their hearts. Already they are writing letters home.

There will be days of playing cards. Hearts and solitaire, patience and poker. Paperbacks will be read and traded and discarded. The tired books will be thrown overboard into the sea, their pages sinking slowly until the words become water, food for the grin of Leviathan. But now, the ships are waiting, their engines a dull thunder. Gulls wheel above slicks of bunker oil and crows cast their dark eyes on whatever is lost, dropped, or forgotten.

On the street are the women and children. They fill the sidewalks and gutters. The young women have a kind of crazed happiness on their faces, all smiles and tears. Their happiness is full of a wild remorse, anger, and something else. It is a whisper in their eyes. It says there will be no men. Not for a long time. A whisper is among them. It joins them each to each, a thread of sound, a murmur in their minds. The old women, the mothers of these men, do not wave and they do not weep. They remember the last war that took their husbands and so few came home. Their gaze rests on nothing. They are sending their sons now. They know what is to come from this leaving, this abandonment, these boy-men who will not return.

The young wives know without knowing. In the years to come they will sit among their kind around kitchen tables and listen to the radios sing of the war and England, Churchill, and the white cliffs of Dover. The women will sit on wooden chairs with their rations of coffee or tea or, if it is a Saturday night, the bottle of rye they share with each other.

The soldiers are marching. A small child breaks from the crowd and runs to his father in the ranks. He takes his father's hand and stares up at him as he goes. The mother walks the edge of the crowd with her older sons. Women point. Some laugh, some cry. When the lines of men reach the harbor she breaks from the gutter and takes the child back. Her husband does not look at her. His eyes are on the man in front. He follows the back of the man up the gangway into the ship. When the ranks are broken he walks to the white rail and looks out upon the crowd, but she has gone with her sons. In the thick heat of morning, there is no one he knows.

This is not my memory. It is a story my mother told me when she was dying. I don't remember running beside my father. I think, if I did, it would be a happy memory. But I don't. What I had was my mother on her deathbed. I sat with her as the cancer quietly ate her. Somewhere inside her faded flesh with its grotesque slash of bright red lipstick and powdered cheeks was a pretty young woman with three small boys. I can see her walking up the hill to her rooms above the pool hall with the three of us in tow.

She spoke from her dying in a fierce whisper: *I did not turn around.*

❧

A frosty morning, a car going by playing its strange, majestic tune to an empty street. I put down my mug of coffee and lean into my hands. My life seeps from me like the light from the risen, milky sun.

Yesterday I wept for memory and now, a day later, I buy a Jelena witch hazel and plant it against the fence put up last year by the neighbor. To do is all. The spidery, orange-yellow flowers glow against the new cedar boards. A perfect spring color to match my mood, which is resolutely optimistic. The war has been put away again in the place where memory sleeps.

The day is the day, no more, no less. This morning I couldn't get past the shrubs at the nursery. I fell in love with a campanula and bought it. Late spring will see a myriad of bell-shaped, red-veined, creamy-yellow flowers in clusters and in the autumn the leaves turn fiery shades of red and orange. I've planted the campanula near the witch hazel. The spot is shady until noon, but both shrubs don't mind the lack of morning light. After taking out a diseased cherry tree last summer I have eyed the empty space. I imagine their roots exclaiming at the rich soil, the abundance of earthworms.

Nothing in the garden gives me as much pleasure as planting. I talked to both shrubs as I moved them into the earth, telling them they would love it here and not to be afraid of anything. The cotoneaster across the path seemed to join in the discussion, nodding its long branches with the red berries the robins and thrushes love.

It will be bare soon if the birds have their way and they will. The shrubs seem content with my assurances.

This is the time when I have the best view of the garden. The earth is bare around the stubbled perennials. The early bulbs are up and their first intense colors are everywhere. Now is the time to sit and feel my way into the garden. I know already what will appear and fill in the vacancies. Much is happening under the earth. The roots of the plants are pushing out their feeder tips in that living layer called dirt.

Everything is alive in the skin of this planet. The worms and nematodes, the bacteria and fungi are spreading their lives beneath the surface. They are breaking things down and building things up. The plants feed off their living and their dying. Without this crust of earth we have nothing. I think of pure sand. I love to hold it in my cupped hands. The grains shine and shimmer, each one a singular stone. Yet most people hesitate before picking up a clod of damp earth. It is full of secret life and that worries them. There is something inside the dark, moist granules and it unnerves them, makes them uneasy. What is in there, they ask?

I go to the compost bin and run my hands through what was once kitchen waste, leaves, and flowers. Over the past year it has been turned by the worms and bacteria into a soft, fluffy substance that I will spread across our garden. I will work it into the soil beside the many perennials, the shrubs, the bamboos, and the ferns. It is alive with worms. In another month I will find them in great writhing balls in the waste. I will hold a thousand worms in my two hands, some of them six inches long and others tiny red whips all twisting and turning on my palms.

Basho watches me rummaging in the earth and like any good cat thinks I am digging a hole in preparation for my toilet. He happily comes alongside, scrapes a hole beside the one he thinks I'm digging, stares down into it, and then changes his mind. He glances up at me as if to say the dirt here isn't quite the right consistency, moves over and digs another, this one obviously just right. He squats and gets that dreamy-eyed look cats and humans get when they are relieving themselves. Done, he turns and looks into the hole for a moment just as we humans do. Satisfied with it all he busily scrapes the tossed earth over it and then looks inquiringly at me. I take my hands from the earth, scrape my palms together for a moment if only to reassure him that what I've done is equally satisfying, and we both walk over to the compost bins, Basho with his tail high and me ruminating on the lives of cats and men. Roxy watches us balefully from the edge of the deck.

My feet have known the earth since I could stand. When I leave sidewalks behind I can feel the world give under the weight of my body. I remember when I ran barefoot across beaten clay or sand, the times I stood in mud and felt the earth squeeze through my toes. I was in touch with the earth when I was a child. The thick mud along the banks of Coldstream Creek, where I hunted for turtles, toads, and frogs, was warm and welcoming. It made me want to lie down and roll in it and sometimes I did. I would take off my threadbare T-shirt and shorts, lie down in the mud, and roll until I was covered with it, my skin, my hair, my finger- and toenails. When I was done, I would wade out into the creek. The mud would slide from my skin and slip away in thick clouds in the running waters.

Childhood is a strange paradise. I remember my father's return from the war. I can see myself in the bedroom on Fall Street, see the small boy I was. There were stars in the night that bloomed like flowers in my eyes, mountains fell in blackness to the water below. The lake was rippling silver, a fierce gentleness I tried to understand, it was so hard and soft at the same time. The air slipped into the room through the open window like a quiet thief and touched my face, my hands, and narrow chest. My elbows rested on the sill. I was standing on a small cot in the corner of the room.

In the bed behind me was my mother. She was moaning softly and her bed moved with the sound of her voice. It was the kind of sound an animal made when it was in pain or a cat when it was roaming through the bush below the house, a night-cry I had listened to many times. It was a hurting sound. It cried through my skin. I was afraid.

I had been moved from my mother's bed and now, sleepless and lonely, I stared from the window at the night. My father was back. He had been gone three years. I have no clear image of him. All I remember is the silver of the cold waters below and the sound of my mother in the bed. I thought my father was hurting her and there was nothing I could do. There was a shape on the bed, an animal like the black bear I had seen by Cottonwood Creek, humped and dark.

I stared across the bands of my arms. The bed shuddered and grew still again. My mother was saying my father's name. She said it in a way I had never heard her speak before. *Red,* she said, *Red.*

In the night sky were all the creatures I imagined. While living things slept I left to fly among the mountains in the faint light of the moon. Below me small axes glinted upon the waters. Deep below the whitecaps, there were great fish, wide-eyed and sleeping. Only the mountains were still. Their skirts of fallen stone fell gentle beside the long dark lake. Somewhere under the rubble of rock a marmot slept in my thin arms, a nighthawk cried in my eyes. In the sky a last swallow quavered. Its bright beak breathed my flight.

Flying dreams stayed with me for years. I loved entering the sky on bright wings. Yet my going back into time is only another kind of flight.

I am trying to know who I have been so I will know who I am. I can't fly from what made me. The air I breathed, the stones I touched, the dirt I rolled in, entered my pores and my body learned the good earth. A garden grows in me.

The fear I had of my father was not one of violence. I didn't fear his punishment any more than I feared my mother's. It was a fear of love. From the first day he returned I watched him as if from a great distance. I searched his body for the signs of love. The hair on his forearms, the tilt of his head, his laugh, his frown, the way he leaned back in the weight of his weariness at the end of a day of work were measured by me and by my brothers. He had returned, but though it was from a war and that his absence was a holy thing, still I was unsure of his presence. A touch from him, any small acknowledgment, a word, a smile, was enough to make me come alive with happiness. He had seen me and that was sometimes enough even though I might have wished for more. The garden that grows in me is full of many kinds of flight. One was the flying toward my father and the other was my leaving him. I was afraid of love for what I knew of it in those early years was that love was a kind of loss and that to hold on to it was to prepare my body and spirit for pain. Did I know that then? Yes, I knew that, though the understanding of it was another matter.

If I want to understand my garden, then I take myself into the forests and meadows, the bogs and swamps, the wild fields and hillsides and there I watch and listen. How a plant lives, where and why a plant grows are some of the lessons a gardener must learn. Much can be learned from a patch of forest or an open meadow. Much can be learned from a backyard.

I find myself on my hands and knees crawling around naming the different mosses in my garden. Their colors are an endless variation on yellow and green with a bit of gray or red thrown in here and there, a dark blush of blue or black at the base of their leaves. Under the canopy of red cedars and Douglas firs the ground of much of my garden is dark and acidic, perfect for coastal lichens and mosses. I love their names: awned haircap, juniper haircap, cranesbill, tall-clustered thread, Menzies' red-mouthed minim, ribbed bog, lover's, false-polytrichum, Menzies' neckera, golden short-capsuled, Oregon-beaked, lanky, step, twisted ulota, hairy screw, bottle, red roof, wet rock, black-tufted rock.

I might as well search out the lichens too: bull's-eye, cladonia scales, bark barnacle, lungwort, lettuce lung, frog pelt, pimpled kidney, orange pincushion, questionable rock-frog, tattered rag, beaded bone, forking bone, tickertape bone, waxpaper, antlered perfume, devil's matchstick, false pixie cup, blood-spattered beard, and common witch's hair. Nineteen lichens and as many mosses. There are probably others if I search diligently.

What wonderful names are blood-spattered beard and common witch's hair. How much more delightful than the tiresome nomenclature of the Latin taxonomy, necessary as it is for scientific identification. Ideas of order, yes, but not a feeling among them. Questionable rock-frog is far more interesting to me than *Xanthoparmelia cumberlandia*. These plants live everywhere in the garden, innocuous and largely unnoticed, but everywhere I look there is another one sharing a bit of rotting wood, a shaded spot beneath a fern. The twenty-year-old shakes on the roof of the old child's playhouse I use for storing kindling and empty planters have seven mosses and five different lichens growing on their gray wood.

The world of the mosses is small, but their pervasive presence is like a mass of exploding galaxies in the garden. There is no better time of the year to find them. The winter rains bring down nutrients from the air, and the wood, soil, and stone they grow upon is awash with water. Their sporophytes are impossible forests. The mosses and lichens creep imperceptibly over everything in the garden. Surely they must go back beyond the Jurassic to some earlier time when everything was new.

I have trifocals now and the only way I can really see anything up close is to take my glasses off and get to my eye's focal point, which is six or seven inches in front of my nose. I must look like some grazing animal here on the ground with my head down and my ass in the air. At night I take my glasses off and streetlights become Van Gogh's stars. They are swirling balls of nova light. This seeing was how I learned the world in my first seven years.

They are very beautiful, these mosses. All year they are a canopy for sow bugs and pill bugs, slugs, fleas, flies, worms, ants, and whatever else crawls under their forest cover. In winter they are the soft green blanket that shelters the sleeping beetles as they wait for spring. I have spent my life in the intimate world of infinitesimal things.

I lie on my back, the moss softer than my bed, the water soaking into my sweater. Above me Canada geese ride on their way to Georgia Strait, where they are sure to find food in the tidal swamps or the bog behind the beaches. Theirs is a constant, reassuring gabble. I am told they are always led by an older female as they drift back and forth above this narrow peninsula. When I was young I was led by my mother.

Nineteen mosses and nineteen lichens? I'm sure there are more. I roll over and peer through the misting rain. There is more than meets the casual eye here on the floor of this garden. I look up for a moment at the fir tree and there on a branch is some speckled horsehair. It is a hanging hair lichen. Up or down, there is something growing everywhere. By the old cherry stump, scarlet waxy caps have appeared in the moss. The bright orange caps glisten in the rain. The mushrooms are tiny. They appear here every late winter. I could eat them but what for? There are so few of them. Like the lichens and mosses they occupy this quiet place and are easy to miss or ignore. It is only up close they take on their beauty. They feed off the debris of the years. Things return to the soil and on the way they are the dinner for a thousand creatures, the scarlet waxy cap only one of many. It is the first mushroom of winter I've seen. The year will produce dozens more.

My presence on this half-acre is only that, a presence. What is here now has been here in some form or another for many thousands of years. Fifteen millennia ago this bit of land lay buried under three miles of ice. I am a passing stranger, one who has stopped here briefly to play in the fields of the lords and ladies who govern all things.

A short month ago I stepped back into the world after an absence of forty-five years of addiction. Those years were the life I lived, but I am seeing this old garden now with new eyes. This search through my garden is for the naming of things, but more than that it is renewal and endurance, patience, knowing, and acceptance. My hands are feeling again what they last felt when I was little more than a child. When I place my hands in the earth my fingers are like the tips of the first root of a seedling sprung to life. What I feel is wonder.

Plants

Big laughing Gym (mushroom) – *Gymnopilus spectabilis*
Bigleaf maple – *Acer macrophyllum*
Bracken fern – *Pteridium aquilinum*
Bunchberry – *Cornus unalaschkensis*
Campanula – *Campanula alliariifolia*
    "   – *Enkianthus campanulatus*
Caraway thyme – *Thymus herba-barona*
Clematis – *Ranunculaceae clematis montana "rubens"*
Corkscrew hazel – *Corylus avellana "contorta"*
Cotoneaster – *Cotoneaster divaricatus*
Crocus – *Crocus* spp.
Couch grass (quack grass) – *Agropyron repens*
Daphne – *Daphne laureola*
Day lily – *Hemerocallis*
Douglas fir – *Pseudotsuga menziesii*
Forsythia – *Forsythia spectabilis*

Giant redwood – *Sequoia gigantea*
Golden bamboo – *Phyllostachys aurea*
Holly – *Ilex aquifolium*
Hosta – *Hosta sieboldiana*
Japanese iris – *Iris laevigata*
Lenten rose – *Helleborus orientalis*
Ponderosa pine – *Pinus ponderosa*
Siberian iris – *Iris forresti*
Sitka spruce – *Picea sitchensis*
Skimmia – *Skimmia japonica*
Snowdrop – *Galanthus*
Sword fern – *Nephrolepis exaltata*
Valerian – *Valeriana phu "Aurea"*
Viola – *Viola canadensis/labradorica*
Western anemone – *Anemone occidentalis*
Witch hazel – *Hamamelis japonica*
Yellow glacier lily – *Erythronium grandiflorum*

ANIMALS, BIRDS, AND INSECTS

American robin – *Turdus migratorius*
Black bear – *Ursus americanus*
Black-capped chickadee – *Parus atricapillus*
Bobcat – *Lynx rufus*
Chestnut-backed chickadee – *Parus rufescens*
Cooper's hawk – *Accipiter cooperii*
Cougar – *Felis concolor couguar*
Coyote – *Canis latrans*
Eastern gray squirrel – *Sciurus carolinensis*
House finch – *Carpodacus mexicanus*
Nighthawk – *Chordeiles minor*
Northwestern crow – *Corvus caurinus*
Oregon junco – *Junco oregonus*
Pine siskin – *Carduelis pinus*
Raccoon – *Procyon lotor*
Red-breasted nuthatch – *Sitta canadensis*
Red-shafted flicker – *Colaptes cafer*

Rufous-sided towhee – *Pipilo erythrophthalmus*
Sharp-shinned hawk – *Accipiter striatus*
Slate junco – *Junco hyemalis*
Townsend's vole – *Microtus townsendii*
Varied thrush – *Ixoreus naevius*
Western rattlesnake – *Crotalus viridis*

2

Come before rain;
rise like a dark blue whale
in the pale blue taffeta sea;
lie like a bar in the eyes where the sky should be.
Come before rain.
　　　　—P. K. Page, "Emergence"

"I will play the swan, and die in music," said Shakespeare in *Othello,* and I can understand his wish as I watch sixty whistling swans pass over the garden. Their white feathers shimmer with a ghostly light this early morning. They are on their way to the fields of wintering grass where they will feed among the fresh green shoots. Their long honking cries flow among the low gray clouds this early February day. Only the loon can evoke the same shivers. If I listen closely I can hear the faint whistling whip as their strong wings cut the air. They call endlessly to each other, the cobs and pens making great joy of the day, a late breakfast ahead in the far fields.

The cry of the swans is among the great beauties and their grace in the air is as mysterious as it is magical. I could dream my way into their flight. How I have wished that my life and perhaps my struggle will find its shape in imagined feathers, wings to allow me flight.

As a child I flew in my sleep. Why did such dreams leave me? Addictions and obsessions drape a shroud over the child, but now that I am older and no longer clouded by drugs and alcohol perhaps I will find that early place where I knew the sky. I had petit mal when I was a child. I loved the deep swoon of the seizure, the darkness rising like wicking water in my skull.

There is no answer for the losses of a child, just as there seem to be no answers to my life these days, only questions. Yet what will come will come and be welcome, no matter its shape. Perhaps my poetry has been a flying dream for me. I can recreate in poems the paling forests and valleys I saw in my dreams sixty years ago as I flew in the night toward a thin light I never reached.

The fragments I remember come unbidden. The anecdotes and stories arrive from nowhere. Why a cairn of stones and why a dead child at the dump? Why, of all the possible memories, are they the ones that came to mind? Yet I will let them come. Somewhere there is a story that needs telling.

The ancient tale of the dying swan's song drifts through the morning as I watch the great birds' flight against the gray skies. Their song follows down the west-bearing wind. Seeing the swans slip from my sight I could say with Virgil, "Now I know what love is."

The swans are beautiful, yes, and so is what I feel for the things around me, but depression still creeps like a mouse under my skin. The lack of light, the cloudy days, and the nights without stars lower a dull helmet over my skull. Swans can lift my spirit for a morning, but swans alone can't heal a grievous mind.

Daily I feel amazed I am not drinking or taking drugs. When I climb into bed at night I'm astonished I've come through a whole day without them. The quiet *thank you* I say into my pillow is sometimes the smallest of mercies. My addiction consumed me three months ago. Every waking hour was spent trying to figure out how I could get enough alcohol, where to hide it, and how to consume it without anyone knowing. From the first sips of whiskey or beer my mother gave me as small child to the inch of beer my father let me finish, I knew what I wanted. As a child my body craved alcohol. What was it in me that needed to be caged?

There is neither grace nor pleasure in the life of the addicted. My drinking transcended the ordinary world of a glass of wine at lunch or a couple of beers in the evening. I needed forty or more ounces of vodka every day in those last years. That was maintenance drinking for me at the end. That's what left me flopping around like a beached salmon on the hall floor. My flesh and bones had a life of their own. My self was gone, only my spirit remained to watch its body trying to die.

It takes an effort each day for me to go to the store or the mall, for everywhere I go my truck wants to turn in to a liquor store. I know where each one is within thirty miles. I wince each time I pass certain corners or drive down familiar streets. My body quails as if it is being threatened by a pit bull. I still twitch and shiver uncontrollably. Small hallucinatory creatures slip along the edges of my sight and I glance here and there as if I could actually find them beside a tree, on a bench, or down an aisle in the grocery store. Loud music hurts me.

This morning I was cleaning ivy away from the side of the compost bin and found two empty vodka bottles tucked behind the vines. Vodka still pooled at the bottom of the bottles, a translucent liquid jewel behind the glass, a thimbleful, no more. I thought of the day I must have lifted the bottles and drained them, held them to my lips until the last vodka slipped down the glass. A thimbleful left, a narrow swallow, a lip, a tongue away behind the glass walls, the metal cap.

Addiction is a disease that is my body. It lives in me, a creature with the same cells as mine, the same blood and bones. I stared through the glass and I was so frightened I thought I would die. Then I walked around the house, opened the garbage can, and dropped the bottles in. As I walked away I felt I was leaving behind the oldest, closest friend, the dearest lover I ever had. I walked away, and I am still afraid.

Weldon Kees, the American poet and alcoholic who committed suicide by jumping off the Golden Gate Bridge, had a couple of lines in one of his poems: "Whatever it is that a wound remembers / After the healing ends." Sometimes I think every poem I wrote in this life has a death in it. Everywhere my imagination looked I found violence. The people's lives I had been witness to as a child and as a young man were brutal, swamped in aggression, suffering, and despair. Their occasional joys were always fueled by drugs or alcohol. A grinding week found its miserable release on a Saturday night at the local hall. A dance always ended in blood.

Yesterday the sun broke free for ten minutes and I ran downstairs from my office and stood in the driveway with my arms outstretched. My body ate the sun. I knew I needed to do something, go somewhere, leave the house and garden, so I phoned my friend Brian Brett and told him it was time we made our annual spring trek for slate. He immediately said yes.

Yellow Slate Mountain is what we call the tumbling mountain slopes of the rain forest near Port Renfrew, the last stop on the highway west along Juan de Fuca Strait. We have made this trip four times in the last five years. He searches for yellow slate and I search for the pearlescent mica-sweated slate. I also would love some of the yellow, but have given it up simply to enjoy his pleasure at finding yet another piece to add to the ones he has from previous years.

Our journey is for slate but is as much for friendship as for stone. We've known each other thirty years, since he was a teenage rebel on his way to being an adult one. Back then I was deep in the wandering, drinking, and drug life that took me across two American continents. I was lost, riddled with guilt, and tormented by the death of my brother, the murder of my father, the collapse of my marriage, and the loss of my children.

My brother Dick, who died of a cerebral hemorrhage when he was twenty-eight, was a poet like myself. He suffered from confusion, self-doubt, bravado, alcoholism, and depression most of his young life. His death blew my family to pieces. It was the beginning of the end of everything I had known, trusted, and understood. I've spent much of my adult life trying to understand why his death caused such ruptures though perhaps they might have happened anyway and he wasn't a catalyst, only a first tragedy among many tragedies. He was my blood. We had shared the same womb.

He quit school at fifteen, drifted into trouble with the law, drank too much just as I did, joined the air force under my father's urging and, upon returning home three years later, slipped straight into deeper trouble with drugs, alcohol, and crime, until finally getting married. His was a shotgun marriage, the same for my other brother, Johnny, just a year older than I. Both their weddings were a few months apart in the summer of 1957. My own shotgun marriage followed six months later in the slush and bitterness of February 1958. Children, poverty, boys married to girls, none of us old enough or responsible enough to recognize anything other than the prison we found ourselves in. We turned to our parents for help and understanding and were refused. *You made your bed, now lie in it,* my father said to each of us. My mother was silent.

Back in the late 1950s and early 1960s, while I struggled with my early poems, I lived in a trailer park in Merritt, a wretched, dusty mill town in southern British Columbia. My two children were three years and one year old and my young wife tried and failed daily to be happy in the miserable trailer the bank owned. I left that flaking aluminum prison each morning for a job in the sawmill, the only life I knew then, though I labored late into the night on writing my poems. I think it was poetry that saved me from killing myself or killing others. There were times when I sucked the steel barrel of my Lee-Enfield rifle or, worse, aimed it at a passing pickup truck. What saved my wife I do not know.

In December 1964, there was a phone call late at night from my sister telling me my brother was dead. I borrowed my boss's car and drove crazily over the winding mountain roads to Vernon, where my birth family huddled, waiting for his ashes to be shipped up from Vancouver.

In four more years I would be gone, my wife remarried and my children lost to me. After my divorce I lived in a fury. I ranged from woman to girl, friend to stranger, bar to barrio, city to village, all designed with one end in mind, to kill myself or at least kill whatever it was that daily ate me alive. I made women fall in love with me and then discarded them like chaff. Guilt, fear, self-pity, self-loathing, self-destruction, all and none of them. I remember little of those years. Much of them is blacked out by depression, alcohol, and drugs. I remember waking up in a car wreck in a snowbound field south of Prince George and wondering why I was still alive. I pried the barbed wire off the door and walked away in search of a bar.

What I do remember has little joy in it, beyond the writing and the publishing of my early books. I hurt anyone who came close to me and sought safety with strangers. There was always a drink or a drug and usually at the end of a months-long bender a pretty woman I'd wake up to who had been crazy enough to take me home with her for the night or the week until I left her for a place called anywhere else.

I would stand on Fourth Avenue, Queen Street East, or Avenue C and drain the last of a bottle of whiskey before pulling out. I had no plans other than to go. Driving nowhere numbed me. The long road across the country was the same as all my journeys. My dead brother with his bloody brain sat beside me and my dead father with the hole in his chest where the bullet had blown apart his heart sat behind me, both of them whispering in my ears the lyrics to poems and songs I didn't want to hear but wrote down anyway. Drugs and alcohol, rock and roll, the Band, Dylan, the Stones, and Woodstock. When I tired of the eastern summer heat I drifted northwest to British Columbia, to Highway Sixteen and my friends who were squatting on a deserted farm north of Smithers. We drank our way through the summers in the local bars, went hunting for goat in the mountains, or sat around with a stick of Lebanese gold and smoked ourselves into illusory satories.

Socrates said, "The unexamined life is not worth living." I think I ranged through those years looking for innocence and examining nothing. I think I wanted to be a child again. I think I wanted to kill someone.

I shake the years away as Brian gets in his truck and we start out in our separate vehicles for our trip to Yellow Slate Mountain. We need two trucks for our booty. Journeys and quests are for the maddened young and both Brian and I have chewed on the years. Now our trips are as much companionship as nostalgia and we can both joke or cry a bit about the times we had together and apart in the bars and cars, rivers and lakes of this land of mountains and plateaus.

The long drive along the southern coast of Vancouver Island is replete with vistas of long beaches of sand and stone. Logs and the broken shards of trees lean from stone cliffs or lie partly buried under a seethe of rocks, shells, and sand lifted into dunes by the winter storms. Every day the beaches shift and change and every day the waves heave their burdens onto the land only to bear them away again the next.

Partway down the coast we stop in Sooke, an old-time logging and fishing village now dependent on kayakers, whale watchers, sports fishers, and beachcombers who drift through here in the spring through summer looking for a taste of paradise before returning to their offices and apartments in the cities.

Our stop here is as much anticipated as the slate we are journeying toward. It is breakfast at Mom's Café. Steaming coffee; loggers, fishers, and highway workers talking about the day ahead and the early morning behind; a waitress who looks like she eats what she serves; and then three eggs over easy, four strips of thick, crispy bacon, three fat sausages, enough fried potatoes to feed a family of five, four chunks of dense toast smeared with butter, and all piled on a plate the size of my imagination, served with seconds and thirds of coffee and the thought of following the whole thing up with a wedge of lemon pie and meringue five inches high.

After Sooke, the Pacific beaches begin and while we are tempted to turn off and wander them in search of nothing more than the crash of waves without the interruption of a host of tourists, we don't. Our journey today is for slate. The stone is back in the mountains a dozen miles up a narrow bush road that's so rutted and potholed it is a danger to walk it, let alone drive.

Hanging over the scar of road are salmonberry, evergreen huckleberry, and salal. They are reaching for the scattered bits of light that filter down through the canopy of hemlock, Douglas fir, and western red cedar. Bigleaf maples and red alders crowd the edge of the forest. Their leaves are yet to come. Around them grow licorice, maidenhair, sword, and deer ferns.

I pull over and watch a banana slug make its slow way around a puddle toward a belly of moss at the end of a rotting alder stump. These slugs are the largest mollusks in the world. This particular one is eight inches long, a pale yellow with a leopard's black spots dappled down its body. Herbivores, they graze the forest floor and grind down the leaves and stems of plants, bracken fern, and anything else that grows low to the ground. Each time I see one I think of the poet Buson's haiku about the slug's cousin, the snail, "One horn long, one short, / I wonder what's on his mind?"

At the quarry we turn in a wide area of road and park. The slate has been taken from here for years by gardeners and stonemasons. Each time they remove some, more slides down, leaving the trees above precariously perched. Thirty-year firs hang umbrellas of roots in space as they wait for just a bit more slate to slide or a heavy Pacific wind to blow contrary and tilt them into oblivion. We both look up and the same thought crosses our minds: Is this the day that one will fall or that other one beside it? The thought flits by and we climb up the slanting slope of shale and push the larger pieces down to the trucks, ignoring our imminent, possible deaths.

Both Brian and I are two testosterone-riddled teenagers when we do things like this. It's not a job, its an excursion lifted to the level of a treasure-quest. One piece of slate the right color, texture, and size seems worth our lives. Working such a piece out from under hanging roots is a joy that passes understanding. Trucks loaded down to the springs and below, we sit on the tailgate of my truck and eat pork-chop sandwiches, pickles, Lorna's magnificent chocolate-chip cookies, and ripe Bartlett pears, all of it tamped down with hot tea. Neither of us is dead or injured. We haven't destroyed our already vulnerable lumbar vertebrae or Brian's knees, which are nothing more than bone grinding on bone, the cartilage long gone. Our hands haven't been crushed and we haven't dropped a chunk of slate on a foot. A few scrapes, a couple of scratches, no more. All told, a good day with very little blood to show for it, but a ton of fine slate to decorate our gardens with.

Tomorrow Brian will send me a poem about our journey. The slate will still be in our trucks, he on Saltspring Island and I on my deck. "Going blind, limp, and weak," is how I will feel when my muscles and joints sing their song of outrage at what I have put them through again. But what are sore muscles compared to the camaraderie of the journey, the treasure carried down and stacked in seams on the truck beds?

ONCE AGAIN, YELLOW SLATE MOUNTAIN
    —*Brian Brett*

When was the first time we traveled together?
Thirty years ago, yet here we are on the road again,

back to the mountains, collecting slate for our gardens;
though these should hardly be called mountains,
shadowed by the shimmering glaciers of the Coast Range.
Say they are hills, hummocks, rises, ridges, earth forced
into stone. How many have died since the first day
we walked into the wilderness, adjusting our packs,
you with your rifle, me with my fishhooks?
A day that began years of arguments over dinners
and whiskies and women and wild rivers that
neither of us will ever see in our lifetimes.
How many of our friends are gone now?
One walked into water. One spiderwebbed his brains
with heroin and cocaine and an odd sense of adventure,
and another had her brains scrambled by her husband.
Several boiled in their fiery alcoholic blood.
The cancer chased most of the rest. But some were unique,
you remember them, the ones who surprised us,
discovering spectacular ways to die in foreign zones.
Yet every year we return to this cliff-face, taking slate
released by the freeze-and-thaw of mild winters—
pathing each of our gardens like the countless other
gardeners who know the secret home of this generous stone.
We're a joke now, getting old, staggering around
under the big slabs, laughing, just avoiding squashed fingers.
Why have we survived this long while the others died?
The doctors said I would go first, yet here I am, stumbling
down the rutted road with my share of the mountain.
If we keep surviving like this, our arms full of rocks,
two aging men, laughing, going blind, limp, and weak,
we might end up taller than Yellow Slate Mountain yet.

※

"You will find something more in woods than in books. Trees and
stones will teach you that which you can never learn from masters."
St. Bernard of Clairvaux said that ten centuries ago and it is still true.

I learn about friendship when I gather stone with a friend. Brian's poem reminds me once again how fragile I am, how like a wisp my breath moves.

Friends have been rare in my life. Staring through the thinning fog of my addiction I can see how afraid I was and how little I trusted anyone's overture toward friendship. I look back down those far-off years and realize I gave to the men and women I knew the illusion of friendship even as I withheld it from them. Yet there were many times I gathered myself into the arms of friends. As my journey to Yellow Slate Mountain is a measure of the happiness that can be had when a moment is shared, so were there moments in the past.

What happened to the men I went fishing with up on the North Thompson, the men I wandered into the mountains with? Such trips were spiritual as much as they were physical. I remember standing up to my knees in snow on a plateau west of Merritt with my Lee-Enfield in my gloved hand. Somewhere to the south of me, perhaps a hundred yards off, my friend Jerry was circling down on a moose whose afternoon sleep we had disturbed. I knew the moose would make his run toward me and I stood there under a young fir tree waiting for it to come as soon as Jerry made his move below.

The hunt was for winter meat, but it was more than that. We were two young men out hunting in the cold morning of October. We were companions, having shared our coffee with each other and shared as well the common stories of our daily lives. A friend, yes, and yet gone like snow is gone from a March meadow. The moose came as I thought it would. I listened to its huge body break through the brush of young alders grown up in the clear-cut we were hunting in and I lifted my rifle and waited for it. When the moose burst through the cover I saw a huge bull with a great rack of horns, the swing of drool from its black lips, and its huge eye catching mine as it took its giant steps through the open space before me. I remember standing still with my rifle raised, its sight on a heart shot I knew I would have as the moose passed by me. I didn't shoot. I simply stood there in awe at the beauty of the great creature of the forest. It passed by me in long strides and disappeared again into the alders to my right.

Jerry never understood my not shooting it and there was no explaining why I didn't. I'd killed before and would kill again. Yet our friendship didn't suffer because of it. There was only a kind of questioning of me in Jerry's eyes. He didn't understand. And where is he now? Those years passed. He stayed in the mills and I went on to Vancouver and my life as a writer. The loss of a friend, yes, but sometimes the loss is one made up of time and not intent. We were friends back then, though had you asked me if we were I wouldn't have known what to say beyond shrugging my shoulders. We drank together, partied together, lusted after each other's wives, and spent many hours playing cards and laughing together. The wisp of my breath as it slips from my lips is as fragile as the memory it brings to me. Laughter, yes, there was that, and friendship too.

The garbage truck had come and gone by the time I got home, the two vodka bottles buried under trash at the dump. I would have recycled them, but I couldn't have borne looking at them in the blue box for a week before the truck came by. I know I will find other bottles in the garden. I feel like the Consul in Malcolm Lowry's *Under the Volcano,* wandering through his garden in Mexico searching for a hidden bottle of gin. I know Lowry's garden well. I have lived there. I remember Lowry's words as he stood in Mexico, drunk and staring at a sign in the middle of his overgrown Mexican garden.

¿LE GUSTA ESTE JARDIN?
¿QUE ES SOYO?
¡EVITE QUE SUS HIJOS LO DESTRUYAN!

The Consul stared back at the black words on the sign without moving. You like this garden? Why is it yours? We evict those who destroy! Simple words, simple and terrible words, words which one took to the very bottom of one's being, words which, perhaps a final judgement on one, were nevertheless unproductive of any emotion whatsoever, unless a kind of colourless cold, a white agony, an agony chill as that iced mescal drunk in the Hotel Canada on the morning of Yvonne's departure.

I watch a brown creeper climb the bark of a cedar, his small, curved beak slipping into the secret places where insects sleep. The tiny bird with his tail straight up like a wren's pecks and chirps at me, someone he knows in this little forest of his. The creatures of this world go on about their lives. Other than a glance or two the brown creeper ignores me as he searches out his late lunch in the bark of a cedar tree.

I stare at the sheets of slate in the truck and imagine the path I am going to build. It will be an irregular walkway along the narrow part of my lot on the west side of the house. It is heavily shaded there by a cedar and an apple tree that was allowed to grow too high for any remedial pruning to be done. In front the way is partly blocked by a bigleaf maple on one side and a holly tree on the other. A few sword ferns line the side closest to the house.

This passageway where I usually pile fallen branches and excess leaves and cuttings is perhaps twelve yards long and four yards wide. It is just right for hosta, ferns, and other shade-tolerant plants. The path I build will pass through just off-center. The cedar's roots in the middle show like knuckles and I will scrape the dirt away from them and lay shale between their splayed fingers. A person walking there will have to look down to guide their feet and will see the ferns and other plants. A larger stone near the middle will allow them to stop and look up and see the natural arch the holly forms. That and the moss-covered trunk of the bigleaf maple with its invasive skirt of ivy that grows inexorably upward.

The maple is old and has been topped several times. Suckers push out from the trunk, all of them dead white molars sheathed in scabrous bark and all of them hiding sleeping beetles and insects. It is a feast for pileated, hairy, and downy woodpeckers as well as the red-shafted flickers. The pileated woodpeckers always startle me when they come in winter to feast on apples or to break chunks of bark off the maple. They are a rare bird and their annual visitation to my garden is an avian blessing. I take this thought to the house for dinner and a quiet night.

❧

It's three in the morning and I'm a little stiff. I get out of bed unable to sleep. I stretch and take my glass of water outside, the cats following me down the lawn to the fishpond, deep night and a distant siren, then silence again, a breeze in the apple trees, the firs shifting their branches.

Quiet, a sip of water, the cats sitting on stepping-stones as they gaze into the ferns and bamboo, wondering what I'm doing outside at this time of their night. Their pointed ears twitch and quiver at sounds I can't hear, a rat in the ivy, a screech owl fluffing his wings, a raccoon's slow walk. I sit in silence, uneasy, worried about the anger I feel in every memory. I am crowded by stories too many to put down.

In the first few summers after my father's murder I stayed with my mother in Vernon. She told me the story of her life through the dreary mask of rye whiskey and television test patterns. I was there for the fruit harvest, picking for a month or two to make a winter stake. My mother still lived in the family home. Drunk, lonely, and depressed, we both sat late into the nights as she talked. It was all a long monologue, ramblings, anecdotes, and snatches from her past. Many of her stories were more than a son should hear, more than I should have known. Those late-summer nights were a lengthy, confused confession.

She left out only one thing, the sexual abuse she suffered from her father. It had gone on from before she could talk until she was sixteen and met my father. I had to learn about the abuse after her death. It changed everything I knew. It gave a new shape to her life and to the family's lives and every story she had told before became something a little bent. Her stories were like circus mirrors, every narrative both reality and illusion. There were strange twists I saw that turned everything she'd said into something sad and lonely.

When she was giddy and drunk, she took on a southern belle voice, a strange mix of Virginia and Alberta, an accent out of the antebellum South with a Canadian, midwestern, prairie drawl thrown in. She said more than once to me: *Titsworth! No wonder all of us girls married young. A name like that!* Her voice was slurred, provocative, and sensual. She'd sit on the couch and pull her dress up to her thighs and, scissoring her legs, say like a Mississippi coquette, *Daddy always called me Hairless Joe. He loved my legs.* She'd wait a long moment and then peer at me out of her sixty-five-year-old eyes. Drunk on the whiskies she called Zem-Zems, she still thought she had the power to charm a man, any man. She'd say to me, *It was Daddy loved me best. He loved me best of all. I was his Dixie.* Then she'd break into one of what she called nigger songs, "Old Black Joe," "Swanee River," and the rest. They were songs she'd sung to me and my brothers when we were little boys. She'd learned them from her father, who had brought his arrogance, intolerance, and racism with him from Kentucky. When she was a little girl her father had hauled her off a streetcar in Nelson when he saw a black man riding on it. He forbade anyone in his family to ever ride the streetcars again. *Can you imagine?* she'd say. I think I've spent my life inside her question.

The salamanders and frogs keep close to my pond over the year, but now, in this almost-but-not rainy season, the tree frogs are spread around the garden, their early-spring croaks tiny, hoarse calls in the early morning and evening. They are as small as my thumbnail, some a livid green the color of rich moss, with parallel stripes following the contours of the body from the eyes to the tip where the frog's tail was. Each frog carries its own tattooed dream on its flesh. One I found was a pale gray with an undercurrent of rose beneath its skin. Its small breathing was a blessing in my hand, its song a wilting in the late afternoon by the pond where a red-backed salamander waited on a stone. Without rain this place of shade and light with its mosses and ferns will be silent. Frogs cry loudest in the wet world, not the dry.

I get up early and look out the window. It is snowing this late February day. Yellow crocuses are bright suns in their cups of snow, the *Pieris japonica* with its pendant ivory blossoms as much falling snow as flower. A junco leaves his delicate tracks, stops and looks back as if what he has left is signature to some wrong spring, then cocks his black head as if imagining the tracks his wings might leave in air. I see his path in the falling snow, that disturbance of snow petals, that swirl of flakes his wings leave behind. The junco moves on toward the fallen seeds scattered from the feeder. They lie on the new snow like a fetal alphabet, a code only the snow can decipher.

How far the cold travels! I can taste the far reaches of the northern mountains; I can smell in it the salt of the Bering Sea, the brine of ocean drying on dark stones, a Steller's jay hooting at the morning as he practices his imitation of the snowy owl who almost killed him on the breeding grounds at the edge of the tundra.

Last night the stars burned high and sharp. I stood on the deck before bed in my monk's robe and watched a high plane drift across the night sky. Another day sober. Orion was tipped back on his heels as he stared at Venus and Jupiter, both brighter than I've seen them for a while. Two wandering gods, and Orion watching as he falls toward the southwest. The neighborhood was quiet except for the steady drums from the Houses on Top Reserve. The far drums and the men's voices came faint across the land. What stars did they sing to and are they the same stars I watched? What names are theirs? Their drums at night are the far joy of a people singing. I love the high chanting of the men as they cry their hearts.

And then the stars went out and the moon became only a glow as the clouds moved down from the north and I went back to a winter sleep.

Three days and the snow is gone. While the snowdrops and crocuses seem to have loved this late blessing, the bees didn't. They had spent the past week or so busy in the throats of the viburnum, *Pieris japonica,* and heather. Now these solitary bees are hunched down, hiding and waiting for the wind to turn the weather around.

The first bee this year was the blue orchard bee. It's also called the mason bee because she seals her egg in a tunnel with a plug made from clay or mud. She's a native bee here and her arrival is a true sign of spring. She's a friendly little lady and so busy with gathering food she has no time to bother me. I've had them rest on the back of my hand and flare their wings as they lay their thorax flat on the warmth of my bare skin. I love it when the great bumblebee mothers appear from their tunnels, their bodies impossibly large for such small wings. The heather's white blossoms wait for their foraging just as I have waited for the earth to return from under its carapace of crystals so I can turn it over and mix in the compost and manure I have piled in the bin behind the house.

The solitary bees cruise the garden beds until the bare earth cools them and they come to the stucco wall by the deck to warm themselves. The heat from the wall eases through the plates of their bodies until, warm again, they drop into the air and begin anew their cruising for nectar. In the brooding caves under the earth bumblebees are being born and these mothers of spring have off-spring to feed.

This three-day snow was evanescent, a transitory glory, a passing that illumined the garden, making the limbs of the contorted hazel a maze only a thread could lead me through. As the snow settled it began its return to the dark earth. When I placed my ear to the garden's white skin, I could hear it singing as it turned itself back into water, a faint crickle of sound. A tree frog croaked from under the hanging leaf of the bamboo by the pond. This was not winter, this was the pearl necklace on the throat of my lover, the sound it makes as it swings above her breasts. A tree frog sang his oldest song above the snow of early spring. As he did, bushtits flittered among the shrubs and trees. What great pleasure they take in each other's company. They are a friendly gang who play forsythia tag. I watch three of them chase another who is carrying a yellow petal in her tiny black beak. When she drops it one of the others picks it out of the air and the chase resumes again, the petal changing beaks every few seconds. They are a tumbled gathering of brown sparks in the air.

When Lorna and I first moved here the lot on the narrow western side of the house was a pile of rotting stove wood, a sullen hive of sow bugs, wet wood termites, slugs, and every other pest I could imagine. The pile leaned against the skirt of siding below the stucco and had rotted it away. It took two weeks to dig through the pile. I salvaged the top wood that still had resins fit to burn in our fireplace and piled the few pieces behind the house. The rest was a punky, damp mess. I hauled four pickup loads to the recycling dump and the rest I dug into the soil.

Now, nine years later, I'm digging the soil again to make a fern and hosta bed for my shade garden. The old wood has turned into an almost-earth, the fir and hemlock chunks are a kind of rough, clumpy dust mixed with glacial till. The soil is acidic and will do well for rhododendrons and ferns. Still, I must add some good earth for balance.

The earth is finally turned and I've transplanted foxgloves from various parts of the garden where I seeded them a year and a half ago. Their flowers vary from a dark pink through pale yellow to white. The spots on their petals are as mysterious as their name until you imagine the tracks foxes leave in sand or snow and then you understand. The gloves of foxes, what a metaphor to start this late-month day where my reward for digging for a week is to place in the ground the coming summer's glory.

In the garden today I find the squirrel. She rests upon my palm, her small claws like limp black hooks not grasping. We have spent three years arguing over bird feeders, sunflower seeds, clouds, rain, sun, the color of a moss, a stone ill-placed, indeed almost everything I can think of. There is no fear in her eye as she looks at me, only an odd, questioning look, querulous and still. She stares up at me as if to find some kind of understanding, not of death, but why I hold her. I am not trying to transfer to her my human attributes. Squirrels are squirrels and humans are humans. Yet creature speaks to creature in gesture, look, and sound. I'd be a fool not to know that. I may not speak this squirrel's language, may not know her words, yet we have known each other over the years. She has been my troubling com-panion of the garden for a long time, alone or with her spring con-sort who comes for love then leaves. I saw him a week ago, his sprightly urgency, his arched tail quivering. Each year, after he's gone, she brings to the garden her two or three surviving babies who grow if they're lucky and the crows and cars don't get them. By sum-mer the one or two left who have lived wander off to find their own territory.

Only she has stayed to argue with me. She has scolded me daily, her tail jerking in an arch above her back as she lectured me on deco-rum, my abrupt entrances and exits, my preoccupations with seeds, baths, and bird feeders. Now she lies on my palm, not confused, but wondering at our close conjunction.

I have seen enough of the dead and dying in this life to know she has only a few moments left, an hour at most to live. She is not the hawk who died in my hands a few years ago after flying into her own terrible reflection in the living-room window. The hawk's death-scream was a cry against the falling light. Her talons gripped my index finger at her death as if she could take my life with her when she died. The same scream is not in this soft creature I hold, this squirrel who has been struck by a car on the street and who I found in my driveway. Her crawl across the pavement to the fallen needles of the redwood must have seemed an impossible journey to one so quick. To move so slowly now. What a thin trail of blood.

I can feel the plump swelling of her belly and I know she is pregnant. I do not try to probe her sides. The swell of warmth is enough and there is nothing I can do. Thinking has never been a stay against the dark. She is only dying as all things of this earth must, her split rabbit-lip curled above her long yellow front teeth. She has no tail today, that plume that balanced her like a wing as she leapt from fence to tree. There is only a bloody stump. What rests in her womb will die with her this sunny morning.

There was a time when I would hasten such a death with heel or club, knife or gun, but not any more. Now I'm unsure whose suffering I was trying to relieve when I was young, the animal's or mine. I think I was merely trying to be a man. Today all I can do is hold her for these few brief moments, whisper a whisper, a hush that might be solace to her and then carry her to the sanctuary she was trying to reach when I found her.

I leave her tucked under a mound of redwood needles beneath a rhododendron. She seems relieved, her bright eye blinking, happy I have left her to the privacy of her death.

As I walk away I wonder what it is that makes me argue with the ordinary appearances of animals or birds. What makes me irritable at the presence of starlings as they crowd the suet block, stopping the other birds from getting their due? What makes me feel I must argue daily with a squirrel who now lies dying in a dark of pale red needles? What idea of order do I have that it must exclude a starling, crow, or squirrel? How human I am sometimes, how petty. There is an absence in the garden today no creature fills. It hurts me.

Another day and the birds are singing. A winter wren flits from bush to shrub to tree, his barred tail flicking up and down. His trill is loud among the leafless branches. I've not seen his mate but am sure his clear, high song will bring one from another yard down the block. If not, his cries will turn into a scolding prattle and he will disappear to search her out in some patch of brush, some bit of woodland nearby.

An hour of meditation by our bamboo on the cedar stool by the pond. The garden has started to heal my body. I never knew how tired I was until I began this slow dance. The first moment of injury does not bring pain, only shock and numbness. The forty-five years of drinking have been a cold detachment. Feeling has come back on tentative feet. I swing my head at times with the quiet pain of it. I feel at times like a clear-cut on a hillside, a damaged piece of ground that will never be itself again. The hurt body gives the bones and flesh a message. I listen to it, each day another day of slowly returning to myself. Like my body and like my spirit, the garden goes on without me.

PLANTS

Deer fern – *Blechnum spicant*
Evergreen huckleberry – *Vaccinium ovatum*
Heather – *Ericaceae*
Japanese andromeda – *Pieris japonica*
Licorice fern – *Polypodium glycyrrhiza*
Maidenhair fern – *Adiantum pedatum*
Purple foxglove – *Digitalis purpurea* (var.) *alba*
Red alder – *Alnus rubra*
Viburnum – *Viburnum tinus*
Western hemlock – *Tsuga heterophylla*
Western red cedar – *Thuja plicata*

ANIMALS, BIRDS, AND INSECTS

Banana slug – *Ariolimax columbianus*
Blue orchard bee – *Osmia lignaria*
Brown creeper – *Certhia americana*
Bushtit – *Psaltriparus minimus*
European starling – *Sturnus vulgaris*
House mouse – *Mus musculus*
Pacific tree frog – *Hyla regilla*
Screech owl – *Otus asio*
Snowy owl – *Nyctea scandiaca*
Steller's jay – *Cyanocitta stelleri*
Striped chorus frog – *Pseudacris triseriata*
Western red-backed salamander – *Plethodon vehiculum*
Whistling swan – *Olor columbianus*
White-tailed ptarmigan – *Lagopus leucurus*
Winter wren – *Troglodytes troglodytes*

3

For winter's rains and ruins are over,
And all the season of snows and sins;
The days dividing lover and lover,
The light that loses, the night that wins;
And time remembered is grief forgotten,
And frosts are slain and flowers begotten,
And in green underwood and cover
Blossom by blossom the spring begins.
  — ALGERNON CHARLES SWINBURNE,
    "ATALANTA IN CALYDON"

FROM MY SKYLIGHT I can see the top of the Douglas firs and the paper birches. The birches are pushing down their fledgling catkins, still closed, but another week will see them dangling in full bloom from the black branches. The contorted hazelnut has already opened with its male catkins, and the bumblebees of spring gather the floury pollen. The magenta blossoms of the hazelnut are very tiny and I have to look closely to see them at all. Just down the fence the forsythia is, at last, in full bloom. It is a yellow breathing beyond the apple tree whose flower buds have begun to show pink tips to the sun.

Spring happened overnight. Three days ago I stood by the pond at sundown and I could feel it arrive, sudden as the breath taken after a deep dive when the mouth first opens above water. Spring was a taste in the air, a smell, a weight as light as a child's hand. I feel the flush that wasn't there before; a touch as if a brush of fine silk slipped across my flesh; a touch so sharp it was almost not there.

Fifty years ago I drove into the spring night. I was a teenage boy, just sixteen years old. I had dropped my girlfriend, my future wife, off at her front door. We had spent much of the Friday night pulled off the road in a quiet cul-de-sac out on the BX Ranch. The spot was a quiet one a hundred feet off the road near a small creek with willows and poplar trees obscuring the car. There we had stripped off our clothes and made love for hours in the spring night.

I remember our bodies. How young we were! How beautiful that night and all the nights of my sixteenth year were. Images stay with me. I remember her body in the dim light and the way I touched her and the way she touched me. It is so strange to think how immortal we were then and how sweet that night was that we spent together. Was I happy? I think so. Such a night as that one in spring was the kind of happiness only young people can know.

It was so long ago. I remember stopping the car at the head of the driveway that led down to my home where my father and mother slept and my brothers and sisters slept. I remember sitting there with my hands on the wheel and my foot touching with the gas pedal as I played with the engine, the quiet roar of the eight cylinders of my father's hardtop Chevrolet. What did I think? I don't remember thinking. That boy is far away from me, yet I know he was perfectly lost in the quiet sensual pleasure of his flesh. He was almost a man, that boy.

❧

I stare at the garden through the glass sheet of the back door, my addiction a creature awake on its wet paws. It never sleeps. Quiet and cunning, it watches my every move for a sign of weakness. I look out at the apple tree and think, *if* I could choose to be sick, then I could choose not to be. It would be like choosing diabetes or choosing cancer and experiencing it with a kind of perverse pleasure. As if that were possible, as if a man could ask for a disease and then unask it at will.

At the heart of an alcoholic is a drink he can never find. It is the first of the last of many thousands of drinks, each one almost, but never quite, as beautiful as that first one he had as a boy when his world spun away. Every addict I know speaks of that first knowing when they met the monster and found it their closest friend, their sweetest lover. I was twelve and had filled a water glass with a mix of rum, rye whiskey, gin, and vodka. I'd raided my father's liquor supply while they were out on New Year's Eve. The sudden rush before I passed out on the kitchen floor was indescribable. I've never forgotten the feeling and never achieved the same bliss since.

Malcolm Lowry, who died of alcoholism, called addiction "a colourless cold, a white agony," and that is as close as anyone I know has come to describing what a drink is to an alcoholic. "A white agony," yes, and walking outside onto the deck into the soft touch of spring I know that the *feeling* I have of spring this year is something I haven't had in a long time. I feel its thin touch in the air. My skin shivers as if at the sound of a knife sliding across a whetstone, that same hiss making of an edge in me. Change. I feel it.

Feeling before feeling is what makes you turn and lift your head and smell the wind. Something new is in the air you breathe. Spring turns the body out of darkness into light. It takes the past away and leaves you breathing in the present. The earth begins to grow fruit long-buried in the dark. Water thickens to sap in the cambium layers under the bark of trees and buds begin to swell.

Night passes and the dawning sun betrays the rain I wish for. Light flutters on the volcanic folds of snowbound Mount Baker. Whistling swans pass over and Canada geese, all of them calling the north to come and whisper them into the long flight to the breeding grounds of the Arctic. Winter loosens on the mountains and ice and snow recede.

The sun is broken among scattered clouds; there will be no rain again today. The drought looms larger every morning. February is gone and this next month will not succor the season. March's rains, if they come at all, will come lightly without the drench of winter. The summer lies ahead. It will be dry and the garden will suffer.

Months away, I say, with the hope and optimism of a gardener. This is a good day to move the woodpile. The ax has been out there all winter, its blush of rust a testament to my neglect. Two or three times a week I've noticed it and meant to move it to the shed, but there always seemed to be something more urgent to do. I put it with the other ax and hatchet in the shed, promising myself I will clean all three next week. Rust lives on steel out here. An implement left out a few days grows rot like measles on the cheeks of a sick child.

The woodpile I am making is a history of my time here. As I load each wheelbarrow I can count the trees I've taken out of the yard in the past ten years. It's like digging down through layers of my life, all the trees I've reduced to sixteen-inch logs. Three small cedars, four firs, a birch, six Lombardy poplars, two plum trees, a diseased cherry tree, and the remnants of the bifurcated top of the redwood tree that blew down twice in windstorms. Each chunk I pick up is a story. I have handled each of them at least twice, and now three times.

The first wood I ever stacked was in Nelson. I helped my two brothers stack the wood under the long veranda of the old house on Fall Street. Being small, I probably only carried one piece at a time, yet I can still smell that sawdust and pitch as I stack this new wood fifty-seven years later. Smell stays with me. The faint, acrid bite of pitch hurls me back into the past.

The Kootenays in winter are a dark place buried in the south-eastern heel of British Columbia. The mountains are places of shadow, deep snows, and little sun. The valley is narrow, just a cut in the stone of the Selkirk and Purcell Mountains where they jut up against the Rockies to the east. In the valley Lake Kootenay is a long blue wand, its water sliding south into the Columbia River. My brother Dick threw one of those pieces of wood at me and missed, hitting my mother in the belly. She was five months' pregnant and miscarried that afternoon in the kitchen, helped by an alcoholic friend whose husband was also away in Europe. It was my father's child, I think, though it could have been her lover's. I remember her shoulders curved, her head pitched forward by the blow.

After the war we moved from the Kootenays to the Okanagan because of my father's silicosis. That valley for me will always be the smell of the sun as it rides through hanging dust. The town itself was nestled in desert country and the wood we burned was the brilliant white of Jack and lodgepole pine, the pale pink of ponderosa pine, and the occasional mix of hemlock or fir, whatever was available, whatever was cheap at the time.

My mother cooked on a woodstove. The house was warmed by wood fire. There was a Queen Heater in the bare living room, but it was never lit unless there was company and I don't remember company for those first couple of years after my father came back from Europe. There was no furniture except in the kitchen with its wooden table and four chairs. There were five of us back then and one of us, me as I was smallest, sat on a wooden stool. The stove there went out only when my mother and father went to bed. It was relit in the early morning by my father and woe betide which one of us it might have been who had forgotten to top up the kindling and the wood box.

Each summer truckloads of wood were dumped in the back of the yard, sometimes pine boxwood, trimmer ends from the box factory over by the railway yards and other times fir and hemlock rounds my father split. My brothers and I toiled at the job of stacking it, or at least we thought we toiled. Likely we just complained. But there was always the dust and the smell of the sun in it. It choked my nose and throat, a pure cloud of heat and dust entering me. I would stand for hours with a hatchet splitting wood for kindling. The thin wands of pine sprinkled away from the blade in high clear tones, a music I loved as my hands turned a block into the morning fires to come.

The kitchen stove was our refuge from winter. The bathroom froze during the cold months. My father drained the pipes and baths were taken in a galvanized tub in the middle of the kitchen floor. The stove was the heart of the house. It was where we could always find our mother. She worked there from seven in the morning until nine at night and sometimes later if there were fruit or vegetables to put up in the jars that were stored in the earthen root cellar. She ironed and mended there, made bread and biscuits, simmered stew, and began the new marriage with my father after the long hiatus of the war.

My father wanted more children. I think now it was because he didn't know the ones he had. If he was a stranger to us, so were we to him. His joy when the next child was born, a daughter, was a wonder to see. He came home from the hospital up on Mission Hill and woke the three of us. He whooped and danced around the room. We danced with him, but we were afraid. Who was this new child coming into our home? Did we belong to this new family?

The root cellar under the house was the home of mice, rats, black widow spiders, recluse spiders, huge, solitary wolf spiders, termites, beetles, blacksnakes, and striped garter snakes, all living in a place of both fascination and terror. I was sometimes thrown or forced down the steep stairs to the cellar by my brothers. I'd be imprisoned for what seemed hours, the trapdoor sealed by the end of the wood box, until my mother rescued me from the cobwebs and the pale, trailing arms of the sprouting potatoes as they reached out to hold me forever in their terrible, blind embrace. The potatoes had a fetid odor, part rot and part the smell of earth. It clotted my nostrils like sickness did. It was what white smells like when it's left too long away from the sun, a smell of inchoate mould, something that grows in tendrils and crawling branches, things without ears or eyes.

The darkness of the root cellar was a reflection of a darkness that lived like a silent mouth in the little town. I spent days and nights running away or toward whatever nightmare I could find. I loved the nights when I was a boy. I was always the last to return home to the shouts of my father or mother. *Time to come home!* was both a plea and a demand I ignored as long as possible. The bedroom I shared with Johnny was over the back porch roof and I would often slip out alone at night to wander the streets. I ranged like a small questing animal for hours through the back alleys. I loved to look through windows at families, but most of all I loved to head downtown to Main Street, where the nightly drama of the loners and drunks played out their lonely song.

One Saturday night when I was seven or eight years old, I saw an Indian woman in the vacant lot behind the fire hall. A man grabbed her arm and pulled her into the shadows where the back of the hotel met the back of the fire hall. The woman staggered against him and he put his arm around her shoulder with his hand under her armpit to hold her up. Her red shoes glinted dully in the light streaming from the back door of the hotel. Another man, heavy with sweat across his forehead, walked over to the fire hall and, reaching up, smacked the Exit light with a beer bottle. The alley and lot were dark now but for the glow of the hotel light bound in heavy wire, a faint rose that reached weakly through the thick air. The woman stuttered something to the man who was holding her up and he laughed.

A third man, his friend, was behind them and he leaned down and put his arm under her skirt. Standing, the skirt of her dress hanging from his arm, he pushed his hand between her legs and she almost fell. The man stiffened his arm and lifted her off the gravel. Her feet flailed in the air and then he put her down again.

I remember her begging them for the drink they'd promised. Her voice was slurred and slow as if she was talking out of some deep pool in a lake where the water was dimmest. Her head fell forward and the man behind her pulled her hair so her head rose back into the darkness. The men laughed as they walked her deeper into the lot. The man who broke the light moved after them heavily, his boots crunching the coarse gravel. I squatted among scattered stones and broken glass, one hand touching the wall, my fingers spread there ready to push me outward into a run that would save me if they found out I was watching. It was eleven o'clock, long after my bedtime.

I slipped along the bricks of the hotel wall and then crossed the alley and faded into the shadows where trucks and cars were parked. Somewhere out on Main Street, a fight had started and I could hear the yelling and a woman's voice high and shrill. Bottles broke. There were more shouts and the sound of feet running in the night.

The man had taken the woman to a dark place where a wall held back the light from the far street. She was very drunk and pushed at him as if her hands could make him stop. The man pulled hard at the front of her dress. It ripped open in a panel of red cotton and came away in his hands. The third man stood aside, drinking his beer.

I lay under a rusted Dodge truck. I could see the men, but only up to their shoulders. Their faces were cut off by the running board. It was as if they had no heads and were only bodies in the night.

The woman was draped facedown over the fender of a car, one man holding her arms above her head while the second pulled her dress to the side. As he banged against her, he struck her back with his fist. It was a striking without intent as if he was striking meat.

The third man said nothing. There was nothing in his body. It was impassive, as if he were a piece of machinery gone wrong, something that needed fixing. The woman was crying. I could see her face bent to the fender, her one eye open and staring at me. It was bleeding, but now I know it wasn't blood she saw.

I pulled myself deeper into the shadow of the truck. I could tell by the man's legs that he was finished what he was doing. The legs stepped away and then his friend pulled her off the car, dragged her across the gravel, and propped her against the running board of the truck where I was hiding. All I could see were her naked legs kneeling and her two red shoes, torn and scuffed, the high heels worn down. I reached out and touched her ankle with my fingers. Her skin was warm.

I didn't know what he did to her. I couldn't see. When he was done her body fell onto the dirt and I could see the feet of two men going away. The third man's boots were still there, the heavy man, the one who put out the light. As he stepped toward the woman I rolled over and out from under the other side of the truck. My shoulder was stained with grease and oil.

I ducked down and scuttled beside the cars, checking to see if they were unlocked. Sometimes the men who'd gone into the Allison Hotel left them unlocked and sometimes there was money to be stolen from a forgotten purse, something a woman had left behind as she scrambled out of the truck following a man.

Behind me was a faint sound, but exactly what I didn't know. As I checked each car door, I thought of the woman, the way she had seemed to fall out of the air slowly as if there was nothing in her to hold her up, no bones, no muscles, nothing at all.

I ran home and climbed up on the cracked rail of the porch, shinnied up the corner post onto the porch roof, and pulled myself through my open window into the room I shared with Johnny. He wasn't asleep. He just stared up at the ceiling as if whatever he saw there would save him from the night. My mother had bathed him again, the bathroom door closed. I got out of my clothes and crawled into bed. The memory of the woman being raped was yet another secret I had to keep. I stored it away just as I had stored other things I'd seen and done. That I would someday write about them would have made no sense to me then.

Days like this live too much in my mind. It is like the memory of fishing trips my father took us on after the war. At my mother's urging he tried to reconnect with us boys after the years of being away. Those few summers after the war were the happiest of my young life in Vernon. July weekends my father would borrow a jeep from the shop where he worked and drive us into the hills. Aberdeen and Haddow Lakes. Of all my memories, the fishing trips to the lakes were the happiest. They seem far away and the boy I was seems another person. When I try to remember it, it's as if I'm standing on the Aberdeen Lake dam and looking down at my father and his three sons.

The boy I was stands in the shadows of the trees and watches his father and brothers fish in the outfall from Aberdeen Lake. Johnny is standing as close to his father as he can and Dick is on the other bank. The three of them flick their rods at the same time. The Royal Coachmen flutter through the air like small, immaculate butterflies and drop on the moil of water. The flies dance on the foaming rivulets. Their red wings toss and twist. They seem tormented insects trapped by the rush of water. There is a sudden flash as if a silver knife has rushed up from the dark waters and Dick's rod bends sharply. He braces himself delicately, one foot on a clump of pale green grass, the other on a flat stone that juts from the bank. He sets the fly in the fish's dark mouth and begins to play it down the creek. His father yells something to him, but he can't hear it over the noise of the falls. His whole body is concentrated on the fish he is playing into the great pool where the water circles in a huge eddy before dropping into the tumble of the creek.

Johnny casts again and then again and then he too gets a strike and begins to play the same moves as his brother. The tip of his rod bobs and bends as he keeps his line tense so the fish can't slip the fly. Suddenly his fish lifts into the air and thrashes there for a brief silver moment in the sun before falling back into the waters. The fish still holds and Johnny has him now at the edge of the pool. The two brothers play out the rainbows. Their father watches them. He has put down his rod and is lighting the stub of a cigar. Smoke wreathes his face. He is smiling. It is a day as good as any day can be. The smoke slips through the air like a shining bit of mist and then it is gone. The boys at the pool below have landed their fish. A finger hooked in the gills, they lift their fish to their father and he nods at them as he would nod at something impossibly beautiful. The turn of his red head is both grace and blessing.

The boy in the trees stares at his father on the far bank of the creek. He studies him in the way he would study someone he's never seen before, someone he doesn't fully understand or comprehend.

His father is bathed in light. It glints on the red hair and flickers among the hairs on the wrists and arms. It slips in and around his loose shirt like it was alive. Mist from the creek eddies around his feet. His father's eyes that were staring at his sons are now lifted up to the horizon of trees that cuts the edge of blue sky. He is seeing something and the boy turns his gaze to where his father's is and sees a bald eagle circling above the lake. It is a young eagle because its head has not yet turned silver. Streaks of bronze spread in ripples out to the tips of the wings. Every few moments it turns its head sideways to cast an eye at the lakeshore. It circles and circles there above the boy's father.

The boy thinks his father has created the eagle. It is as if his father imagined it and then the bird was there. He knows it is a crazy kind of thought, one that he can't tell anybody. But it is true. His father has imagined the bird into the air. As he thinks this his father turns his head and stares straight at him. He knows his father can't really see him, he is too deep in the shadowed trees. Then he understands. His father knows he's there even if he can't see him. He has felt his son in his hiding.

The boy looks where his father's eyes are and lock on his. They hold each other there and for a moment they are one seeing. His father lifts his hand then and holds it out to this boy in the forest. The hand is held palm out. It is a kind of wave, a kind of benediction. When his father's hand drops, the boy steps out of the darkness and into the day. His brothers are once again casting their lines into the creek. They are wholly there by those tumbling waters. The boy walks slowly up the trail to the dam and then across it and down to where his father is waiting for him.

His father puts his huge arm around his son's shoulders. It rests there for a moment. The boy can smell the cigar smoke and the sweat of his father's arm. There is another smell. It is like his own smell but there is a deepness to it, a thickness. It is something he will have someday but not yet. He is still a child. He breathes it in. It is father-smell. His small arm is around his father's waist, one finger hooked into his father's belt. At their feet, in the wooden box lined with cool green grass, there are twenty fat trout. They don't look at them. They are watching the boy's brothers as they fish. Neither has caught anything for a while, but they are persistent in their desire. The boy looks up at his father's face, the red hair, the whiskers, and for a moment the eagle circles above in a wheeling bronze ring that is a part of the sun.

It is night now and the sky is alive with stars. They shine through the holes in the world's tent. They shine there as if flung from a hand that loved light so much it could not keep it. The lake flickers with their light. Somewhere by the far shore a loon utters a cry. It stutters across the water to the sandy beach and the fire that burns there.

For a moment I step down from the dam and enter their world. I lean against a single spruce tree and stare at this man with his three sons. They are gathered around their fire. It is a flutter of rubies. My father squats on his haunches and holds a frying pan over the dense heat. In the pan are four fat rainbow trout, caught only a few hours ago. They have been dredged in flour and now seethe in melted butter. A battered steel pot is wedged into the edge of the coals. Coffee purls in the blackened steel. The smell drifts over the sand and wreathes my face.

I would join them if I could, but I know that if I tried they would vanish. The only clues I would find to their being here would be blackened stones, wet ashes, and the tracks of a crow in sand.

My father grunts and shifts his heavy legs a bit. He pulls the pan out of the coals and turns each trout, then returns the pan to the fire. His three sons sit around him. They are watching him cook the fish. Their eyes are intent upon his huge hand as it shakes the pan a bit. The fish slip in the butter. They are almost done. The white flesh of new potatoes gleam in a pot beside the coffee. No one says anything. There is no story now, no fight, no cry, no laughter. The smell of frying fish has filled them with hunger. Each boy has a tin plate and a knife and fork clutched in his hands. The man watches as the fish bellies curl open to reveal the red flesh inside.

The brothers say nothing. How to fry a fish will be stored in their minds along with every other thing their father does. They don't know that what knowledge they will have of their father will be spare and made up only of small fragments such as this.

He pulls out the pan, rests it on the log beside him, and takes the plate from each boy. He places a fried trout and chunks of potato on each one and the boys smear butter on the potatoes and then begin to eat.

He sits back on the log and balances his plate on his knees.

He takes his knife and slits the trout's back, works the blade between the bones and the flesh and strips the fillet. The bones come away. They are a filigree of lace. He holds them a moment in the firelight, then drops them on the coals. A small puff of sparks swirl into the night. He spears a chunk of potato and puts it in his mouth. The boys watch each move he makes and do the same.

From where I stand beside the spruce tree he looks content to be there and that is enough. His sons, I know, are growing up. They verge on their lives. These are the last of the creeks and lakes and meadows, these are the last years of their boyhood.

In twenty years, my father will die. A bullet from a Winchester 30-30 will enter his chest and blow his heart to pieces. He will fall from the top of a parts bin at the shop where he works. He will fall ten feet into his own blood and lie on a concrete floor. There will be no breath in him then. Whoever he is will go away where no one can find him.

I stare at him intently.

This is my father. I can't hear the sound of his voice. I remember when his voice left me and it was as if someone had struck me in the belly. How old was I when sound left me?

My brothers and I eat our fish as if they are the first meals of our lives. We smear our plates with hunks of bread our mother made that morning. We stuff it into our mouths. Later our father will lean back against the log and tell his spare stories.

It is long ago now in another time, another place.

The loon's cry rides like a blacksnake on the silver waters.

Soon I will leave them there by their fire. They are full now, the hunger gone. Tomorrow they will get up into the squint of dawn and pull on their clothes. Their father will start the fire and heat up the coffee left over from the night before. He will make the boys steaming cups of cocoa and they will have fried fish again and then they will go back to the creek to fish through the morning before getting in the jeep and returning home where their mother waits for them. It is one of the last times they will camp with their father.

I stand by the spruce tree and watch them until they climb into their blankets. The last to sleep is their father.

He will stare long into the stars before his eyes finally close.

Not even the loon can wake him now.

I've gone far from the garden this morning, wandering off into broken things. This afternoon I stood up, stretched, my back aching, and saw my mother on her hands and knees disappearing into a bed of ferns. I wasn't afraid, only startled at her appearance seven years after her burial by my father's grave on the grassy slope under the trees in the Vernon Cemetery. She should be in the black walnut coffin I made for her ashes. She should be at rest.

Her spirit visits are unpredictable and I'm unsure whether they're brought on by my uneasy soul or hers. This afternoon I stared into the ferns where she had crawled and told her quietly to go to spirit. There was no answer.

My mother was not content in her life and she is not content in her death. The place she might have gone to beckons, but she has refused to go. She doesn't haunt, for her presence in my garden, though full of frustration, is not malevolent. She unsettles and confuses me a little. When I saw her she seemed distracted and busy as if there were things left unfinished in this present. I wished her peace, but that is something I can't give her as she wanders between the worlds. Would she be here if I wasn't? Has she returned because there is something she wishes to give to me?

Today she knelt among the sword ferns with her red babushka tight around her head and the skirt of her print dress dragging behind her in the dirt. Oddly, she was wearing high heels. Her dress dragged in the dust at the edge of the driveway in that Okanagan yard of years ago. I think she may have been content there, but I wonder if she was ever really happy. I don't remember her ever laughing.

I remember my father driving me down to school when I was fifteen. When he stopped to let me out, he told me I shouldn't speak to my mother for a while. When I asked him what he meant, he told me not to worry about it, just not to speak to her. It was six months before I spoke aloud to her and even then she reciprocated with a deep silence.

That was the year she began to paint the rooms of the house. She began in the kitchen, moved on to the dining room and living room, and then to the bedrooms and the hall till she got to the bathroom. All this was done with a furious intensity. When she finished the bathroom she began again on the kitchen, this time with colors more wild and flamboyant. We all watched but said nothing. It was only when, on the third time around the house, she painted the walls charcoal and the ceilings a blood red that my father took the paint and brushes away from her. A few weeks later she started to speak to us again. She was forty-one years old.

None of us ever talked about what had happened. My father told us nothing of what was wrong with her that year. She cooked the meals for us all, washed clothes, and cleaned house as she had always done. We lived in the charcoal and red of the rooms for months until she suddenly began to paint the walls and ceilings over with the soft pastels they had been before. That too was a quiet time.

I was mostly afraid during her silence. There was an impenetrable barrier between us. Dick was in the air force that year and Johnny had only been back a year from the Chula Vista deportee prison in California.

He had run away from home, tried to join the marines, been arrested as a minor, and then placed in a deportee prison for Mexicans by mistake. No one had spoken of him when he was gone. Like my mother's sudden muteness, my brother's disappearance was left unexplained. I didn't ask where he was and I wasn't told. He disappeared from our family. To my mother and father, he didn't exist.

When he arrived back months later he was sent to school for part of a year before he quit forever. His months in prison is his story to tell, not mine. He was fifteen, a red-haired boy in a hard-core prison, where the authorities simply pretended he didn't exist. His novel, written years later, tells what truth of that time he could bear to reveal. The silence in our home and the denial of any kind of trauma were how we understood things. The words or touch that might have helped us understand anything emotional, spiritual, or physical was never there.

I tried today to approach my mother there in the ferns, but like a bone-wracked, crippled goddess her spirit slipped quickly away. The ferns shivered, their long swords hanging above the swollen buds of a rhododendron, buds promising dark red flowers in a few more weeks. Like blood, the blossom of my mother's passing; like burned bone, the dried hull of her presence.

Her next life will, I hope, have less suffering in it. Whoever she returns as, I pray she is not the abused child she was in her life. I also pray she abuses no one else in her life to come. What her father did to her was done by her to others.

My mother was an alcoholic and so was my father. When I helped clear her apartment after her death I found a hundred or more empty whiskey bottles in her spare room. I think she was too proud or too ashamed to carry them out in the garbage for fear of them rattling. Alcoholics fear such things. I too have squirreled empty bottles away and surreptitiously hidden them or dropped them in strange garbage cans. Like father, like mother, like son. Today I'm sober and have been for almost four months. That's enough for now.

☙

The snowdrops are in full bloom. In another week the white blossoms will fade and it will be time to take them up, separate the clusters of young bulbs, and transplant them to the beds. The bulb irises are splendid with their rich blue. The tulips will come, but the March rains will torment them and the flowers will probably not open. Every year I watch them do their best until they finally bend over and die under rain-filled skies. The daffodils are everywhere now, their bright yellow splashes of intense color against the dark earth.

Red-winged and tricolored blackbirds have returned and the males sing in the scrub beside the dugout by the daffodil fields where I walk each day. I find their *kwong-kay-re* rich and wonderful as they cry out this spring to their more drably colored partners who are busy building nests in the bulrushes. The crows will rob their eggs and late spring will see the blackbirds fight the larger birds. The flash of red on their shoulders is a bright sign of maleness in the bare branches of the wild brush.

My garden beds have been turned and dressed. The weeding goes on as I move around the garden and pluck the first green dandelions for salads. The perennials have sent up their first shoots, a promise of late spring and summer. The manure and compost is already leaching down into the soil, feeding the roots. There is still not enough rain and the drought looms. The reservoirs are barely half full and there will be no sprinklers turning on the lawns this year. All my watering will be by hand, a laborious job awaiting.

A beautiful garden shines. It doesn't have to be some huge display over an acre or two of grounds. It can be a couple of flower beds in a small backyard, a vegetable plot in the heart of a city. When I lived in Montreal on St. Urbain Street in the early 1970s I loved to look at the vegetable gardens in front of the row houses. The few square feet on either side of the cement walks were filled with tomatoes, scarlet runner beans, peppers of all kinds, a squash plant with huge yellow flowers in a metal washtub, and always an older woman, overweight and wearing the prescribed black dress, caressing the flowers, hefting young tomatoes in her palms. The first ripe red tomato on the block was a sign of the best gardener, and the envy and joy others on the block felt was palpable.

The plum blossoms are beautiful today and the apple blossoms that will follow them in the next weeks will be an additional blessing. The flower beds are alive with young green shoots. The ferns have begun to push up their rolled clubs and are ready to begin their unfurling. It's time to plant my salad vegetables, the lettuces, green onions, and spinach. I don't bother with cabbage, broccoli, or cauliflower. My vegetable plot is too small and there are so many fruit and vegetable stalls at the local organic farms that I find there is no need to grow my own. What I do want is the freshness of bok choy, radicchio, arugula to grace my stir-fries and salads in the late spring and summer.

In the far corner of the garden the *Clematis armandii* has put out its stunning white flowers from among its oval evergreen leaves. In the evening it is rich with scent. I have it mixed in with honeysuckle and the two balance each other beautifully, the clematis blooming in early spring and the honeysuckle in early summer.

Outside my parent's bedroom window was a honeysuckle. It climbed the front wall of the house and lay its long tendrils along the sill of the second-story window. The window was always open in summer as was the one at the back of the house where I slept. The upstairs was impossibly hot in summer and the spare breezes from the north played through from front to back, bringing with them the dense bloom of the honeysuckle's scent. The flowers were the sprung mouths of a thousand thousand birds whose call was smell and smell alone. There were many nights I woke to them.

The south wall of the house stared straight at the summer sun and the heat bathed the wall all day. Wasps lived there and in my bedroom. From early summer on they gathered in ever-increasing numbers so that by fall there were thousands of yellow jackets festooned on the walls in sagging drapes of living insects. When I went to bed I would brush their bodies off the covers onto the floor and crawl under the sheet to sleep in the drenched perfume of the honeysuckle vine. I remember the summer when I was sixteen and woke to a full moon. I lay on my back and stared down at the white sheet. It was alive with slow wasps. They had formed a second cover for me and their many wings fanning had cooled me as I slept. I lifted my arm and the wasps upon it rose with it. It was as if my hand were covered in rings with yellow stones polished smooth by the moon's bright light. I let my arm fall gently back. I was not afraid. I had lived among the wasps for two summers and knew that if I did not disturb them they would not disturb me. What a strange joy that was to sleep among their deadly bodies and know there was no danger. I fell back to sleep, the drift of honeysuckle sweet in the night.

Basho said once that in the end we are all the bamboo's children. There are many bamboo thickets in and around the temples of Japan, just as there are many here on Vancouver Island. The bamboo is one of the most revered plants in Asia and stands with the pine, plum, willow, lotus, and chrysanthemum, all of which represent the deep virtues of lasting peace. The bamboo stands for endurance. We are what resembles us, in the garden as in our lives. The bamboo's leaves stay green all year and its culms bend and move with the wind. They symbolize the strength of the compliant. They give way to the forces around them, but after the wind they lift back straight again. Having this kind of flexible strength is to have a *bamboo mind*.

In Japan the most noble plants are the bamboo, pine, and plum. They are called the *three friends*. Bamboo symbolizes the Buddha, the emptiness at the center, the strength that conquers through yielding. How many times have I not yielded and how many times have I paid the price for such obduracy? Now I try to move as the bamboo moves. How many years it takes to learn the simplest things and how difficult my life has been because of my refusals. It's called doing the same thing over and over, expecting a different result.

A few years ago I spent some time in Kyoto and Nara in Japan. I wanted to visit the temples and gardens there. It was a humbling journey. The peace of the garden at Ryoan-ji will stay with me forever. I went very early in the morning to the Zen temple and was led to the garden by a kindly little woman from the Christian nunnery across the road. She meditated each morning in a bamboo grove at the temple. She was serene as all such monastics are. Her smile was gentle and without rancor or guile.

I had an hour alone at Ryoan-ji, a gift of solitude I treasure yet. The garden's simplicity of stone, moss, and raked sand is a great beauty. My own garden is not Ryoan-ji, but it is my garden and I have made small rooms in it for quiet and meditation. A garden can only be itself and the gardener must travel by instinct as well as knowledge to allow it to be so. A garden should never be an imitation, only a variation on the thousands of years of gardening. Imitations are always less. There is only one Ryoan-ji.

Tonight Gemini perches on Orion's sword tip and gazes across the sky at Libra and Virgo. There is a bit of glow from the city just a few miles down the highway and its slow weight dims what is above. The stars as they were before the city put them out. I remember writing that as I thought of my youth. The city's glow hazes the night sky with artificial light, yet I can still see most of the larger stars, however faint, in their classical arrangements. Everywhere on this earth the stars have been a blessing to me. I used to know most of their names, but time has dimmed my knowledge and I need a star map now to identify many of them.

I allow myself wonder as I always have. The pleasures and pain of childhood have never left me for long and I can still lose myself in the dark infinities. Would that I could make wondering a part of my daily life. I remember that moment at the treatment center when I said, I surrender, to the starry night. It was such a simple moment, yet one I'd yearned for all my life. I'd searched for such surrender in the jungles of Peru and Brazil, in the thunderstorms of Saskatchewan and Montana, in all and every place, from mountain peaks, deserts, and oceans, and I had never been able to let go of myself.

My surrender was just a moment, perhaps a few seconds of looking up into the night sky, and then I walked on into the treatment center and started to live. It had everything to do with my addiction

and, more, everything to do with my life. I changed that early morning and I knew I could never go back to who I'd been before. I have
had visions and moments of transformation before, but this was
unlike any other. Strange how the simplest things cannot be
expressed. I had struggled against surrender all my life. It took sixty
years of dying to finally be alive.

I have begun my sixty-second year. As I do, I feel at peace for the
first time in many, many years. Old days and old ways swim through
me and though they can be a torment I ride the memories through,
reminding myself I am here, not there. I try now to learn.

PLANTS

Arbutus – *Arbutus menziesii* (Pacific madrone)
Bamboo – *Bambusa* sp.
    "   – *Chusquea breviglumis*
    "   – *Hibanobambusa tranquillans "Shiroshima"*
    "   – *Phyllostachys aureosulcata*
    "   – *Phyllostachys nigra*
    "   – *Pleioblastus fortunei*
    "   – *Sasa veitchii*
    "   – *Shibataea kumasasa*
Bulb iris – *Iris reticulata*
California lilac – *Ceanothus* spp. "Puget Blue"
Clematis – *Clematis armandii*
Day lily – Barbara Mitchell – *Hemerocallis*
    "   – Hyperion –   "
    "   – Jungle Princess –   "
    "   – Purple Down with Gold – "
    "   – South Seas –   "
    "   – Sun on Red Cloud –   "
Foxglove – *Digitalis*
Heather – Glenfiddich – *Calluna vulgaris*
    "   – Hammondi Aureifolia–   "
    "   – Silberschmetze –*Calluna vulgaris*
Honeysuckle – *Lonicera periclymenum "Graham Thomas"*
Jack pine – *Pinus banksiana*
Lodgepole pine – *Pinus contorta*

Lotus – *Fabaceae (Leguminosae)*
Paper birch – *Betula papyrifera*

ANIMALS, BIRDS, AND INSECTS

Bald eagle – *Haliaeetus leucocephalus*
Black ground beetle – *Pterostichus* spp.
Black widow spider – *Latrodectus mactans*
Pill bug – *Armadillidium vulgare*
Recluse spider – *Loxosceles reclusa*
Red-winged blackbird – *Agelaius phoeniceus*
Sow bug – *Oniscus asellus*
Striped garter snake – *Thamnophis* spp.
Tricolored blackbird – *Agelaius tricolor*
Western diamondback rattlesnake – *Crotalus atrox*
Wet wood termite – *Zootermopsis angusticollis*
Wolf spider – *Lycosidae* spp.

4

Thou art thy mother's glass, and she in thee
Calls back the lovely April of her prime.
 — WILLIAM SHAKESPEARE, "SONNET 3"

A MOTHER'S HAND still lives in me, the one that turned the soft soil on an April day and planted flowers, pushing at the season long before all fear of frost was past. Her urge to trouble just-warm ground is brought back to me and I can turn upon another phrase from Shakespeare ("Sonnet 30"), "When to the sessions of sweet silent thought / I summon up remembrance of things past."

I was a child in my mother's prime and I still can conjure her up on the porch of our wartime home in Nelson, legs sheathed in silk, a tartan skirt, a sweater, and a simple necklace at her throat. She leaned back with an enigmatic smile for the photographer who might have been my father, but is more likely her lover who gave her solace during those lost years. Where is that image now but in my mind? Has it gone to crisp and dust like her? And where are they who sang—mother, lover, father—and what of the three small boys who smile so roguishly in the same memory? Too many years ago to tell.

While my father was away in Europe my mother took a lover. The years were long and my father's return was farther away at times than her heart. My mother's friends were all mothers of young children and like her, their husbands had gone away to fight. They sat around the kitchen table listening to the war news on the radio, talking and taking drinks of whiskey that one or another had bought with her monthly ration stamp or had as a gift from some soldier who had passed through and spent the night. I think my mother's lover was Czechoslovakian. My mother called him our uncle, just as other women explained their lover's presence to their children. Some of the children I knew had many uncles during the war.

When my father returned from Europe, her lover disappeared. My mother told me later he wrote her one love letter. She answered it and he never wrote again. She told me she had loved him but had chosen my father instead because of us. She told me she learned again to love my father and that she had a few truly happy years with him. I realized when she told me that those years were the four between my brother's and my father's deaths.

The early years in Nelson seemed happy ones for us boys as were the few years that followed. In the Okanagan after the war, the summers were golden. Our days were spent in the hills and at Kalamalka Lake, where we played and swam from eight in the morning until we returned home for dinner. My father gave us a tractor inner tube for the lake. We played with it for weeks until it was punctured, stolen, or lost.

Swallows threaded the air above the lake. Their slender bodies made a calligraphy in the air as intricate as the brushstrokes of the old men who sat in the sun outside the Dart Coon Club across from the Goon Hong restaurant. Every few moments a swallow skimmed the still surface of the lake and drank, leaving a thin wake that spread outward. The water was covered with pollen from the trees in the mountains. It seethed on the surface. It was gold dust suspended in blue.

The swallow's young had left their mud nests under the railway trestles and bridges. Miniatures of their parents, they were wild in the freedom of the air. They were tiny dark jewels flung against the sky. Their mothers searched the air for insects, mosquitoes, flies, or the rare moth that had stumbled into the day and lost itself over the waters. When a swallow took a moth it carried it in its beak for a moment or two, the moth's wings spread on either side of its beak so that it was if two creatures flew there, one within the other. When a breeze lifted from the south, the birds doubled upon themselves in pure pleasure.

The pines and firs and spruce on the mountainside above the lake felt the first touch of the breeze, and their long branches swayed with the air that moved them. The branches' sound was a soughing wheeze as millions of needles clicked against each other. The trees were ready to give off their pollen to the waiting cones, and yellow clouds drifted from the high branches in rivers of seed. They boiled slowly in the breeze and reached out like golden banners from the mountain's side. The sky filled with pollen. It was like a living breath that rose from another kind of fire. As the breeze lifted, the pollen clouds stretched out across the lake and then began their long, slow falling into the waters below.

We swam out from among the cattails at the edge of the lake. We were brown with summer. Dick straddled the huge inner tube while Johnny and I hung on and beat the water behind us with our thin legs. The tube floated farther and farther out into the lake as we played our tumbling game, each of us trying to climb up on the tube and each of us falling off in unison or alone. Our falling was mostly laughter. Nothing was as beautiful as our young bodies. We had lived our weeks in the sun until our skin had turned into bronze that shone in the slick of water.

My brothers had red hair like my father, but mine was blond turned silver by the sun. In the water world we were one animal, our flesh one flesh, our bones one cage holding all our hearts. We fell, flew, and twined among ourselves like young otters. Dragonflies hovered near us amazed at this creature thrashing in a lake of aquamarine and turquoise and a blue so deep it was a darkness below us where trout and kokanee swam in our other world.

The pollen from the mountains settled out of the sky. Suddenly tired, we climbed onto the tube's back. We sat so the tube was balanced, each with our legs on the inside so that we faced each other. We said nothing because there was nothing to say. Our heads were down as we breathed slowly and deeply. After a few minutes, one of us would suddenly flip backward and the tube would turn over and throw the others into the lake. But not at that moment. As we rested there the pollen cloud settled upon us turning our skin from bronze to gold. Our hair glinted with a thousand points of light and our shoulders and backs became the carapaces of golden water beetles.

In a moment or two we would return to the waters that surrounded us. High on the mountainsides, pollen drifted among the branches of the great trees. Swallows darted among cattails at the lake's edge. Red-winged blackbirds screamed at a single crow who searched out their nests. A coyote, fat from eggs and nestlings, rested among the grasses on the slope above the lake's edge. She watched us as we drifted among the amber waters. Her ear flicked once and a fly lifted and settled again on the black-tipped hairs. The coyote lowered her head to her paws and began her first sleep of the day.

The afternoon stretched out under the sun. On the lake we took breath after breath and then we slid forward in unison into the tube's center and down into the cool waters, pollen lifting away from our skin in flakes and scales. We rolled on our backs in the deep and stared at the opening above us, a circle of light we would swim toward when we could no longer hold our breath.

❦

Summer at the lake is in the far past, but it is spring here on the coast and April has come with a mix of storm, sun, wind, rain, and all the vagrancies of this tempestuous time of year. The buds on the Japanese maples are open and the first leaves push their way into the air in soft, furled points of the palest green. Their colors are as delicate as the fabric they are woven of. The young maple leaves are diaphanous, a trembling so fragile I think they cannot live.

The leaves are the same as a butterfly's wings when it first crawls from its hard carapace. The wings are crumpled and if you did not understand their fragility you would think them dead. Then the butterfly pumps blood into its wings and the frail sails expand into the colors we love to emulate in our fashions. Leaves are the same when first they lift into the air.

I have just come into the house after gathering dandelion leaves to mix with our salad tonight. Washed, they rest in the colander, a tonic for spring. They will be a little bitter now. Only the very earliest of leaves are sweet, but a wisp of bitterness is good in spring. It clarifies the blood. A little vinegar and herbs, some extra-virgin olive oil, garlic, and the leaves of spring augmented by some early red-leafed lettuce. Was there such pleasure in spring before I quit drinking? Did I kneel in wonder in the garden then to pick dandelion greens, arugula, and herbs?

What this healing has done is bring the past from obscurity into light. It appears in me in stunned cameos, in anecdotal fragments. Each memory seems colored like some mad child's painting of spring. What is it in me that can make of a memory joy and of others regret and shame?

The simple task of going to the garden for fresh salad makings has brought back old ways this morning. It's hard to lift myself out of the past. I find I have to go back with a will toward remembering and so understand not only why I was alcoholic and sick but also who I am now that I am sober. I can remember looking around like a feral dog as I lifted a hidden bottle of vodka to my lips and drained it of thirteen ounces of alcohol. This garden was the garden of a drunk. Now I can sit on my haunches and pick single leaves from an early arugula plant and not have my arms and hands tremble with the effort.

Everything is up and growing. Hostas push their hard tips through the damp earth. They are fierce spears much like Cadmus's teeth in the fields of ancient Greece. I think of warriors rising from the dead to do battle with the turbulent air. Would they came to battle the ubiquitous slugs. I've spread benign bait around the hostas in anticipation of the annual scourge. The invasion has already started but hasn't reached its peak yet. The baby slugs are hatched from their eggs where they have rested under stones, boards, logs, and leaves, and they slide, voracious, across the garden in search of midnight meals. Like the snails, they will eat triple and more of their weight in a night.

The snails' spiral shells are a coruscating spin of mottled yellows and browns, and a single one can carve a hosta into an emerald filigree. I hate killing snails, but if I didn't there wouldn't be a hosta or a primula left anywhere. Their blossoms are frayed stars in the garden, their fringes tattered.

I was up an hour before dawn this morning and stood on the deck in the dark with a cup of coffee when Roxy came bounding up with a half-dead siskin in her jaws. Where would she have found a bird at this hour? Aren't the birds safe in the branches of trees when it's dark? Unless this is a siskin left over from yesterday, one who smashed its head against a window of the house in some futile flight from a hawk or in a fight with another over who is dominant and who gets the latest girl. Roxy played with it in a desultory manner, bored by the bird's refusal to struggle. The siskin was locked into the stillness brought on by fear and shock.

I have tried to rescue the occasional bird from her. Like all cats, she loves to play with her prey before killing it. I gave up when I tried to wrest a white-crowned sparrow from her jaws. When I gently tried to ease the tiny bird from her, Roxy looked directly into my eyes in much the same way the lion did that I watched eat a gazelle on the veldt of South Africa. She clamped down her jaws on the bird just as the lion did on her gazelle. I gently pulled and heard the crunch of her teeth on feather and bone. She let the bird go, then gave me a look of disdain and walked away, leaving the dead sparrow on the grass for me to do with as I willed. I've never tried to save a bird from her again. The cats are acting as they should and it is not for me to prevent them.

I am finding it easier in these spring days to leave the confines of the garden. The larger world outside, the fields, woodlands, beaches, and islands have not been a problem for me. It is the busier, frenetic human world that disturbs me. I think it always has. It is only now, sober and still vulnerable, that I feel the madness of activity that surrounds me, cars racing up the street, the muffled beat of sound from three teenagers passing with their music turned as loud as their hearts.

Anxiety, the close neighbor of paranoia, isn't good for me, especially now in these early months of recovery. I'm able though to go to the grocery store and walk the aisles without twitching at every quick movement, jumping at the sudden sound of a can of creamed corn dropped behind me, the appearance of some harried mother at my shoulder with a rattling metal cart piled high with a week's groceries and a desperate child who feels exactly as I do. I can go to the bank now and drive past the local mall with its liquor store and not have it bother me too much. That I notice it is there each time I drive by is indication enough of my past and my going there sometimes three times a day to buy liquor as my tolerance for alcohol rose higher and higher.

86

The garden has been a sanctuary for me these past months. Inside the high fences I feel safe with the plants and birds, our cats, and my woman whose love for me surpasses understanding. Her tolerance and patience have been remarkable.

I know the need to impose solitude upon myself will pass, but for now I treasure the peace and quiet it offers. My daily life is a reflection of my need. Birth and death are practiced here daily by all living things and I participate in that cycle as I step into the simple round of plants, animals, insects, and birds.

The golden northern bumblebee and the red-tailed bumblebee are both busy in the garden now. They feast on the nectar of wallflowers and *Pieris japonica* blossoms as they await the largesse of the apple blossoms to come. They are huge females and now that they are foraging they will have expanded their tunnels in the earth. There are smaller females looking after things underground as they wait for their mothers to return with nectar.

I am aware of how much and how little I have paid attention to their presence here in the garden. Like the spring winds, they are ubiquitous. Here it is sweet April and the garden is awash with perfume. The bees, drunk with the surfeit, work the spring blossoms. Their hives double in size each day as eggs are laid by the queens and grubs poke their heads above their waxen cribs.

The blue orchard bees have been around since mid-February. They are a common spring bee and are essential island pollinators. In the wild world they build their nests inside holes in trees or fallen logs, but in the garden I have set up a few condominiums for them. Blocks of wood drilled with holes three inches deep are perfect nesting places for the bees so long as they are given a sunny southern exposure. Each hole will hold one egg. These bees are solitary and by June they're gone.

The western leaf-cutting bees haven't appeared yet. I only notice them when I see the circles cut in the delicate, lime-yellow leaves of the acacia tree. They line their nests in the earth with the fragments of leaf they carve. Bee wallpaper, something to delight the young when they are born.

Later in the spring I will keep my eye out for the virescent green metallic bees. They live in burrows communally and begin with one over-wintering female. Their thorax is a bright metallic green with tiny hairs that become decorated with golden pollens when they are at work in the garden. They are one of our most beautiful bees.

I saw my first sandhills and bald-faced hornets today and wondered where their nests were. Last year one was in the fir above the pond and the other in the redwood above the driveway. The hornets chew their way along the cedar boards of my fence. The gray, weathered wood is what they are harvesting. They leave behind red trails of fresh cedar. The fluffy wood, mixed with their saliva, is turned into the paper they build with.

There are five apple trees in our garden and I don't know the varieties with the exception of the Spartans. The trees were here before we arrived. An hour ago I watched a short-tailed ichneumon fly hunting the trunk of the apple tree. Its thin, coral body searched relentlessly among the crevices and lichens for caterpillars. The apple tree is always active with caterpillars, particularly now that the first tender leaves and blossoms are appearing. As the caterpillars appear, so do the ichneumon flies. On finding a caterpillar, the fly will lay a single egg high on the insect's thorax where it can't reach it. The caterpillar then carries its own death with it as it feeds. Once the caterpillar spins its cocoon, the parasitic-fly egg hatches, and kills and feeds on its pupating host.

The ichneumon flittered its long antennae over the bark. Its movements were quick and nervous as it searched the tree branch for prey. It feeds on nectar like all the ichneumon flies. Today it had enough to eat and more important work to be done. I watched it for half an hour, but no caterpillar was to be found. They will appear in numbers soon.

The garden is almost ready. It has suffered this past two or three years because of my neglect. I let the garden go a little bit each year, only watering and doing some desultory, necessary weeding. At Christmas this year, fresh from the treatment center, I looked out and saw a garden in trouble, overgrown in places and dying back in others from too much shade or sun, insect predation, or crowding.

A raccoon is in the garden, attracted by the pond and the flower beds where worms rise close to the surface. Raccoons are beautiful but are also obnoxious predators and can wreak havoc in the garden. The mossy lawn and beds had several dozen holes dug down four or more inches. Still, I love their presence, the delicate way they walk, as if they were ballet dancers with wrestlers' shoulders. I was out for a quiet moment under the stars and watched her walk across the lawn. Such a burly wanderer.

The raccoon follows the stepping-stones, leaving damp tracks on the blue granite. Her long toes splay slightly and her claws like slender knives scratch the stones with the sound of whiskers on a tender palm. She stops by the water's still edge and stares at an element she knows better than she knows the air she breathes.

Her button-black, upturned nose catches at the night. *What is alive and what is dead?* she seems to ask. Her nose tells her everything as she dips her paws into the pond's water and begins to wash with an obsessive wringing motion like a woman who has lost everything. The slide of her curved claws on naked stone is movement without mind.

She takes the iridescent body of a tiny tree frog from her mouth and places it in the water. She washes it with a kind of praise as if the frog's body were a jewel found after journeying across the yards of night. The frog's body, its legs extended, turns over and over in the water until it is finally clean of the imagined sand and grit. The raccoon rises to her haunches and lifts the body to her mouth. Her bites are made slowly, each one precise. First the head and then the front legs, the body with its minuscule organs of heart and liver and lungs is next, and last the long back legs, until there is nothing left. Done, she places her paws back in the water and cleans them.

She seems always to be in a dream place, as if her mind is far away. I watch her drop to her front paws and amble over to investigate the iron pot at the foot of the fir tree. It is an ancient pot, one I bought in Japan years ago. I keep it full of water for the birds. She looks into it for a moment and then tips it onto a stepping-stone beside the blue iris. She rolls the pot off the stone and courses the air with her nose. The peanut butter and bread is what she moves toward. The frog was only a small appetizer. It is the open sandwich I have made that interests her. That it sits on wire mesh in the cavern of a live trap in the corner of the yard seems only a small concern to her. She meanders over to the trap and circles it slowly. She has been trapped before. Hours of planting can be turned into a wreckage in a single night as she digs for beetles and worms under the young foliage of a new garden bed. I set the trap an hour before nightfall and decorated it with a slab of fresh bread and peanut butter.

I watch her in the moonlight as she circles the cage with its inviting open end and the spring-loaded trapdoor that hangs above it. All she has to do is walk inside and step on the trip-plate just in front of the bait. First she digs around the perimeter of the trap in hope she will find an alternative entrance, a safe exit. Finally she walks, a humpbacked little bear with a ringed tail, up to the mouth of the trap and peers in. The peanut butter is just a few feet away. She stretches her paw inside and then withdraws it.

Finally, after stepping up and down in impatience she moves inside the opening. Nothing happens and she takes another slow step and then another until finally she is only a long reach away from her prize. One step more and she comes down on the trip-plate, the trapdoor slams shut behind her. She turns and attacks it as if she could eat her way through the wire mesh and back to the open night. She thrashes around and, finding once again there is no way out, picks up the sandwich and begins to eat what she got trapped for.

The sudden clang lifts me off the step and I go down and squat beside the trap. She stares at me with her fine, bright eyes, but she doesn't stop eating. She is a female and her belly is slightly swollen. The kits she is carrying are a week or two away from birth. I have caught her just in time. The cats have followed me down, but they stay a respectful distance away. A chirring growl greets us all. The sandwich is finished and she warns us all of her keen claws and bright, needle teeth. Her brawny little bear body thuds against the cage and then she settles into a corner.

I will leave her there until morning when I will drive her to a beautiful lake where there are golden skunk cabbage and freshwater clams and a plethora of beetles and eggs for her to feast upon. Lorna and I will stand at the back of the truck and watch her scramble out of the open cage and down to water where she will splash in and hide under a fallen alder log or run to the nearest tree and climb to safety. The last we'll see of her will be two sharp black eyes staring at us from the water weeds or from a high fir branch. Our nocturnal guest will have found a new, wild territory.

Regnavit a ligno Deus, "God reigned from the wood." The raccoon in her slow perambulations was like a small, nocturnal god as she visited. In the wild wood there are many creatures, each one a part of who I am, each one an extension of myself like spirit arms extending from my shoulders and touching what cannot be touched by flesh.

That is what I think of as I climb into bed beside my woman. The raccoon will sleep fitfully in her cage as she awaits morning. She is a little god of the garden and I lie on my back and think of her as I stare at the ceiling. Roxy has curled up against Lorna's belly and Basho sleeps in the blue easy chair in the corner of the living room by the fireplace. I have trapped one of the little gods and while I did not kill her, still, I have trapped her.

Somewhere in the future of another life I will have to pay for this and the many other interferences I have made in the natural order of things. I think of this as I begin to fall asleep. I offer a small prayer to the little bear-god in her cage and ask her forgiveness. I hope she knows she will be the god who reigns on the margins of the mountain lake that will be her new sacred glade. There are visitations and departures. Everything moves just before stillness, just before sleep.

As I lie in that place between this world and the dream, I think of a night in a cabin near Old Hazelton on Highway Sixteen. It was back in the spring of 1969. I was living temporarily with Ken and Alice Belford under the shadow of the mountains on the high valley floor above the Skeena River. Ken and I were loading boxcars at a little sawmill down the road.

I half-dream the late afternoon of an April day back then when we stopped the truck and rescued a thrush that had been running down the narrow bush road in front of us. Its wing had been broken, perhaps by a hawk attack or an owl's or in some battle with another male in the late days of mating. I remember carrying it back to the cabin. Ken and I drank whiskey and built a cage for the bird out of woven willow wands we'd cut from the swampy side of the creek bed just beyond the cabin. The thrush lay wrapped in a blanket in a cardboard box behind the kitchen stove where Alice was making a stew. She would appear and disappear, finally going to bed in the lean-to.

The two of us wove willow wands and were, for that night, entirely happy in the dream that we were somehow making a place where the thrush could live until its wing was mended. That the broken wing of a wild bird would never heal did not occur to us. All we wanted to do was make some kind of reparation, give something that might resemble love back to a wilderness that was slowly being torn apart by the loggers and the mills, the clear-cuts, and the mines.

It was dawn when the cage was done. It was an artful thing, perhaps six feet high and swollen out at the middle in a woven platform. We both lifted our glasses to the empty bottle and the night and our friendship, then we went to the box behind the stove and lifted out the bird with its bound wing.

It was dead, of course.

I remember our bewilderment, our sudden sorrow.

Ken went to bed in the lean-to where his wife slept fitfully and I sat in my chair and stared at the cage that was now a kind of strange artifact. The sweet contentment we had when we were building it was no longer there, yet I remember looking at the woven willow wicker cage and thinking how beautiful it was. I sat there in a sad wonder at what we had wrought, the dead bird lying on the table's edge, waiting for the grave I'd dig for it come afternoon.

I lie here in the half-sleep and think back on that time, the arrivals and the departures, that spring running to summer and my leaving the north to head back east on another crazed quest that I knew, even as I drove it, led nowhere, nowhere at all.

❧

I have moved three large boulders into the new shade garden. Ferns and rhododendrons and other plants are in the ground. The pebble path needed some large boulders to balance it. The largest of them weighs over three hundred pounds and the only way I had of moving it was to get on my knees and wiggle it slowly forward to its spot halfway down the path. It took two hours. The other boulders were slightly smaller but no less awkward. My back hurts now and will for a week. Lorna will give me an admonishing *I-told-you-so* look, but there is nothing to be done about that. I've wanted large stones for this part of the garden for years and when I saw these three in the pile beside a farmer's field I knew they were the ones. They sit in my side garden, looking like they've been there since time was imagined.

Now, there's another rhododendron to be moved, five more sword ferns, and an azalea I've had in a pot for a year and which did not set buds last fall. It will when I put it beside the largest of the three boulders. The sun will warm the stone all year and the warmth will be passed on to the moist earth. The azalea will benefit from it and some acid fertilizer. This fall will see new buds, next year white flowers.

That is the eternal optimism of the gardener. The struggling plant of spring will find new reasons to bloom the following season. The gods of the garden are always on the gardener's side so long as he pays obeisance to them. Fortune comes to those who worship in the green worlds. As Virgil said, "Fortunate is the man who has come to know the gods of the countryside."

We must cultivate the gods of stone and water, plant and animal. How else to explain the sickly rhododendron that blooms profusely after being moved to a different spot? How else to explain what moves a gardener to choose a particular spot? He cannot know the exactness of the right soil, the right light, the right everything. How else but mysterious instinct? And it is the gardener's instinct the gods direct. That occasionally the move does not work out is only a momentary problem, the fault lying in the gardener and not the god. It is not a judgment by the gods but, rather, an acknowledgment that sometimes magic simply will not work. The sky gods often mis-judged old Gaia, the goddess of the earth. Hubris, that Greek excess of pride, is a grievous fault in both gods and men.

I've stood in the gathering dusk and seen in the shadows Shake-speare's "elves of hills, brooks, standing lakes, and groves." The lit-tle gods dance their dance on the stones by the pond; they sleep beneath the bracken by the fir. Already they've woven their fans among the vines and lilies.

The shade garden lies just outside our bedroom window and the night scents should rise and flow across our bed at night. Like the honeysuckle and the viburnum, these plants smell the richest at night. I reel when the moisture in the air is just right and carries the heavy perfumes into the house. Tomorrow I will put in the path.

I've decided on pebbles rather than slate. For one thing I don't have enough slate to do the whole ten yards and, for another, I think a pebble path will echo the path that goes around the pond in the main garden. The slate will find a place elsewhere. I do want to add to the slate stepping-stones that lead from the deck down into the garden. The largest piece will become a garden bench. Yes, pebbles are the answer. I like the sound of them under my feet, the crunch as stone grinds soft against stone.

The cedar tree in the middle of the shade garden has pushed its roots out of the soil. I get a small hand scraper and, back on my gardener's knees, I carefully lift the earth away from around them. The gravel will be three inches deep and I want the roots to show above it. The job takes hours, but I am unaware of time as I lift the dirt away from the pale red roots. This is when I am most content. It is like making a poem or drawing. Time ceases to exist and hours are only imagined things. The simplest physical task takes us out of ourselves. Like weeding, the most mundane endeavor is sometimes the most rewarding. In my addiction I forgot this simple pleasure.

What is it that brings such joy to me? I feel like a child who has come newly to the earth. I look at my hands with their cuneiform lines and wrinkles, their spots and scars, and wonder at their pleasure in returning to simplicity. In the *Tao Te Ching,* Old Lao Tzu said that there were three things to learn, simplicity, patience, and compassion. He said that these were the greatest treasures: in action and thought, to be simple; to be patient with both enemies and friends; to have compassion for yourself. If I can learn this practice I will begin to live in harmony with all the beings in the world. I repeat his words like a mantra. It is as if I have been a closed, locked room and suddenly windows and doors have been cut into me. I reach down and pick up a pebble and lick it clean of earth. The striated lines of quartz among the granite shine as if they had only now seen a sun lost to them ten thousand years. I place the pebble in a declivity of the second of the great stones where it gathers light like a cup gathers water. I turn back to the garden path and carve the earth around the roots of the cedar, my hands slowly and with care preparing a place for my feet to walk.

The path cleared of impediment and flattened, I lay down cloth to cover the dirt. It is a fabric that allows water to pass through. It breathes, but the grass and dandelions will die beneath it and I will be saved many hours of pulling weeds from among the pebbles. What I am striving for is a stream of stone. I want it to be the illusion of slowly moving water.

Two truckloads of gravel and the path is done. I sit on the first stone and stare down the wander of pebbles as they flow gently among the ferns and hostas. Where the path comes up against a large stone, I have tried to recreate a stone in a stream. The pebbles slide up against the stone and then curl round it, just as water does when it meets a water stone. I sing to my path a hymn to stone.

Sea stone, water stone, stone of scree and mountain, valley stone, grass stone, outcrop, ledge and whisper stone, tooth of hill and desert, moss stone, moonstone, the many stones of this and there, vision stone, entrance stone beyond the place of bone where small lights shine with crystal stillness, hand of stone and eye of stone, knuckle stone and tongue of stone, all these and more as you walk the pebbled path, stand beside the trunk of a Douglas fir and imagine it by the sea. At your feet is a single perfect stone with striations of pale pink quartz that was your journey. You pick it up and turn and turn its many sides to your eyes in wonder. Do you remember the day you found it in the sea's wrack?

It is your stone, the one you have waited half a century for. It is a stone worn by the sea and sand. You hold it in your hand. This is what treasure is. This is the child in you, the one who drew maps of ancient islands with trails that twisted and turned until they ended in the maze of directions with a single X that marked the place where every story you have been told begins.

There is no one in this garden but you. You are between things. Do you hold the stone or does the stone hold you? How did this pebble, this bit of crystal ice, find you among the millions who have wandered here? Why have you been picked, plucked, taken to this moment? The tide beyond your garden is far out. It has left you bereft. It plays its susurrous song among the flotsam and jetsam, the floating world of traveled things, things lost, things forgotten, things. The stone you hold knows every story, has heard the dolphins mourning, the salmon's greed for death, the flick of silver the dust mote knows in the moment of falling into water so deep it will take a thousand years to find its way to stillness. How many times have you come here and left with nothing but quietness?

Now the stone travels with you. It rests in its pocket against your thigh. Your body keeps it alive. Kyoto stone and stone of Nara, Machu Picchu stone and stone of Sahara, Nowlan stone, MacEwen stone, Purdy stone, stone of Stikine and stone of Miramichi, Amazon stone, Euphrates stone, Nile stone and stone of Zimbabwe, field stone, sea stone, Lorna stone, stones of the deserts and the mountains, Cordillera stone, Ural stone, stones my father left me, my mother left me, the dead and the dying, the living stones, the stones of Haida Gwaii, of Nass and Fraser and Coldstream, creek, rivulet, stream, river, water moving slow as wrists, Saskatchewan stone, the stone my lover gave from her mouth polished white by her tongue, into my mouth, the stones of stillness in the garden you have made of air and water, of fallen, fragile leaves, the red of autumn, this dying into snow. The stone that waits, the carved stone, the emptiness stone, the skull at Chichen Itza, the sacrifice at Narle, the carved stone in the heights of the Andes, the one you welcome in your hand you found at last in the Ithaca you searched for, the poem stone, the Neruda stone, the one you write like life into the world in this garden of thought, this green and terrible place where you stand forgotten and alive.

PLANTS

Bamboo – *Pleioblastus chino*
Bleeding heart – *Dicentra "Luxuriant"*
Cape gladiolus – *Watsonia pillansii*
Double bloodroot – *Sanguinaria canadensis "Plena"*
May apple – *Podophyllum peltatum*
Shield leaf Rodgersia – *Rodgersia tabularis*
Shirobana akebia – *Akebia quinata*

ANIMALS, BIRDS, AND INSECTS

Bald-faced hornet – *Vespula maculata*
Golden northern bumblebee – *Bombus fervidus ferridus*
Red-tailed bumblebee – *Bombus ternarius*
Sandhills hornet – *Vespula arenaria*
Short-tailed ichneumon – *Ophion* spp.
Song sparrow – *Melospiza melodia*
Virescent green metallic bee – *Agapostemon virescens*
Western leafcutting bee – *Megachile perihirta*
Western yellow jacket – *Vespula pensylvanica*
White-crowned sparrow – *Zonotrichia leucophrys*

5.

Rise up, my love, my fair one, and come away. For, lo, the winter is past, the rain is over and gone; the flowers appear on the earth; the time of the singing of birds is come, and the voice of the turtle is heard in our land.

 — SONG OF SOLOMON 2:10–12

THIS MORNING a snail moved like a wet tongue down the long leaf of a day lily and brought to my mind John Donne's lines:

> And seeing the snail, which everywhere doth roam,
> Carrying his own house still, still is at home,
> Follow (for he is easy paced) this snail,
> Be thine own palace, or the world's thy gaol.

And so I wondered at this tiny mollusk's journey down a leaf blade. He didn't eat as he went, but slicked with a steady will along this green path that ended in space. When he reached the spear-tip, the delicate leaf bowed under his infinitesimal weight until it touched another frond, whereupon he slid calmly off the one and continued his journey. A stroll or quest, who knows? "This bed thy centre is, these walls thy sphere," said Donne, and I carried his thought with me as I left the snail to his slow devices.

Coming back to myself I was, for a moment, like Chuang Tzu who upon waking from a dream that he was a butterfly, said, "I do not know whether it was Chuang dreaming he was a butterfly or a butterfly dreaming it was Chuang." So the garden and I dream each other and everything here is one harmony.

How many times have I walked across this earth and been brought back into clarity? That's what my body knows beyond thought. When I remember the past it is alive and it is as if it is dreaming me. Without the past I can't learn to live in the unfolding present. This bit of history called the new millennium wants to forget, but forgetting means having to repeat everything that came before. While the past can be a burden, it is also a gift out of time. The clear moments of memory must be understood. It is only then they can be let go.

The early sun catches the viscous trail on the lily leaf and turns it into a pale opal, a thin slick that makes me think of semen. I have left thin trails on the thighs and breasts of women. I think of my lover's breasts and for a moment my fingers reach for a pen and paper, something to draw with, the snail, Lorna's breasts; I try to catch the snail's spiral house, the leopard markings on his skin, the faint freckles on my lover's flesh.

The first artist I knew was a child in a passing carnival. The carnivals, Gayland Shows and West Coast Shows, among others, came to Vernon every summer in the 1940s and 1950s and whenever they came I was drawn to the sideshow tents. I was too young to go into them, but in the evening freaks were paraded on the stage in front of a tent in hopes of getting a crowd to buy tickets. That's where I first saw the Bearded Lady and the Tattooed Man. They were dream creatures to me, not men and women, but mythic beings, lesser gods. The summer of 1949 is as clear in my mind as the lilies by the pond.

The carnival that year was a whirl of color and dust. I watched the carousel as it turned in its endless circle of music, the painted horses rising and falling on their silver stakes. Their mouths strained as they reached into the darkness around them, small children hanging on desperately in their small circle of paradise, in the center a painted unicorn prancing to calliope music.

I loved the night of carnival. Families walked the midway. Many had traveled in from Falkland, Armstrong, Enderby, and Canoe, tiny villages tucked away in the mountains around the valley. Mothers held their children's hands tightly or let them go to run among the many legs of the men and women who surrounded them. Hysteria was as close as a barker's cry, a swarthy man leaning over, exhorting a man to step right up and throw darts at balloons or brass rings over the necks of bottles. Little children stopped a moment and stared at the stuffed bears and dolls that hung from the canvas walls. Men placed their dimes and quarters on the anchors, crowns, and hearts of the gambling tables. Somewhere a woman shouted bingo and dried corn was swept from cards as a prize was chosen, the losers buying new cards and settling in for the next game.

I watched a young man throw baseballs at piled iron milk bottles. He was drunk and the girl with him was trying to get him to stop but he wouldn't. He pushed her away and she stepped back, her pink dress fluttering in the light. I knew he wanted to win something for her. It was his fourth try at knocking the pile down and he was angry, convinced he was being cheated, the game rigged. His girlfriend grabbed at him. He swore and pushed her again, hard, so that she fell. He said, *I'm trying to win you something here.* She got up from the dust and brushed at what must have been a handmade dress, the crinoline billowing out. People moved away from her, embarrassed, ashamed, and were replaced by new people who wondered at the crying girl and the young man throwing baseballs so hard.

I stared at them a moment and left as quickly as I had come. I skittered through the drifting folk. Children clutched cotton candy and apples drenched in thick caramel, their eyes as large as the Tilt-A-Whirl. My small, hard body seemed to shift its shape as it moved among the huge noise of the carnival. It was nine o'clock at night. My mother and father were at the Royal Canadian Legion drinking beer and I had been left alone to wander. I had five dollars in my pocket.

I had stolen the money on my regular run through the crowds of men and women on Kalamalka beach that afternoon. I always looked for young men with girls. They were the men who left their blankets unguarded, the ones who picked up their girls and carried them struggling into the water, the girls thrashing as they screamed at them to stop, in laughter and in panic. It was their blankets

I watched, the young men's wallets lying there by their pants and shirts.

Slim as a swift I would run through the sun, flicking sand in people's faces. At the empty blanket I would drop my towel on the wallet. It took only a sudden stop, a grab for the towel, and then I would have the wallet in my hand concealed in the folds of thin cotton. I would escape down the beach to the cottonwood groves and willow brush where Coldstream Creek emptied out of Kalamalka Lake.

Five dollars. I buried the wallet under a stone with the other leftover pillage I had stolen that summer. I pushed the five folded one-dollar bills into my red bathing suit. Gayland Shows was on for its last night at the Mac & Mac parking lot. I needed money. The twenty cents a week my father gave me for an allowance was not enough. A comic book was ten cents, the Saturday movie at the Empress Theatre fifteen.

The night before had changed my young life.

I had snuck into the Sideshow tent where I was not allowed and there I had seen a strange boy on a stage in the corner. He had no arms, only buds growing out of his shoulders. He sat alone on a small stool. His skin was very dark and his hair so black it shone with blue lights. It was as if he existed in a world where no one could touch him. I pushed and squeezed my way through the crowd until I was at the front.

The boy with the shining black hair was naked except for a cloth over his hips. He sat very still and then, the people waiting, he reached out a foot and pulled a piece of paper toward him. With his other foot he took a stick of charcoal from a jar and began to draw the face of a woman in the crowd. She was pretty and standing right in the front. The man with her told the boy to draw more than just a face but the boy ignored him. The face came alive under his swiftly moving foot. Each arc, each delicate touch of shading was done seemingly without effort. For one moment, hesitant, the boy's foot hovered like a dragonfly in the air and then it touched lightly down to draw a shadow under her eye, a small bruise only he could see.

I had never seen anything so marvelous, a child the same age as I was who could draw beautiful pictures, and with his feet. I stood there crushed against the small stage, only my head and shoulders starting above it. But the dark child knew I was there. I could tell.

His quick eyes touched mine for the briefest of moments before slipping away and back to his drawing. Then he looked directly at me and asked what I wanted him to draw. His voice was light and quick with a slight twist in the sound. It was a way of speaking I hadn't heard before. It sounded as if the child was from somewhere far away. His voice was full of pictures, expectations, and somewhere at the heart of it a kind of dream only the dark child knew.

It seemed to me the tent went silent at that moment and no one breathed. There were only the two of us. I told the dark child to draw a boy, a boy like me. The dark one nodded and picking up his charcoal and fresh paper began to draw and it was me he was drawing, me. I could see my eyes and nose and mouth appearing as the dark one's foot moved across the paper.

Look, a woman said, *he's drawing that boy.*

What boy? asked a man.

That was when I reached out and grabbed the drawing. It wasn't finished, but I knew there was no time. I wasn't supposed to be there.

Children weren't allowed in the Sideshow. They weren't supposed to see the Bearded Lady, the Snake Man who was covered in scales, or the Fattest Man in the World. And there was one called a Geek, but I didn't believe the stories they told of him.

The dark child lifted his foot as my hand touched the paper and then I was away, paper clutched to my chest, slipping and sliding through the crowd.

But I had seen his smile.

The dark child knew me.

The next night I ran through the crowd again toward the Sideshow and the freaks. The dark child was who I wanted to see. I wanted to talk to him, but I didn't know how. There was no chance in the Sideshow. They would catch me almost immediately and then I would be sent home to my mother and my father's anger. But I did know something. Behind the Sideshow and the other tents were trailers. I had seen people coming and going from them. Circus people, roustabouts and barkers and the men who ran the Tilt-A-Whirl and Octopus, the hucksters and bouncers. This was where they lived. Somewhere among them was the dark child, the one who drew with his toes, the one who had made the picture my older brother, Dick, had torn up that morning when he found it by my bunk.

I slipped behind the Sideshow tent and hid among the folds of canvas and ropes. I thought that if I waited long enough the child would come. The noise from the midway dimmed and fell away.

One by one men passed by where I hid. They were going into a tent in a far corner of the lot. They walked in a way that said they didn't want to be seen, their shoulders hunched, faces obscured by their hats pulled down low on their foreheads. The tent in the corner was set up under high maples that obscured the light. I thought perhaps the dark child might be there. Like a shadow within shadows I drifted beside the trailers, always watching for anyone who might see me. I knew I had stepped past the midway and past the shows into another, darker world, one that lived behind the fantasy everyone else saw in the glitter and dust. Beyond me the Ferris Wheel turned like a waterfall of night, brilliant with rainbow screams.

Behind the tent straggling Saskatoon bushes sprawled above dusty grass, their leaves mottled and their few berries withered and black. I squatted among them and waited to make sure no one had seen, then I crawled to the edge of the tent. My hands searched the edges of canvas for an opening, some crack in the spiked edge that would allow me to get in. The tent was quiet, but there was light leaking through and I found a spot. A spike of wood was loose and I eased it out of the hard ground. The canvas lifted a bit and I tugged it up until I could push my face through to see.

In the tent I saw men sitting on narrow benches or lounging in the shadows with their hands in their pockets and cigarettes hanging from their lips. On a low stage was the Bearded Lady. She had no clothes on. Her flesh lapped down to her knees and her breasts were pendulous sacks resting on her huge stomach. From between her legs hung a black bush of hair. She was sitting on a low chair, leaning forward into a man.

I looked around at the men who were watching. They were very quiet, their faces still as if part of them had been pulled inside their bodies and hidden there. But it was the dark child I was looking for, not this. I glanced one more time at the Bearded Lady and the man and then I pulled out from under the flap of heavy canvas and backed away into the dark.

Near the entrance I saw two men walking away from the tent. I stopped and waited for them to pass.

The short one said, *That wasn't worth fifty cents.*

The man with him laughed. He flicked his cigarette away and the two of them returned to the midway where their girls waited for them just beyond the shadows. I was just behind them.

When they reached the light I hid under a trailer behind the Sideshow. I sat there in the darkness for what seemed forever. Two of the dollar bills were crumpled in my fist. I waited for the dark child to come. I was going to talk to him. I would give him the money and he would draw me another picture. It would be a picture the dark child would choose and I knew it would be beautiful. I could tell by looking at his face there in the Sideshow tent that he could make a picture so wonderful it would be better than anything in the world. And I would give him the two dollars, three if he wanted, or even four, but the picture would be mine and mine alone. I knew a hiding place where my brothers wouldn't find it.

After the dark child made the picture with his feet we would talk together and tell each other everything. The boy would tell me what it was like to have no arms. He would tell me how he had learned to draw with his feet and I would remember this telling and I would learn it too. It would be like my own drawing and coloring, but nothing I had ever made was anything like what I had seen. A face, my face, growing on paper. For a moment I wished I had no arms and then I wished them back, afraid for a moment, feeling stumps at my shoulders, a sudden emptiness as if my flesh and bones were gone. I thought how wonderful it would be just the two of us together.

I knew it was late. My mother and father would be home from the Legion by now and my father would be calling my name on the dark streets. I had never stayed out so long before. But it didn't matter now. The beating my father would give me would be the same if I stayed out for another hour or two.

I would wait there, I thought, even though I knew the carnival was over. The lights had gone out on the Ferris Wheel and already men were moving over the huge machines. The fretwork of metal was turning into piles of steel stacked on the backs of trucks. Tents were coming down. Far in the distance a fight had begun between some local men and the carnival people. I could hear the shouting and the curses.

I knew the dark child was gone. He was gone even as I had searched for him. The picture the dark child was going to draw for me would never be made. Though I could see it in my mind, I knew I would never have it. It would have to stay in my dream, indescribable, a shimmer of lines and shading, whirls of black upon pale white paper.

As I sat there I vowed I would learn to make pictures like he did. The dark child knew how and so would I. For a moment the Bearded Lady and the man appeared in my mind, but they went as soon as they came, the image of them something I didn't want to think about.

I was already gone from the carnival, walking across the lot behind the legion. Looking up at the summer sky brilliant with stars, I took off my glasses. The stars became distant explosions among the thin clouds. Dust fluttered around my feet as I began to walk again, my face lifted up to the night. I knew the dark child had seen me in the dim light of the stage. He had taken my face and given it back to me. No matter that my brother had ripped it up. It was there in my eyes.

I believe with Borges in the immanence of revelation. Chuang Tzu's conundrum of the butterfly dream is such a revelation realized. I come awake from my meditation on the snail and rest in the equilibrium of now. It is both in-dwelling and out-dwelling and is the snail, the leaf, and me. The dark child too. I can feel his eyes on me still and have only to close mine to see the picture he never drew for me.

❦

The snails are beautiful, yet I put down slug bait and the snails eat it and die. What does it mean to me that I preserve a garden and then kill the creatures who also live here and whose needs are their own, just as mine are? I twist and turn on this dilemma, but there is no clear answer. The spring flowers disappear under the rasps of the slugs and snails. The slug bait I have placed in the garden is exhausted now and I will use no more. What snails have survived may eat what they will. The plants are no longer tender shoots, but have grown halfway to their maturity. What damage the snails do will be little or nothing now. I carry the burden of their many deaths with me. Thus it is for gardeners: life, death, and the beauty that arises from them.

I think of this as I gaze at the holes in the lawn the newest raccoon has dug in his search for beetles and worms. I will set up the live trap again tonight and tomorrow, if he is caught, I will take him like the others into the hills. Another decision made and another creature I wish to banish from the garden, but at least he won't die at my hand.

My drinking years didn't protect me from feeling. The difference now is that I feel more and perhaps this is part of healing. My skin is still a tender sheath covering my body. My liver has begun to grow back, the only organ in my body that can repair itself. The rest of me, stomach, heart, lungs, and brain, injured by the years of drinking, will have to get along as best they can. The doctors say it is remarkable I haven't done more serious damage.

They speak only of the flesh. There are times I feel I am some misshapen thing, a creature who wears his illness inside the illusion of a body that does not betray the damage done. The people I have turned to for help tell me I feel what all addicts feel. They say I must not dwell on the past with all its traps and seductions, its old habits that are designed to lead me right back where I was before, alcoholic and dying. Perhaps what I need to do is learn to accept forgiveness, but who among the dead will forgive me?

Death, alcoholism, and *disease* are words to conjure with this warm April morning. I know I started dying the moment I was born and my life lived so far has been a long path leading toward my leaving. I know that, but I still grieve for time wasted and in meditation do what I can to focus myself and turn away from loss.

Sometimes that focus can only be found in doing. The monkshood need staking, as do numerous other tall plants that a heavy wind or rain could bend or break, and leggy plants need to be pinched back so they can spread out and prosper. The salad garden I planted is well up with lollo rosa and lamb's lettuce, arugula, radicchio, chervil, chicory, bok choy, sweet endive, early spinach, nasturtiums, all kinds of edible surprises.

The tender salad greens that seeded themselves last autumn are now rising like nuns in an abbey, hands raised in praise. I will do a second planting of my favorites in a couple of weeks. I also place seeds in other beds among the flowers and shrubs, anywhere there is a sunny spot. The rich and tender greens decorate the bare spaces with ruffles that shiver when I water them in the early morning. They delight in the bliss of a cool shower, much as I do in the heat of summer.

My main vegetable garden is small, an oval bed of four yards by three, just enough to fill a salad bowl every spring and summer night. Crisp greens picked and plucked are still alive as Lorna and I and our friends eat them drenched in virgin olive oil and fine red vinegar.

The boulevard garden in front of the house is a catch-all for every shrub that bears fruit. I wondered why for a few years until I realized the garden sits under the power and phone lines where birds regularly perch to rest and sing. Of course, they defecate while in that state of tonal bliss and when they do they drop seeds they've eaten, each one surrounded by rich manure. Every spring I am confronted by any number of plants and shrubs, from the salal and Indian plum to red huckleberry and crowberry. I don't bother picking the berries, just allow them to be eaten by robins, thrushes, and the spring swarms of robins and cedar waxwings. This fall I will put a meditation garden here with bamboo fences, a few shrubs, water, and stones. It will be my last project for the year.

The waxwings, Bohemian and cedar both, have arrived and already the holly tree is almost stripped of berries. The birds appeared three days ago and the holly is a quavering whir of sound as they feast. They are delightful birds and love to gossip. No wonder the Bohemian's Latin name is *garrulus*. Their gregarious nature is a wonder to behold as they swirl up in a single, startled flock much as starlings do. The Bohemian has a cinnamon patch on his belly under his tail and yellow, black, and white markings on his wings. What a pleasure to see them again this year. It's very odd to see the two species at the same time and place. They're very affectionate with each other and quite fearless. Seeing twenty of them in the birdbath is to watch an immense shower as they quickly empty it out. They're such sleek dancers in the air.

I think the robins are going mad. I've had a male banging into the window in the dining room for a week now. He perches in the cedar tree and attacks his reflection until he's exhausted. I think he is a young male without a mate. I've seen his behavior before among our own kind, young men who constantly look for argument and fights, the whole of it a frustrated sexuality. The robin like a young man crashes against himself as he delights in the exhaustion of his blood.

He cries as he bangs against the pane, and it is easy for me to make the leap from his madness to my own. I spent much of my time as an alcoholic crashing into my reflection. I can stare through the glass at his frenzied eyes and see in them myself during the years of drinking. I felt the same panic as I made the same repeated attack upon an image I saw as an enemy and who was only myself. It makes me think of friends who are alcoholics or addicts and who methodically and with exquisite malice spent their hours hurting themselves, sometimes with a razor blade or a piece of broken glass, or sometimes with their fists, beating their faces into something broken and, finally, thankfully, unrecognizable. *This is my pain,* the alcoholic says to himself. *It is only mine.*

⁂

I watched the shy appearance of a young woman at the treatment center last winter. The slow unfolding of her beauty was a wonder to see, for she had hated herself and her body for years, hurting it with anorexia and razor blades. She had scored the tender flesh of her arms and the white scars withered on her skin whenever she moved her hand. As the weeks went by in treatment she began to grow a new person out of her old self. I watched her one day as she stared into a mirror. There was a gentle, tentative smile on her face. She had begun to see someone she might love instead of hate. It was her gentleness I saw. I don't know what happened to her after she got out. Pray God, she is all right. She talked a lot about suicide.

I know her story well. I tried to kill myself several times with a gun and many times in the covering illusion of car accidents. The last time I tried suicide I sat on the edge of my bed in the house on the Sunshine Coast. It was deep autumn and raining. My wife and the boys had gone into Madeira Park to pick up groceries.

I was once again deep into drinking. I had found my annual fall depression at the bottom of a bottle a day. It was six months before my wife and I split up. I knew I had to leave, but images of the wreckage of my first family had reared up in my head. Here I was, doing the same thing all over again. I had once more found my life both predictable and appalling. The great ghosts of the past danced in me. I welcomed the grotesquerie. A recurring nightmare of the dark cellar and the blood I had to hide from whoever was coming downstairs had returned. Every night I woke up in a sweat, weeping. Sitting there on the bed I stared down the barrel of my 22/410 over-and-under, the brush gun I'd inherited from my father.

I had the shotgun barrel open and a shell in the chamber. The taste of the gun oil was strange honey in my mouth. I had tasted it before. There was peace in that moment, peace and a great tiredness. I had the stock braced against my foot and my right arm down with my thumb pressed in the trigger guard. My left hand gripped the barrel just below my lips.

A wasp had stumbled into the bedroom and was banging his metal skull on the window. I remember feeling frustrated by his desire to escape and wished him into the kitchen where the door was open onto the deck. My eyes were closed. The wasp kept cracking against the glass.

I heard the car drive into the yard and my wife call out. I could hear my little boy run to the steps. I pressed the trigger down and the shotgun went off and blew a hole in the light fixture in the ceiling above me. I don't remember pulling my head back. I only remember a split second of frustration at their return and the feeling of shame that they might catch me killing myself.

The light fixture flashed sparks and a fire began in the black hole my shotgun had left. Smoke curled across the ceiling in folds. I threw the shotgun aside just as they all came into the bedroom. I told my wife I had been cleaning the gun and it had gone off. In the panic of getting a ladder, disconnecting the wires, and putting out the fire, she didn't ask why I was cleaning the gun in the bedroom, nor why there was no gun oil or rag there. The boys were excited. The oldest ran around the room as his brother lay on his back in his blanket and kicked his little legs in the air, happy to see his father fixing things, making everything all better.

She put the shotgun away on the rack in the front porch. I finished dowsing the fire and sat down at the kitchen table. I poured myself three more fingers of Scotch. She had brought a sack of fresh prawns from a fisherman and began shelling them for dinner. I took my Scotch into the living room. As I sat down, the suicide attempt sank quietly into the depression where I kept such things as death. I held the two boys on my lap and began singing them a made-up song about guns and ceilings, explosions and fire, and the big bad bear that makes it all happen. The boys loved my songs because I always included them in the tale.

In two days it was as if it had never happened. Only a story remained, something my wife would encourage me to tell over drinks after dinner to friends, the one about the time I blew a hole in the ceiling with my shotgun. One designed to make people laugh at my foolishness.

※

A few delicate marsh violets have appeared out of nowhere below the holly tree and I transplanted them yesterday with care, for they can be fragile when disturbed and can die away. As Wordsworth said, "With gentle hand / Touch—for there is a spirit in the woods." I put them in the shade garden. They're a lovely addition to this quiet spot and I hope their spirits prosper there. They spread by seed, of course, but mostly by rhizomes and creeping stolons. Their flower is the most delicate white, although one plant is showing the palest mauve on its petals.

I love it when plants appear from nowhere. I've no idea how the violets came to be here, but they fit into the shady habitat I've moved them to. They love the moist and the damp. Bogs and wetlands are their joy. They complement the early blue violet and the Alaska violet, both of which inhabit my garden. They all flower in late March, but all three are still blooming here and there in garden beds and in the lawns. They appear as if by magic.

All the violets are perennials and are more than welcome. They are shy, low-growing plants and love the dappled, dampness of the semishade. In Europe violets were sometimes worn in wreaths around the neck. It was said they were a cure for drunkenness, something I didn't know before and wish I had. My mother should have knotted a wreath around my neck when I was born.

The scent of violets always takes me back to my mother. Like most women of her generation, she wore powder, perfume, and lipstick, and all the filmy garments that made her think she was exquisite and beautiful in the eyes of men. I loved her beauty when I was a boy. I dressed up in my mother's clothes one afternoon. I was, perhaps, eleven or twelve years old, just around puberty when both child and man ran side by side in my young body.

One afternoon while everyone was out I walked down the hall to the bathroom in my mother's silk underwear. The fragile material felt cool against my hard cock. My hand was behind my back, clenched in the silk and I pulled it tight against me. In my other hand her brassiere dangled to the floor.

In the bathroom I put on her brassiere and then took handfuls of toilet paper and stuffed it in the cups. Satisfied, I went back down the hall to the bedroom and pulled on a pair of silk stockings. They sagged around my skinny legs, but it didn't matter to me as I stepped into her black dress. I squirmed to do up the zipper in the back. My new breasts filled the front of the dress and I touched them. They felt soft under my hands. I turned then to my mother's small vanity and carefully applied powder and rouge and finally lipstick. When my face was changed I stepped into a pair of her high heels and teetered over to her full-length mirror. Her shoes were bright red and they shone on my feet.

How beautiful they were. The leather shone like an animal might shine who first saw herself clothed in glory. The skin I wore was not my skin. It was an other, strange with illumination.

I turned around slowly as I gazed at myself. My thin arms moved in the perfumed air of the room. The smell of lipstick and rouge filled my nostrils. I licked my painted lips, touched my narrow waist and new breasts. You're beautiful, I thought. I reached down to the crinkled hem of the black dress and lifted it slowly until the silk underwear was revealed. My small hard cock jabbed against the pale pink silk. I tried to force it between my legs so I would look more like a girl, but it wouldn't stay there. It kept springing out. I let it stay that way and dropped the dress back down.

I turned then and walked out of her bedroom into the living room where I walked uneasily across the hardwood floor and then began turning in slow circles. My arms floated in the air. My eyes were closed. Even when the heels turned on me and I stumbled in an awkward twist, I never opened my eyes, just kept moving in the beauty of the dance.

Who did I see there in the mirror? That young face was not grotesque. It was comical, a clown's face, a fool's. The lipstick was crooked, the eyebrows too long, too large for such a small, delicate face. I was fierce in my transformations, a small dreamer in the mirror of my desires. I was not a man, not a woman, only a child, one who was growing into the years. I loved my desire to be whatever, whomever I wanted.

Ten minutes later I took off her clothes, hung up the dress, and placed the panties, brassiere, and stockings back in her drawer. Naked then, I turned back to the mirror.

I was a boy again except for my face. I turned my head this way and that as I inspected my makeup. I slipped my tongue across my lips and tasted the lipstick again. For a moment I didn't know what I wanted or who I was, and then I did.

I ran down the hall into the bathroom, washed my face until there was no trace left of what I had worn, pulled on my jeans and running shoes, and slammed out the screen door into the backyard. I raced across the beaten clay to the alley and down the worn ruts toward the fields where I had hidden cigarettes in an old can.

Safe in the shade of a pile of rotting cedar fence posts, I lit a cigarette and leaned back into the smell of dust and wood. My thoughts flickered on the image of myself in the mirror. As it did, a girl from across the street entered my mind. I remembered putting my hand inside her panties. I had been kissing her and she had let me touch her. There was nothing there but smooth skin and the slit of flesh I had seen the summer before. We had pushed against each other and then we broke away, both of us startled by what we had done.

I leapt up and began to run. The air blessed me as it rushed past my mouth and eyes. I was full of my own lean, lonely race through the day. The dust swirled around my sneakers. There was nowhere I couldn't go, nothing I couldn't do. The sheer pleasure of running was alive in my muscles and bone.

❦

I have spent my years here in a great battle with one of the most beautiful little plants we have in this region, the creeping buttercup. This spring is no exception. The buttercup's glossy yellow flowers appear in profusion everywhere in the garden. It spreads by seed but also by long stolons. The stolon end touches down and almost immediately roots. Its invasive nature drowns out such plants as the delicate violet. Once established it is impossible to eliminate entirely and unfortunately it is firmly established in my garden. Its roots are extremely tenacious and I never attempt to remove them unless I've watered the ground well in order to soften their hold on the earth.

They invade everywhere and, if not controlled, will dominate and eventually smother anything else. Lorna and I spend days on our knees methodically digging up the noxious weed.

A plant is a weed only if you don't want it to grow in your garden and I don't want this one. The creeping buttercup is poisonous and can inflame and blister the mouth and throat if it's ingested. Woe betide the gardener who mixes their dark green leaves with salad greens! It's smart to know the deadly plants that live in your yard.

The power of the old lords and gods of earlier times was their ability to harm as much as bless us. That they could destroy us at their whim is one of the roots to the word *danger*. To have power over someone and to control them is the way of witches and warlocks, all of whom used potions and simples to both heal and harm us. A garden has always been a place where both good and evil coexist. Knowing which plant can harm us is only wise.

The commonest poison I can ingest is a mushroom, but there are many others. It's odd that some of the most poisonous plants are among the most beautiful. I watch the monkshood growing tall against the fence in the shadiest part of the yard, a place that gets little direct sun. They have not yet budded and won't bloom until September. I love the nodding flowers with their dark blue hoods. Yet every part of the monkshood is deadly. And what of the rhubarb Lorna makes our spring pie with? We eat the stems and throw the leaves away because it is in the leaves that the toxins are concentrated. The foxglove is poisonous as well. I know its use as a source for digitalis. I have sucked the nectar from the blossoms with no ill effect. The leaves are very bitter. I tried one the other day and while I felt no sudden jolt to the heart, it's best to be cautious. The garden is full of danger to the unwitting neophyte who thinks all nature benign. It is also full of things to eat such as nasturtium blossoms. Their peppery flavor livens up a salad.

I live-trap the raccoons, but I put out spring traps that kill the rats. They're baited with cheddar cheese. The rats live in the ivy that grows around our house. There, and in the woodpile and under the sheds. We had them in the attic and in the walls when first we moved here, but I have managed to rat-proof the house now. The yard is another matter and my battle with the rats will go on until I drop or we move away. The cats catch the occasional one but not too often. Rats are very intelligent creatures but noxious because I find them so, their smell, their depredations, and their propensity to carry disease, though I'm sure my fear of disease is only because of ancient tales of medieval plagues. They feed in the compost bin and forage among the seeds the birds fling from the bird feeders.

I've killed five in the past week. I have to keep moving the traps around for once one is caught, the others stay away. I've had to pour boiling water on them to wash off the smell of a dead uncle, aunt, or cousin rat who died there. A clean trap will catch a rat. These are wood rats and they are everywhere in the Americas from desert to jungle, from Tierra del Fuego to the Arctic Circle. They are sometimes called pack rats or trade rats because of their propensity to pick up shiny objects to take back to their nests.

When wood rats are excited or threatened they do a kind of drumming dance that is, to my mind, a warning to the other rats nearby. It could be celebratory or a show of macho energy, but I doubt it. They drum their hind legs on the ground for a moment or two, then scamper off to safety in the woodpile. I've heard the drumming on dry boards I have laid down beside the woodpile.

I've cleaned out their nests in the wall of ivy at the back of the house. Some are quite large and are made of sticks and leaves and moss. The nests look quite untidy until you open them up. The inner nest is a wonderful cup of the softest mosses and grasses. Threads of wool, bits of cotton string, and oddments of torn fabrics are all used to make a comfortable spot for their brood. Once I found a nickel and two dimes in a nest. I thought I'd keep the coins as some kind of strange souvenir, but they got mixed in with other change and disappeared into a cash register somewhere.

I measure friendship by those who are the friends of spiders and those who are not. To me there is nothing more beautiful than an orb weaver as she makes her web in the early evening in anticipation of tomorrow's feasting. Watching her slow, patient dance as she moves in ever-decreasing circles from the perimeter, pausing at each of the walking strings to anchor her catching-silk. The sticky silk radiates inward in a spiral like a star that is going nova. Rise with the dawn and count the dream-catchers in your garden. You will find them by their jeweled webs festooned with a thousand droplets of dew. The first rays of the sun as it breaks above the far mountains catch their many webs and turns them into the purest form of meditation there is.

I meditate upon orb weavers. What child hasn't dropped a bug into a web and watched the subsequent struggle as the spider darts from her hanging perch at the web's center toward her prey? Who hasn't seen a grass spider dart out from its funnel of web to snare a passing insect that has wandered too close? Everyone should watch the minuscule branch-tip spider guard her spiderlings through the early autumn before the band disperses to find solitary shelter in crevices of bark, anywhere there is a safe place to wait out the winter. The tiny webs of this spider decorate the farthest tips of my fir tree branches, the best place to snare passing prey.

This morning I climbed on top of the old stump beside the contorted hazelnut in its blue ceramic container to check on the *Magnolia grandiflora* I pruned earlier this spring. As I gently pulled a branch close to see if the tree was putting out new buds, I found a nest of baby orb weavers. There were more than fifty of the tiny golden spiderlings all still bundled together as they were in the egg sac.

I breathed on them gently, just as I have so many times in the past. The smell and warmth of my breath alarmed the tiny creatures and while some scattered outward the rest dropped on filaments of webbing so finely spun it was almost impossible to see, until they rested like a living wind chime in the air. I waited and watched as they carefully climbed back up to their brothers and sisters and gathered again into a bundle.

I believe in arachnids just as I believe in snakes. I count them among my closest friends in my garden. As long as there are spiders, then there must be gnats, flies, mosquitoes, wasps, and every other kind of prey. The spiders tell me my garden is healthy. They tell me it's alive. As for the magnolia, it's doing fine.

I have found spiders all over the world. I was once in Xian in China at the Great Goose Temple where the poets Li Po and Tu Fu sat in the heart of the Tang Dynasty and drank and read poems to each other. I stood in the shadows of the temple and touched the stones that those ancient poets touched and I remembered their poems and felt close to them and their struggle to find beauty in the graceful, urgent lines of poetry. Like Chichen Itza, Machu Picchu, or Stonehenge, the Great Goose Temple was a reminder of how the words of those poets, frail and transitory, lived long enough to touch me when I was a young poet in the mountains of British Columbia.

Tired and quiet, I walked out of the temple into the dusty gardens. I followed a narrow path and found myself among weary rhododendrons and willows. It was easy at that moment to find in the poor plants a metaphor for the temple, the poets of long ago, and my own writing. I sat on a stone bench and stared at the temple in the early evening, the sun just beginning its slow fall into the west. As I looked I realized I was staring through the huge web of an orb weaver spider. It was one of the largest webs I had ever seen, easily two feet in diameter. In the center of the web hung a great spider.

What to a passing fly or bee might have seemed a dangerous maze, was to her an intricate knowing, a place of symmetry and beauty. As I watched, my tiredness slipped away and I was content in myself, for a brief hour happy in a place far from my country and my home.

I think that contentment, that happiness, has stayed with me in spite of the many difficulties and confusions my life has offered me. Even during the worst of my addictions I know there lived inside me that same happiness and though I denied it or worse, stared at it through the mask of alcohol or drugs, it made no difference to its presence. I think back to that hour in the garden of the Great Goose Temple in Xian and know I find the same peace in my garden here where the sisters of that orb weaver hang in the breeze of this late spring, their webs growing each day as they grow larger. Such is the life of spiders and such is my life now. Each day is a slow growing that I am only aware of by looking back and remembering how far the journey has been for me. The magnolia is fine, the baby spiders are fine, and so am I.

※

A clutch of western Saint-John's-wort grows with Siberian miner's lettuce just behind the stump. The latter have delicate white flowers and the Saint-John's-wort yellow ones. The stamens of the Saint-John's-wort are very long and resemble fragile needles. The bees roll over and across them in what seems a paroxysm of sensual pleasure as they get covered in the pollen. It is the only way they have of gathering it. The stamens are far too long and fragile to bear a bee's weight. By rolling they accomplish their task of gathering food. Preprogrammed instinct? I don't think so.

Some few-flowered shooting stars have also appeared and are already pushing out leaves and what will soon be flowers. The plants appear, blossom, and then disappear entirely, their leaves dying back once flowering is over. They are aptly named and their swept-back lavender wings seem to float in the air on slender, leafless stems. They poke out from under sword ferns and bracken, and under them the cleavers prospers. It's a spindly plant with tiny hooked bristles on the angles of the stems. It is hard to eradicate as the stems break off very easily when it's pulled, leaving the roots to grow again. It appears, I pull it up, and it appears again. It's not too much of a nuisance. Actually, I like its crooked wandering among the other plants. It leans on them, its tiny bristles supporting its search for the sun above the columbines and other vigorous perennials. I leave a few here and there for the pleasure of their limbs. They remind me of sweet peas and have a similar kind of back-and-forth, crooked stem and pealike flower. It helps in climbing to shift your limbs from side to side. I too have shifted my limbs from side to side as I climbed the mountains of my youth.

The mountains were my home during my childhood, but so was the town. Its alleys and vacant lots were my playground and I watched and learned from the town's strange people, the vagrants and wanderers. My father would give me fifteen cents on Saturday so I could go to the movie at the Empress Theatre, but it was not enough, never enough. There were too many temptations, too many things I wanted. I stole and lied in order to get a few more nickels.

If I couldn't get any, I would drift down to the edge of Main Street near Chinatown where the cheap cafés were.

My favorite was the Victory Café. It was old and worn out. Booths sagged along the wall. The seat covers were some kind of early plastic. Most had been cut with knives, and the stuffing flared out like a flower. Jimmy Woo sat on his stool by his cash register, flies droning in the air around him. He had long ago given up trying to deal with them. They landed on everything. In the glass case in front of him were the candies children bought, jawbreakers and nigger-babies, all the penny candy a child could covet. Jimmy had seen it all. He had built this café when he was a young man. Now he was old.

Once, I watched as his wife shuffled out of the kitchen and yelled something incomprehensible to everyone but Jimmy. He didn't move from the cash register. She yelled again and shuffled back into the kitchen through the swinging doors. A smell of grease and meat slid into the café and settled slowly onto the booths and the long counter with its stools.

At one end a man leaned into a bowl of chow mein. He forked it into his mouth, slivers of pork and bean sprouts and noodles. It was a cheap meal. This man looked at nothing, saw nothing. At the middle of the counter another man sat with me. He had bought me a sundae, a concoction of ice cream and cherries and sauce. I spooned it into my mouth. Under the counter the man moved his hand onto my thigh. I paid no attention as the hand moved down into my crotch. I had my pants on. It didn't matter. The sundae cost twenty-five cents. The change from the dollar the man paid with was in my pocket. I could feel it there. Seventy-five cents.

I shifted on my stool and the man took his hand away.

When I started eating again, the man put his hand back and fondled me through the thin fabric of my pants. I was hard from the touching. The taste of the ice cream and cherries was cold and sweet in my mouth and belly. I knew the man would soon want me to go back to his room in the Angeles Apartments. It was always the same, the man buying me things and giving me money while he played with my cock. He was only one among others. They all gave me money. So far it had always worked out.

When I finished the last of the sundae I asked the man to buy me something else. Something cheap. When the man tried to pay for the candy with a dime, I took a fifty-cent piece from his palm and paid Jimmy Woo with that, pulling the forty-five cents change across the counter and into my pocket.

The man had begun to rub himself and tried to get me to touch him there. I did and felt the hardness pushing against his pants. I told him I had to go to the bathroom. I promised that after I was finished I would go home with him.

I looked at the man's face. It was gray and old. It looked angry and frightened at the same time. There were hairs in his nose and his eyes were a strange shade of blue. There was a smell, a mustiness that rose from him.

I walked down the worn boards toward the bathroom. I knew the man was watching me. I made as if to move into the toilet and then slipped through the swinging doors into the kitchen. Mrs. Woo yelled something, but I ignored her. I slipped under her arm, dashed around the steam table and chopping block, and ran through the screen door into the alley.

I think now of the man in the café. He knew it would happen. I imagine his pain as his desire ran away from him. I imagine his trembling as he got up slowly and went out into the hot, dry summer of Main Street.

But that is only imagining. What I see is the boy fleeing down the street. He runs with the swiftness of a fox, a slipping run that can't be caught by eye. Two alleys and he's disappeared into the trees behind the billboards at the end of Main Street. He sits on a high limb in a twisted maple and counts his money. Men wander in and out of the Vernon Hotel, some drunk, some not. Two blocks away the sun glints off the windows of the Victory Café. Oil and steam have made them almost opaque. A man steps out of the doorway and, glancing both ways quickly, walks east toward the hotels. His hands are in his pockets. His head is down as if he were searching for something on the wooden boardwalk, something he lost.

I had a dollar twenty. A fortune.

The moment I was aware of innocence, I knew I no longer had it. Memory is not continuous. It was not meant to be, and innocence is lost in its small fragments. Each time I remember the past it comes to me in pieces, each an event that expresses something gained or something lost. Guilt and remorse are the companions of healing, just as happiness is. The past is the present illuminated. It is a small house with many windows. I stare from each one at myself.

I stood once with Lorna on the stones at Knossos outside Heraklion in Crete and was struck by how small history is. The ancient palace and temple complex covered only a few hectares and yet this was where Daedalus fabricated the wings for Icarus while the monstrous Minotaur waited for sacrificial virgins in the spiral labyrinth somewhere below, somewhere never found and perhaps existing only as metaphor for the unconscious.

The Knossos of my imagination is far greater than the scattered stones on that little hill in Crete. When metaphor becomes reality, it stops the spirit. Yet somehow I think I am in search of the real. The bits and pieces of the past that have intruded in these last months are only steps toward what I wish to know. The only gift I can take from them is the opposite of innocence, wisdom, and that is a humility I am learning to accept. Perhaps the past does not exist at all and is only an obsessive fabrication.

※

This is the month for rhododendrons. Some can bloom as early as January but the majority flaunt their flowers from mid-April till June. There are two wild rhododendrons native to British Columbia. One is the white-flowered rhododendron and the other the Pacific rhododendron. There is also a false azalea that is sometimes called fool's huckleberry. The false azalea and white-flowered rhododendron are often found together along with the copperbush. There are hundreds and hundreds of other kinds of rhododendrons growing around the Pacific Rim from Alaska and Siberia to Tierra del Fuego and the Philippines.

Across from the three rhododendrons water falls into my fishpond from a bamboo spout. The bamboo is buried among the leaves of a skimmia and a hydrangea. The spout above the pond is a small dark cave balanced upon stones. It looks as if it has been there forever.

This morning I watched a chickadee bathe in the spout as the cool water flowed between her tiny black legs. A private bathing spot, much safer than the birdbath out in the middle of the lawn under the apple tree. Basho hunts there and has been busy catching pine siskins. The chickadee had seen his daily hunt and had decided to take her bath elsewhere. Bathed and refreshed she flitted up into the fir tree, found a sunny spot, and rearranged her damp feathers to her liking. Finally, dapper and pert as ever, she flew to a blue columbine blooming at the edge of the salad garden and perched there a moment. The columbine bent under her weight and she lifted away from the uneasy perch to the feeder, where she busied herself choosing just the right seeds for lunch.

I must always remember to think my way into the space of a garden. I don't run around and throw plants wherever there happens to be a bare spot. When I first came here with Lorna I tried to picture myself in the garden of my mind. That was a good place to begin. The garden I imagined had always been there inside me. It just needed letting out.

I didn't squat in my living room in front of a book. I sat in established gardens. I spent time among plants and trees. I looked at them and felt them. I absorbed textures and smells, observed the landscape, its levels and planes, the way it rose and fell. When I stared into its depressions and stood on its miniature promontories, I imagined a pond or a rockery. I planted a Japanese maple above a rhododendron and added a small bamboo to a corner long before I acquired the plants themselves.

This garden is an extension of my hands and feet, my eyes and ears and nose. Do you like stone? Then search out stones, little ones or big ones, it doesn't matter. Choose them for color, shape, or texture. For years Lorna has picked up what she calls moon rocks. They're stones that have a circle of white quartz in them. Our pathways and garden pond are decorated with hundreds, from rocks the size of a walnut to hundred-pound stones. Why moon rocks? I don't know, she just started collecting that kind of rock. Friends have brought them to her from as far away as Haida Gwaii, Provence, Cape Town, and Kyoto.

In my garden the common spreadwings are already hunting tiny flies and early mosquitoes. These slender damselflies are wonderfully delicate. The blue-eyed darner is huge compared to them. I've read that falcons learn the skills of flying by chasing dragonflies. What a delight it would be to see a peregrine falcon coursing my garden in search of blue-eyed darners so he could improve his aerial arts.

Spring azure butterflies have been cavorting in my garden these past three weeks. They are my earliest butterfly. They're quite small, about an inch long. They will be my garden's companions until the end of May when they will become shabby and tired. It's the males I see. They're out searching the garden for females to mate with. Three males had a territorial battle yesterday. They chased and battered each other until one of the butterflies left the garden altogether. The other two decided to call a truce and share the space. Their wings are the softest of blues. They are the color of the morning shadows that touch Lorna's small shoulders when she is reading in the shade of the apple tree.

A gardener has nothing but time. Stooping to pull yet another creeping buttercup I looked under the sharply serrated leaf of the perennial cilantro that grows by the viburnum near the deck and there, hanging quietly and safely concealed from birds, was a silvery-blue butterfly. It was a gossamer-winged butterfly and normally it keeps his wings tightly closed together when resting, but this little fellow had his wings spread. The underside had a pale gray hue with telltale black spots circled by white around the outside edge of the wings. He rested there out of the sun and I finished my bit of weeding and went back into the house. There are many small worlds in the garden, each one a place to rest.

❧

This morning I found a full mickey of vodka tucked under the corner of the deck in the shade of the overhanging viburnum. My hands shook as I picked it up, doubly so because it was full. The weight of the clear glass bottle, its shape, the color of its red cap, and the dense swirl of slight oiliness in the liquid made me feel I was holding an old and trusted friend. It was all I could do to carry it into the kitchen, break the seal, and watch the alcohol chug slowly down the drain. It was like watching both ambrosia and poison vanish at the same time. How my body yearned to drink it and how, at the same time, it rebelled against the thought.

I dropped the empty bottle into the garbage and went down to the pond, where I sat alone in the slant sun of late afternoon.

Desire is feeling elicited by something or someone else. It is a powerful pain as sweet as Lowry's cold agony as he stood in his garden with his bottle of gin and drank it. The power the body has to go willingly toward pain is something no one understands, not even the addict himself. It was pain that made me empty the bottle in the sink. It was pain that made me turn away. I felt no triumph of will, just a terrible longing as if I were asking for a blade to be held to my own throat.

Almost six months sober and a bottle of vodka can still hurt me. I sat by the pond for an hour before I felt capable of getting up. As I walked across the lawn I felt a dozen other possible bottles beckoning me from the daphne and the bamboo, the woodpile and the toolshed. The whole garden seemed a drinker's minefield, a place of terror. I lay down beside the golden bamboo and closed my eyes. I woke an hour later to shadow and a long evening of unsteady peace. In the morning I rose, shook off the weight of the night, and began to drive to a nursery to pick up some water plants for the pond.

At the side of the road a few blocks from our house a hermit thrush flew up from the gravel verge and thrashed in the chill air of this unseasonable May morning. He rose and fluttered with a kind of hysteria that belied his quiet presence in the brush, which crests in fragments among the intrusive suburbs that have slowly eaten away at his habitat. I pulled my truck over, parked, and got out slowly and quietly. It was a male, a little smaller than a robin with a freckled breast, rusty tail, and olive, buff-colored head and back. Pale rings circled his black eyes. He rose in a dance I've seen before.

A car came and the bird lifted as if to attack the oncoming thunder of rubber and chrome, plastic and steel. The woman behind the wheel saw nothing but the road ahead. She had to get to somewhere in the hurry that is only human. She did not see the thrush with his breast lifted and his beak open. The car passed in a rush of wind and sprayed gravel.

I watched as it ran to the body of his mate. The female had been struck by a car or truck and her body was folded upon itself in the small desert of gravel between the pavement and the yellowed grass at the edge of the drainage ditch. The male bowed to her and cried a new, impossible song. It was not the song of warning and not the song he sang when he was trying to win her attention this past month. And it was not the rare single high cry of late summer and early autumn. The notes I heard didn't carry that rise of hope. This was different. It was a trilling that stuttered into wild squawks. He grasped her wing in his beak, and pulled it a bit, urging her to fly. When she did not respond, he flew up once more, threw his head back, and sang again.

His was a song of grief. There is no other way to describe it. I have heard the same song in the streets of Peruvian villages, in the mountain towns of Mexico and Colombia, Xian and Rome. I have heard it in my own land. It was a cry to God. It asked for impossible answers. It was the song that precedes Kaddish, precedes mourning. This was outcry.

It is one of the oldest songs the world knows and the male thrush sang it and would go on singing it until he was exhausted. Somewhere in the crotch of a tree or shrub was a nest with spotted, pale green eggs. The male would sing and do his dance of death until driven away by the steady rush of traffic or by the ubiquitous crows, one or two of which were already perched on the gable end of a nearby house.

They recognized the dance, they knew the song. The male thrush would try to keep them away with audacious, raging attacks but eventually he would give up the ground and a crow would carry away her prize to the ditch where she could eat at leisure. The male would stay around for a few days and then he would be gone. The nest would be deserted. There would be no incubation there, no further life.

Whenever I see this I am enraged, not at the death by misadventure, for such deaths on the roads and highways are common enough and the bodies left behind are provender for hawks, eagles, vultures, crows, raccoons, rats, coyotes, and whatever else hunts the highway's verge for food. The death of one songbird is not of great consequence. There are many thrushes in the forests and fields near where I live. My cats kill the occasional siskin or junco and I do not grieve their deaths, though I am saddened a bit when I see the cats play with their still-living bodies. I have my own griefs. I understand that.

I am enraged by the carelessness. I wanted to bring car drivers to this stretch of country road and ask them to watch this creature, this thrush, as he mourned the death of his mate. I would ask them to pay close attention as he touched her dead body with his beak as if with his touch he could bring her back to life. I would ask them to be aware of what occurs at the edges of their busy lives.

The hermit thrush rose on flared wings, fell, and rose again. The crows cocked their heads in anticipation and cleaned their beaks on the shakes of the gable. They waited with the patience of their kind.

I got back in my truck and drove slowly away.

✺

I want at times to speak of everything in my garden. How the clematis weighs down the lattice bower and the wisteria in full bloom climbs the front porch and runs from there to the peak of the second-story roof. The wisteria is one blue breath against the red shingles of the wall. The clematis is a bird warren, the house finches with their rose breasts are one with the blooms they play among.

Today I will stand under the eaves and listen to the plaint of the rain in this young garden of mine. I will stare through the mist at the yellow blooms of the Japanese iris by the pond, how they seem to hang like wet suns among the bare stalks of the golden bamboo. I will wish my people well. *Selah.*

PLANTS

Alaska violet – *Viola langsdorfii*
Albida water lily – *Nymphaea "Marliacea Albida"*
Anemone – *Anemone magellanica (multifida)*
Astilbe – *Astilbe* × *arendsii*
    " – *Astilbe japonica*
    " – *Astilboides tabularis* (formerly *Rodgersia tabularis*)
Baldhip rose – *Rosa gymnocarpa*
Bamboo – *Polystichum cristata*
Cleavers – *Galium aparine*
Columbine – *Aquilegia* spp.
Copperbush – *Cladothamnus pyroliflorus*
Creeping buttercup – *Ranunculus repens*
Crested lady fern – *Athyrium filix-femina "Cristatum"*
Crowberry – *Empetrum nigrum*
Early blue violet – *Viola palmata*

False azalea – *Menziesia ferruginea*
Indian plum – *Oemleria cerasiformis*
Lady fern – *Athyrium filix-femina*
Ligularia – *Ligularia stenocephala, przewalskii, dentata*
Monkshood – *Aconitum carmichaelii "Arendsii"*
Nootka rose – *Rosa nutkana*
Pacific rhododendron – *Rhododendron macrophyllum*
Red huckleberry – *Vaccinium parvifolium*
Rhododendron – *Rhododendron* spp.
Rhubarb – *Rheum rhaponticum*
Salal – *Gaultheria shallon*
Siberian miner's lettuce – *Claytonia sibirica*
Spanish lavender – *Lavandula stoechas "Otto Quast"*
Stream violet – *Viola glabella*
Trailing yellow violet – *Viola sempervirens*
Trillium – *Trillium*
Western Saint-John's-wort – *Hypericum formosum*
White-flowered rhododendron – *Rhododendron albiflorum*

ANIMALS, BIRDS, AND INSECTS

Blue-eyed darner dragonfly – *Aeshna multicolor*
Bohemian waxwing – *Bombycilla garrulus*
Branch-tip spider – *Dictyna* spp.
Cedar waxwing – *Bombycilla cedrorum*
Cherry-faced meadowhawk – *Sympetrum internum*
Grass spider – *Agelenopsis* spp.
Hudsonian whiteface dragonfly – *Leucorrhinia hudsonica*
Orb weaver spider – *Araneus* spp.
Pacific forktail damselfly – *Ischnura cervula*
Peregrine falcon – *Falco peregrinus*
Silvery blue butterfly – *Glaucopsyche lygdamus*
Spring azure butterfly – *Celastrina "ladon"*
Swainson's thrush – *Catharus ustulatus*
Wood rat – *Neotoma*

6.

I believe a leaf of grass is no less than the journey-work
  of the stars,
And the pismire is equally perfect, and a grain of sand,
  and the egg of the wren,
And the tree toad is a chef-d'oeuvre for the highest,
And the running blackberry would adorn the parlors
  of heaven.
  —WALT WHITMAN, "SONG OF MYSELF"

A STONE UPON A PATH knows more than I do of the rain. The hummingbird's heart has a rhythm greater than Gilgamesh, the snail's shell more intricate than the stones of Sacsahuaman. When I listen closely in the garden rooms there is a great singing in the earth and in the air that shelters it. The tiniest forms seethe in their immensity. A black ant walking across the pebbled path by the pond follows a trail she and her cohorts laid down a million years ago. There was a time I would have said I was oblivious to the ant, but no more.

Once in Mexico I watched a line of leaf-cutter ants parade toward their underground nest. Each ant carried a green sail carved from the leaves of trees. The cavernous opening of their nest was two hands wide. Deep in the underground chambers a horde was busy transforming the leaves into provender. Like them, the black ant on my path is followed by her sisters, each carrying a grub, insect, or crumb from the bread I ate an hour ago. One bears the body of a moth a hundred times her size. The ants know more than I of intricate stones.

The path to the ant is a great plain, a rubble heap of boulders, which to me are merely pebbles. Like the ant, I have clambered along the screes of mountains. I know how difficult the passage is through a boulder-strewn valley when there is no one to mark my path. These past months have been one such path and I have tried to learn its ways. The ground of my healing is strewn with boulders that once were mountains.

I step over the ants and continue down the stone path to the pond with my cup of tea. In this late afternoon, solitude eludes me. I am no more than a garden monk who walks the green cloisters with his beads and cowl as he ruminates upon the lives of ants and butterflies, fir trees and ferns.

I think solitude is other than peace and more than quietude. It's not a journey to some elsewhere. It's not the wish to be lost within myself and it's not a willful silence. Solitude is presence, not absence. It leaves at the moment of apprehension. The contemplative life becomes a struggle as soon as I'm aware of it. I go here and there thinking this cedar tree or stone bench will afford me quiet and seclusion, but within a few minutes I become restless and go to search out some other spot to be alone. But I am by myself most of the time so what is this other thing I seek?

There have been moments when my body took me away into another world and once there I could not find a way back. My flesh has made choices for me that my mind cannot comprehend. I remember when my body began its great change from boyhood into manhood. I remember standing in the last summer of my family's first home in Vernon. That house is now a parking lot, the only thing left to mark my time there the stump of a tree cut flat to the cement. I climbed that tree with my brothers and practiced throwing hunting knives into a chalk circle drawn on its bark. I hid stolen cigarettes in a hole under one of its gnarled roots. Five years ago I stood on the stump and occupied the space the tree had known. I stood on its many rings and felt I was growing ancient roots and leaves. Among my fingers a small boy played.

We lived in that old house for seven years. In the last week I was there I took wax paper left over from a loaf of bread and went into the woodshed. Against the back wall were rows of stacked wood for the house fires. Thin beams of sun streamed through the wooden walls. Spiders sat in their webs, thin legs poised on silk dream-catchers as they awaited a blundering fly who had fed too long on the body of a mouse slowly decaying under a pile of old kindling. Sitting in the curve of the chopping block, I took the page I had spent the night writing and folded it small, then placed it in the center of the wax paper. I wrapped it around the words, making what I thought would be a waterproof package. No one had seen me, no brother, parent, enemy, or friend. Tucking the package into my back pocket, I walked barefoot from the shed to the broken gate, through it and down the narrow alley past Ralston's Bakery and Kineshanko Motors.

My family was moving to the new subdivision of postwar houses on the hill above Vernon. We were going to live in one of the two-story houses. My father had a better car now. Our lives were changing. New things had begun to appear, a radio-record player that played 78s and 45s, new dresses for my mother, a camel-hair topcoat for my father, shoes and shirts for us, a Mixmaster, a refrigerator, an electric stove. The old icebox with its weekly block of melting ice was gone from the back porch. The iceman with his spavined horse and creaking wagon no longer passed down the alley with his ice pick and tongs. There would be no more of us boys chasing after him and begging for shards of ice to suck in the hot afternoons.

Alders and cottonwoods leaned out from the edge of the deserted field and hung motionless over the roof of the Holy Roller Church behind the burned-out remains of the Vernon Hotel. The church was quiet now after the ecstasy and madness of the night before. I had stood in the church doorway then and watched the men and women and children. Some had torn at their clothing and hair and some had fallen to the floor to thrash and roll. They didn't speak in words I understood. Theirs was an ululation, a speaking in tongues.

A girl I'd never seen before stared at me from the door. Her hair had come undone and hung around her shoulders in wet locks, clotted from her sweat. Her father was yelling at her, her mother slapping at the girl's face with open palms gone red from the blows. The girl knew I was staring at her and I felt ashamed. As I gawked she ran to the back of the church, her father following her.

I watched the people sing for a long time before returning home and climbing up to the porch roof and through the window to my room. The girl stayed in my mind for a long time before I slept. Her eyes had been dark, almost black. When I stared at her she had stared back. Her mother had fallen to the floor, her dress rucked up to her waist. I had seen the woman's swollen, thick-veined legs and the dark shadow that showed through the thin cotton of her underwear.

But that had been the night before. Now, carrying my hidden words, I crossed the field by the empty church and went through the weeping willows to the trail that led down to the creek. The girl slipped in and out of my mind. Oregon grape and Saskatoon bushes crowded the narrow path. I stepped over and around them until I came to the poplar log that bridged the creek. Balancing easily, I walked the white wood. Beyond the log, at the edge of the scree from Cactus Hill was the place I had chosen. I went there quietly and then, squatting, lifted a flat boulder.

The rock was a large crescent shard come down from the cliff above. It was covered in hard, brittle explosions of red and yellow lichens. I tipped the rock up until it balanced on its edge and then I took from my pocket the wax paper package with the words inside and placed it on the scree below. I lowered the stone. I knew the words I had written were safe there, hidden from the world. I knew the paper would stay intact for many years. They would remain there in the darkness under the stone. Other shards would fall, sloughed off by the hill, and bury the words even deeper. What I had written was mine and mine alone.

Now I sit here in the garden and wonder what I wrote back then, what the words said. They are gone, but I don't regret their passing. What secrets they contained I wanted buried and so they are. They were a boy's words and must remain so.

I remember staring at the stone and the others around it. There was nothing to show the ground had been disturbed. Satisfied, I turned and made my way back to the creek, the log, the path, and the last days at our old home. As I passed the church I thought of the girl, her eyes upon me as I stared in at her in the dark doorway. I had smiled hesitantly at her as she stood in the church. She had not smiled back, yet her eyes had touched me with something I hadn't understood.

That night I went back to the church by Coldstream Creek. I knew she would be there, somehow knew she would be waiting for me.

Once we'd eaten, I'd had the usual fight with my brothers over who would wash and who would dry the dishes. My father sat in his chair, tired, his eyes falling into the Luke Short western he had been slowly reading for weeks. My mother, pregnant with her last child, had vanished, gone somewhere, a room, a closet, wherever my mother went. My sister, four years old, had gone to play with her dollhouse. Once our chores were done, my brothers had run out of the kitchen into the early twilight, Johnny yelling at Dick, saying, *Where are we going?* Dick, with his snicker of mouth, his click and snick of quickness, had said nothing.

I was alone. The last plates were dried, the pots and bowls, the steel knives and forks. My mother came back to put more wood in the firebox. She turned to me and said in her tired voice, *Why isn't there wood?* I ducked under her arm as she stood by the stove and ran into the night, my mother's voice trailing behind me, the sound of my father getting out of his chair.

I knew the girl was out there.

In the church, people were singing. I saw that they were poor, like we were. But they were different. They were immigrants, Polacks and Bohunks, Slavs and Wops and DPs, the "displaced persons," come here after the war. I'd heard them called those names and so they were to me. My mother had told me not to go where they lived out by Swan Lake and not to play with their children. I disobeyed her as often as I could.

I knew we were poorer than the families who lived in the big houses on the hill. The fathers there owned the dry cleaners, Mac & Mac Hardware, and the Ford and Chevy dealerships. They managed banks and ran the town council. They were rich. They were not like my father. I was not like their kids. The people in the church were like me.

The church both disturbed and fascinated me. The hymns were strange, nothing like I had heard at the United Church where I'd stopped going after I was seven or eight, preferring to spend my collection dime at Nick's Kandy Kitchen than drop it into the wooden plate they passed around for God. This singing was exotic and new. Their worship was different. The out-of-tune piano hammered out music, and the people inside sang. I went to the front door and opened it.

What I saw was a small boy on the floor just inside the door and a man standing over him, his legs on either side of the boy's body, his boots locked into the wood he stood upon. The boy was silent as he stared up at the light. Around them were women, old and young, some of them falling down and rising, but most of them standing and swaying. I walked in, searching for the girl. An old woman grabbed me by the shoulders and spun me around. She said something incomprehensible and I jerked away. As I turned, the old woman pulled at her shawl and threw it into the crowd of worshippers. It lifted into the yellow light and drifted down, diminishing in folds until it was lost among the bodies. I walked to the back of the church, to the door I had seen before, and I passed through.

The night surrounded me, cool and dark. Coldstream Creek purled muddily beyond me, its slow slip and bubble calling me to the quiet of shadows. I leaned back against the wall. I could feel the wood slats digging through my thin shirt. There were stars everywhere. There was no light that could put them out. I pulled away from the wall, to go home, to go somewhere, and then she was there, by the trees. When she slipped into the willows I followed her.

She had not gone far, just inside the verge of thin willow whips. I touched her arm. There was no sound but our breathing. I could feel her beside me. She reached out and grabbed my hand and I held it and she dragged me to the shade of the creek where walls of clay rose up in a curve above an eddy. I turned to her then, confused, and she touched my face and when I didn't respond, she stood away and stripped off her coarse jacket and her cotton blouse. She stopped for a moment, naked but for the gray skirt above her bare feet, and looked at me with the same look she'd had when she stared at me past her father's outcry. She lifted her arms then and crossed them over her eyes.

I touched her. I unfolded her arms and she felt my face, her palms on my cheeks. I put my hands on her breasts. Nothing had ever felt so soft and warm. And then I became afraid and took my hands away.

She fell down then in the dust and leaves. She touched my leg and I stepped back from her for a moment and then sat down beside her. Her arms were crossed again over her eyes. I simply watched as she lay beside me. The singing from the church filtered through the dark leaves, a distant sound as if from another world.

I don't remember going home, but I do remember never going back to the church and I never saw the girl again. She had never appeared in my school and I never learned her name. What I remember most is my fear. And her breasts. It was the first time I had touched a girl's breasts.

I wonder now at that girl in the night and the words I buried that day, what they said, and what I must have thought back then. Whatever the words were they marked a passage for me that led from one life to another. The girl had also taken me across to another place. That day and night I felt a different kind of loneliness than I had felt before. I now knew there was something in my life, something beyond brothers, beyond family and friends.

❧

I have lived alone much of my life, even when with other people, my wives, friends, and family. I've often disappeared into the backcountry just to be far from people. In the early 1970s after my first divorce I set up camp in the mountains northwest of Adams Lake having followed game trails to a meadow beside a nameless creek. For weeks I saw no one. I lived mostly off the land, shot squirrels, and willow and blue grouse, and cooked them on a spit over my fire. I left when I ran out of dry vegetables, salt, rice, and coffee. It took two days to walk out. When I saw the first house I stopped in the trees, afraid to pass by for fear someone would see me. A logging truck sat in front of the house, its twin stacks pouring out black diesel smoke. When it pulled away, I skirted the house and followed the truck back to the world.

I think most people think of solitude as loss, as loneliness, but my journeys into isolation were journeys into myself, always painful as if I were running away from someone or something. Yet I always chose to return, chastened by my need for companionship and love. The human world always called me back.

There was an old hermit who lived in a shack down Pottery Road near Vernon when I was a boy. I wandered by his place one afternoon. I wasn't trespassing. I was just a kid following the tracks of a bobcat down a dry coulee. I gave no thought to the old man who lived in the shadow of the coulee. I was aware of nothing but a perfect paw-print beside a bit of desiccated sage or balsam root.

I was so intent upon the tracks of the bobcat I didn't notice I had intruded upon the old man's cluttered yard. He had nothing to fear from a stripling boy, yet when he saw me he raged from his clapboard shack and assailed me with threats and warnings to be off. I left as quickly as I could. I think now he lived alone in willful malice. It was as if he were punishing someone who he imagined had wronged him in the past and had chosen to live away from people out of spite. But it was not solitude he had found in that dry coulee, it was suffering.

When I was a young man working in the mountain valleys of central British Columbia I met a number of old men, solitaries who had chosen by will or by chance to live alone. I came across one on Poplar Flats up the North Thompson when I worked in the mills there. He was a man left over from before the First World War, a remittance man sent out by his family in the nineteenth century. He had gone back once to fight in the trenches and then returned with poor lungs to prospect for gold in mountains that held little or none. There had always been men like him in the crooks and crannies of the hinterland, men who had returned from war or who had escaped from family, scandal, or shame. They loved the wilderness. If they feared anything it was man.

Unlike the recluse who attacked me when I was a boy, this one welcomed me but with the reserve of one who lived quietly by himself. He invited me into the one-room cabin he had built fifty years before. The cabin floor was three feet lower than the meadow outside. I had to step down into it. He shared his meal with me. We didn't talk much of worldly things, instead we spoke of our love of Shakespeare. He astonished me by reciting from memory much of *Julius Caesar* and *Hamlet*.

His respect for a young man who had happened by and his sharing of Shakespeare, wood-rat stew, and fried bread was an unforgettable kindness. He was a solitary man, but there was nothing about him that spoke to me of loneliness, anger, or despair. Like Thoreau, he had three chairs in his house, "one for solitude, two for friendship, three for society." From what I saw that day and on the subsequent days I visited him over those years, the old man's third chair was never occupied.

I think I too might someday become like that old man. Perhaps not so reclusive and, no, not a man seeking a gold mine where there is no gold, but a man who is content in himself and sufficient to the day. It may be that happiness resides in such quietude. The torment of the past will recede. I am told it will and while I know and trust that, still it rises in me in this year of healing and I must follow its occurrences, if only to understand where I have been. If I do that I will, with luck, know where I am now.

That old man had something that William Faulkner described in so many stories: honor, respect, and wisdom and something more, a belief in the land and himself as inseparable things. I must always remember that and remember too to honor those who come, the young particularly, and let them sit in a chair and share with them what I have.

I am much by myself in my garden, even though I share it with my woman and two cats. When someone drops by to visit I send them out into the garden. I love to watch them from the deck. Occasionally a visitor will notice some small detail, perhaps a stone Lorna has placed to catch the moon in its coil of quartz. Today a friend noticed the clay planter that was broken by frost last year. A great scoop had fallen from the side of it. I was going to throw it away until Lorna rescued it and planted it with a waterfall of petunias. When my friend complimented me on the artful use of a broken thing I told him it was Lorna's idea. Two people occupy this garden's rooms. We are not alone.

Yesterday Basho sprawled languidly on the new stone bench I built beside the birdbath and Roxy lay at ease in the shade under the cedar bench beside the apple tree. Lorna weeded in the refurbished bed in the front of the deck where the heathers were in their last bloom and the delphinium in their first. I was staring at the deer ferns and vanilla-leaf a friend had dug up for me in the forest behind her home. In a year or so the vanilla-leaf will have spread in a carpet under the Douglas fir and the weeping birch. The ones I planted were already in bloom, thin spikes of white flowers rising above fan-shaped leaves. Some people call it deer foot, but I prefer vanilla-leaf because of its fragrance.

Now, as I write this, Lorna and Basho and Roxy sitting outside in the garden yesterday are thoughts made out of mind. They are instants caught in the mesh of the past. I think of my garden in Saskatoon back in the 1980s and I can find moments that still breathe in me. Lorna will lean forever into a huge sunflower, her face turned gold by its reflected light. There is a blade of grass across a stone by the fence I built there. I can see it clearly. The grass blade and the stone, their textures, their presence, abide in me.

I spoke of this in a poem once: "Memory begins with the small, / a piece of paper lodged among roots / in a garden I no longer remember." The words I left buried under the stone in Vernon are, perhaps, the echo of the poem that came a quarter-century later. The past lives in me, an occult present.

Other people live in that house in Saskatoon now. The garden I remember is not theirs. Marcel Proust said, "The true paradises are the paradises we have lost." If that is true then I have lost many par-adises, and the one I have gained here in my garden on this early June day is paradise only because of what is gone. But I think Proust is wrong, for nothing is lost. The ancient paradise of metaphor and myth grows under my living feet. The past lives under the nails of my hands, is ground into the soles of my bare feet.

My mother's garden informs my motions as I dig with a trowel for a deer fern I am planting beside a vanilla-leaf. My first wife still stands at the prow of our trailer in that tight North Thompson val-ley and stares down at the seedling corn struggling up through the gravel I turned. Her belly is swollen with my daughter, Kathryn. What my wife thinks I do not know. That bleak life ate her spirit every day, just as it ate mine.

North of Sechelt, my second wife still watches as I run through the sword ferns and rain, shouting at the black bear who feasts on my stunted squash in late September. She is frying liver from the deer I shot the night before. My sons play on the scuffed grass under the locust tree. Each garden I have had grows out of the past and each one is only a variation on that first garden.

I think at times that, like Adam, I too was thrown from a garden. I too have known the sorrow that follows when he went out into the world to struggle, procreate, love, and someday die. But perhaps I never left and that original garden is of the spirit only. Here where I sit among the lilies is the garden I was thrown from. I have been given it, not to find innocence again but to learn my self.

The apocalyptic has no place in this garden, where a beautiful woman, my friend, lover, and companion, kneels among delphiniums as she pulls up creeping buttercup. A thread-waisted wasp drags a fleeting, minuscule shadow across her shoulders as it heads to the plum tree to search for caterpillars. Lorna is unaware of the solitary hunter as she weeds steadily across the earth. I love the delicate waist of the wasp with its flush of rich orange on the abdomen. I love my woman's waist, the blue shadow that rises to her breasts, their curve as close to metaphor as love.

※

Henry David Thoreau said, "Here I have been these forty years learning the language of these fields that I may better express myself." I feel much the same. I lament the loss of names. It's as if the elimination of species all over the world is coincidental with a loss of vocabulary. It is a kind of voluntary silencing, a desire not to remember or to know.

Perhaps my father's generation lamented my generation's ignorance. I know my father was confused by my brother and I becoming writers. What he might have wanted me to do with my life, I don't know. When I was in high school I asked him to help me when I was faced with my girlfriend's pregnancy. His response was, *You made your bed, now lie in it.* He was driving me to high school when he said that. A month later I was married. I wasn't angry with him. I simply felt helpless. I was responsible, I knew that, but I also knew I was not ready to take on a family. I tried to make the marriage work for nine years, but it was obvious in two or three that it wasn't going to last. I had done as my father told me, knowing even before the wedding that the marriage was doomed.

I thought at the time that he was casting me aside, just as he had my two brothers when they had their shotgun marriages six months earlier. My mother said nothing. I took her acceptance of his edict and her lack of support as a betrayal. Also, I think my father was a little in love with my first wife. It's strange to say that now. I understand it only because I have grown older. My father then was not yet fifty years old. He was still a man in his prime. But perhaps I am mistaken and what he felt was only a deep affection for her. It was all a long time ago.

Generations change and histories disappear. Language does the same. The names of *things,* like wren and cleavers, disappear too.

Why is the Pacific bleeding heart called steer's head or the vanilla-leaf, deer foot? The common touch-me-not's other name is jewelweed or policeman's helmet and the skunk cabbage's more beautiful name is swamp lantern, a name I love for the way it conjures how the bright yellow bract illuminates the mottled shade of fens, bogs, and swamps; a light to guide the spring wanderer. The origins of names are often lost in folklore yet their meanings are still alive, even if my students likely would not know the policeman's helmet being referred to is that of a London bobby of a hundred years ago and not the one worn by a cop on a motorcycle. Should they know that? Without a knowledge of where words come from, things disappear, history is lost.

My brothers and I vied with each other for knowledge when we were boys and young men. It was a competition arising from childhood and the attention we never seemed to get from our parents. We yearned for something we thought we'd been denied. Dick quit school at fifteen, a troubled boy, and I barely finished high school. Johnny left school at fifteen as well. As the 1950s turned into the 1960s, Dick and John and I lived in Kamloops with our new wives and kids. The three of us worked and lived close to each other for two years. They were the happiest years of my young manhood. On the wall in my cold-water flat I had nailed a list of authors I wanted to read and understand. One list survives from that time.

Anacreon, Pindar, Euripides, Socrates, Plato, Sophocles, Theocritus, Aristotle, Catullus, Virgil, Ovid, Juvenal, Taliesen, Caedmon, Aldhelm, Li Po, Tu Fu, Liu Tsung Yüan, Han Yü, Po Chu Yi, Bragi, Jehuda Halevy, Su Tung-po, Basho, Issa, Abelard, Bertrand de Born, Beroul and Thomas, Dante Alighieri, Petrarch, Boccaccio, Hafiz, Chaucer, Villon.

These were names and behind these names were thought and knowledge. I yearned for both. I gave this list and others to Dick. We had decided we would read our way through history, from the beginning. I searched out translations. The local library had a single copy of a truncated *Beowulf* buried in an obscure textbook. The *Elder Eddas* took weeks to come from the National Library in Ottawa. The *Kalevala* couldn't be found in Canada. The librarian at the Kamloops Public Library despaired of my demands for books. The *Saga of Gilgamesh* finally arrived after months of waiting. It was a muddy, incomplete photocopy from Washington, D.C. The librarian said she found a translation of *Taliesen* at the Bodleian in England. I remember her staring hard at me when I gave her a new list. She had never heard of the things I ordered. *Are you sure there's a book called the* Kalevala?

I exchanged books with Dick, but I knew he wasn't reading them. He liked the idea of it but lacked the discipline or, perhaps, his life was simply too depressing for him to concentrate on anything but his own hapless dilemma of being married too young with children. He had read *On the Road* in the late 1950s and he yearned to go and do likewise. He wanted to be a part of Madison Avenue's creation. My brothers' lives and mine were far wilder than Kerouac's and Ginsberg's had been. We had all climbed more mountains than Gary Snyder.

After I got home from work I would read the smeared photocopies of bad translations, the leather-covered books from nineteenth-century England and America. I read Li Po and Abelard, Plato and Taliesen. I couldn't find anything by or on Hafiz or Rumi, except a mention in an obscure book that said they were the greatest Persian poets of their day. I found *The Golden Bough* in a used bookstore in Kelowna when I was sixteen and read it like a Bible, a sacred text, a great mystery revealed. Of all the books I read as a boy, it was the most important. It drew me into the common weal. It made sense of a world.

And there were new lists to make.

I told myself I had to read all of British literature and then go on and read all of American literature. I told Dick we had to start at the beginning of language and read ourselves into the world. It did not occur to either of us that there was a Canadian, East Indian, African, Australian, or New Zealand literature in English. They were not places of the imagination then. I found no mention of my country in any reference books on literature. Canada didn't exist and therefore neither did I.

I wanted to exist.

I read the Bible out loud to my first wife as we lay in bed in the first months of our marriage. It wasn't religion I was interested in. It was words and rhythms, patterns and cadences. She lay curled into my shoulder as I read Ecclesiastes and Job aloud. There was something in the language, some secret code I had to break. I knew even then that what mattered was not necessarily what books said but how they said it. I did the word quizzes in old *Reader's Digest* magazines with my wife and we competed to see who knew the most definitions. I made lists of words out of the books I was reading and looked them up in dictionaries. I invented pronunciations because there was no one to tell me how the words were said and I didn't understand the accented syllables in the dictionary. I read the local library's *Collier's Encyclopaedia* like a novel.

With my first paycheck I bought the 1958 edition of *The Encyclopaedia Britannica*. My father took over the payments three months later when I couldn't keep them up. Three dollars a month was more than I could afford. He took the encyclopedia away from me but left me the two-volume dictionary. I still use it, the covers long since broken off. I was nineteen years old. I was beside myself with words. I was beside myself with sound. I read aloud, I read alone. I wanted to be a word.

Poetry was more important to me then than food or sleep, my wife or my children. I found my place in the world with language. I was certain that with language I could heal myself and control what surrounded me. If the house should burn down what would be most important was how I would describe the flames the next day. Love for me lay in imagined places, not in the real world. Death's only dominion was in a poem.

Henry David Thoreau said, "I once had a sparrow alight upon my shoulder for a moment while I was hoeing in a village garden, and I felt that I was more distinguished by that circumstance than I should have been by any epaulette I could have worn." I too have had birds on my shoulders and on my head and have, like Thoreau, felt privileged in the extreme. The bird landing on me this morning did so out of accident as much as by design. Perhaps it was because I was standing still and the bird mistook my balding head for a large pink stone fringed with yellow moss. The benign gardener is no threat to birds.

Hummingbirds are another matter. Our resident hummingbird is the rufous. He guards this garden and ruthlessly chases other males away. He is there to attract a female and he wants no competitors. His dance once a female arrives is wonderful. His mating dive from fifty feet in the air is an awesome display of pyrotechnical skill and verve. He dives from the heights and comes to an abrupt, curving stop three or four inches from the female where he squeaks his mating cry and hums violently, his wings a blur as he tries to impress her with his aerobatic skills. He is obviously intoxicated by her demure beauty. In his flights of glory I'm sure he dreams only of mounting her delicate body and touching her sumptuous feathers, her exquisite chrism.

I like to watch the minuscule, jeweled birds hunt among the plants for honeyed, red blossoms. They will give a nod to a blue delphinium but a bright pink foxglove or red fuchsia is their pleasure.

Their tiny nests are mossy cups lined with spiderwebbing. The babies' bodies are no larger than half of my little fingernail. Both the female and the male make endless, swift trips to fill their chicks with nectar and the occasional mosquito or midge. I once saw a hummingbird's skull. It was more delicate than the rarest petal, so thin I could see through it. The beak was as fine as a needle.

Today I watched the resident bright-feathered fellow shower. I was sitting on the deck by the umbrella pine when he perched for a moment on a plum branch above the container pond. For a moment I thought he was simply resting, but then he flew to the pond and hovered over a small patch of open water. Then he came down until his tiny breast touched the surface and beat his wings furiously, sending showers up and over his back. His head was raised, his beak pointing skyward as he reveled in the fine mist he created.

Beneath him rose four small goldfish who live in the pond to rid it of mosquito larvae and to provide a flash of secret color to the casual observer. The fish nibbled at the hummingbird's threadlike toes but the little fellow ignored them. Perhaps he enjoyed the tickle of the fish's mouths, I don't know. Paying the fish no mind, he bathed until he felt he was adequately clean and then rose straight up to the plum limb he had dropped from, sat and preened his green wings and russet-red breast feathers. Bright again and like a living jewel, he flew back to the fuchsia for a late breakfast and perhaps an early dalliance with his ladylove.

✖

The apple tree is showing its first fruit. It needs pruning. In autumn I will cut away the suckers and trim the longer limbs. The tree is drooping at the ends and I run into branches when I cut the grass. I am reminded of the apple trees on the small acreage my father bought when I was fifteen. Its fruit trees had been much neglected. That summer I was given the task of scything the grass that had grown up around the house like a hayfield. I was a teenager and lost inside the boredom of the task and my own dreaminess.

The tall grasses were just beginning to head, the seeds still cling-ing in clusters. The tangled, old fruit trees still grew spare fruit. But the coddling moths had been busy and their grubs had riddled the apples with tunnels and holes.

My family had just moved in and that day, before he left for work, my father told me to cut down the long grass so a lawn could be put in. I had gone out into the hundred-degree heat with the scythe my father had sharpened. He had showed me how to bind the scythe in the vise and draw the stone in long sweeps along the blade. Its edge now was as fine as a razor's tongue. How he knew how to do that, I didn't think of at the time. I didn't think of my father at all. He was simply there, the man whose family I belonged to; the man I obeyed when he was around and disobeyed when he wasn't.

I watched my father's car leave the driveway and immediately leaned the scythe against an old tree and went back inside to bed. My mother said nothing to me as I passed her in the kitchen. She had become more and more silent in the weeks since we had moved.

My father had told me to stay out of my mother's way. *Don't bother her,* he'd said. *Why?* I had asked, and my father said, *Just leave her alone, that's all.* I glanced at my mother as she stood on the stool stroking paint onto the walls of the kitchen. She had painted the room two weeks before and then moved in a circle through the house, painting the dining room, the living room, the two bedrooms, the sewing room. Now she was back where she'd started and she was repainting the kitchen walls a deep red and the ceiling charcoal. Her hair was pulled back tight and sweat shone on her slender arms as the paint went on. I went up to my room, swept the resident wasps off my bed, and slept.

At midday I got up and ate three fried egg sandwiches and drank a quart of milk. I didn't see my mother. I had to begin scything. The heat was a living thing, two cupped hands of hot metal holding the whole valley. All I wore was a pair of shorts. I took three passes at the grass and then leaned the scythe against the wall and lay down among the thin stems.

I felt hidden from everything but the sky. I lay there for a moment and then reached down and pulled my shorts off. My groin was a pure white and I took myself in my hand and slowly stroked myself erect. The hair between my legs was the color of gold. I came onto my belly and chest, my back arching.

The heat of the sun bathed my body. My eyes opened and I stared up into my mother's face above me at the window. She gazed down at me, a paint brush in her hand. There was no expression on her face. She was there and not there, a ghost in an empty room. I knew she had watched me yet, strangely, I didn't cover myself. I lay there, my hand on my chest. Something passed between us at that moment, but exactly what I did not know then and do not know now. I wasn't ashamed. I was simply there, a young animal taking what pleasure there was in the heat of the day, and somehow I thought my mother understood that. Yet there was a knowing in her I didn't understand. It was like pity or grief, though I did not say those words to myself as I stared up at her.

Then she was gone and I closed my eyes against the bright sun and stared through the blood of my eyelids.

I look back to that moment and wonder at it now. Why didn't I cover myself? What was the complicity between us, what did the look that passed from mother to son and back to mother again mean? It was as confusing as the look that passed between me and the girl at the church. Both had a kind of woman's knowing that was alien to me.

My mother had gone a little mad that year, perhaps the whole family had. She was isolated on that small acreage. She didn't know how to drive, had no friends I knew of, and no visitors. The farm was my father's dream, my mother's prison.

❧

My garden is a living place, not just a showroom for flowers and plants. A thirteen-spotted ladybug does not mind me watching while it feasts on aphids in the honeysuckle. Their ant-shepherds carry the aphids up the vines and place them at the flowers where the honey is sweetest. My favorite plant has begun to bloom in the garden. The common foxgloves have opened their first blossoms, and today I saw a hummingbird hover at the mouth of one of its thimble-shaped flowers. He slipped his long, slender bill inside the pink blossom and drank the sweet nectar.

The foxglove is a biennial and this year's fresh plant will bloom next year. The colors range from the deepest purple to linen white with every range of subtle reds between. I love to see them on their tall stalks above the columbines and feverfew. The feverfew grows willy-nilly everywhere, and I allow it to prosper selectively for the flush of white blossoms that begin now in June and continue to the end of summer. If I cut them back severely after the blossoming I get another flush of the white, daisylike flowers in early autumn.

The columbine appears here and there as well in its many variations, from deep purple to yellow and white. There is a kind of stately delicacy to the columbine's thin stalk. The bees love them. The native Haida people called them "red rain-flowers." Their sharp tips look like blades of rain striking a puddle. I wish we had kept more of the native names for things. The Nuxalk people called the columbine "grizzly-bear's den." The sharp spurs on the blossom must resemble the claws of a grumpy bear who's just awakened in spring after long sleep. How much more interesting this place would be had the first settlers accepted the names that were here before them.

These months have been a naming of things, not so much for memory's sake, though alcoholism left great rents in my mind where words used to play, but rather to find myself among the things of this world. Nouns are among my favorite things and, beside verbs, are the most important objects in my creative life. My own name has begun to come back to me. In the ancient Celtic tongue it meant "the old gray trout." The Celts placed a fish in the bottom of a well to keep it clean. It came to symbolize the deep and hidden knowledge of the earth. The coin thrown into such a well and the wish made, was to the trout who swam deep in the dark waters. I whisper my name in the fragility of this ordinary day where I am free from drinking. I speak of this day and not of days because I can be free of alcohol and drugs only today. Tomorrow is a mystery and if I promise I will not drink tomorrow I will surely fail. Today I am sober and still alive. Perhaps, if I live long enough, I might live up to my name.

The compost is turned. It is rich with worms. The last of it must be moved this week and used for mulch around the rhododendrons and the bamboo. The new compost is a steadily growing pile. I've made sure not to throw in obnoxious weeds like morning glory, ivy, or the mint I pull up from the main flower bed. I planted it ten years ago in a drunken enthusiasm and I've been paying for it ever since.

The chusquea bamboo grows just behind the perennial fuchsia, which is now in full bloom. The fuchsia's curving branches are rich with clusters of pendant blooms. The blossoms have a scarlet outer leaf and a rich, purple inner cone from which hang long stamens. The hummingbirds feed upon the nectar, tipping up the cones with their beaks and quaffing the honey with their tongues. The chusquea will be a lovely companion to the fuchsia's florid excess.

The irises are also in bloom. Thutmose III of Egypt conquered Syria in 1479 B.C. and of all the treasures he plundered from that vanquished state, the irises were considered the most valuable. He treasured them above gold and when he built the Temple of Amon in the sacred city of Karnak, he had sculptures of the flowers carved into the walls. The iris was spread throughout the Nile delta and worshipped as the queen of flowers. Louis VII of France took the iris as his symbol when he conquered Egypt. It was incorporated into his coat of arms and was called the "fleur de Louis." The fleur-de-lis has remained the symbol of all things French. Greeks, Romans, the Chinese and Japanese, the Indians and the Spanish, have all bowed to the beauty of this exquisite plant. It is grown everywhere in the world.

Like Louis VII and Thutmose III, I am undone by irises. I have at least two dozen of them growing in my garden. They bloom in every shade, from pale white to mustard yellow, incandescent blue to royal purple, magenta and copper, peach and orange. Some grow from rhizomes and some from bulbs but all of them are glorious.

An iris of the palest blue just flowered in the sunniest spot of the new shade garden. Early this morning I watched a bee climb, one flower at a time, down the three-branched styles and drink from the blossom. The sun shone through the pale flesh of the style and I could see the bee's soft shadow inside the standard. I wished for a moment that I could do it too. The throat of the iris is ivory and the pendant petals are fretted with black lines that look perfect against the blue. There are times beauty is a thing apart. The poet goes there carefully for beauty is a word much abused. The sentimental is always a failure of feeling and I have lived in fear of it, so much so I think I have sometimes deprived myself of simple things. The iris I looked at was beautiful and such moments of apprehended beauty are rare. They quiet the noisy doubts that arrive each day to pester me, and with doubt banished, I go to the back garden and pull up ten volunteer poppies that have enshrouded a hydrangea I saved from neglect earlier this spring. I left a few of the poppies to blossom. I must remind myself to pull them after they flower or their seeds will scatter and cause the same problem next year. When in doubt I go into the garden and the garden heals me.

The pond is fringed with Siberian and beardless irises, both of which are now just past their peak, but their reflections in the pond are still beautiful. The koi and goldfish rise to the surface as soon as they catch the sound of my feet on the gravel path. I feed them twice a day now. After a long winter of living off the stored fat in their bodies, they are ravenous and growing.

The big koi consume almost everything. They are violent feeders and frighten the smaller fish away. They push through the water-lily pads and batter the water hyacinths as they try to shake loose the occasional pellet that gets hung up on a leaf. The smaller goldfish sneak out from under the leaves and grab at a floating flake or pellet.

Oxeye daisies are in full bloom now everywhere. The roadsides are ablaze with them. They share the same gravel verges with wild lupines. In the garden its shocks of white flowers balance the blues of the last bachelor's buttons and the thick, clotted red of the alstroemeria that lean out from under the apple tree by the north fence, a place where I don't mind their invasive ways. Should they dare expand it can only be toward the lawn where I can mow them down. The feverfew is everywhere as an accent to the other perennials. I pull it up as it appears in spring, leaving them only in corners that need a brightness.

The cascading fall of the *Wisteria formosa* with its huge breathing of pale mauves, lilac blues, and china whites is over. The front of the house is now a flare of green leaves from the ground to the peak of the roof. The wisteria has rambled more than twelve yards. Its trunk at the corner of the house is four inches in diameter where it begins its slow and steady twining upward, bifurcating here and there until it is a many-branched hydra. In bloom it is a wonder to see.

Below the wisteria is the ivy that will plague me until my death. A former owner, in some misguided desire to emulate an English cottage garden, planted it around the house. He must have been drunk when he did so, for only an alcoholic would visit such a scourge on his own garden. When we moved here ten years ago it had climbed to the top of the chimney and across half the roof. The cedar shakes underneath the ivy had rotted and after I removed it, a task that took days, I had to get a roofer to come in. A baby ivy twining around a miniature trellis is cute in a kitchen window, but on a wooden house it is a disaster in the making. I curse it and the gardener quietly each time I look at it.

A little yellow spider hangs from the corner of my glasses as I type these words. Each letter struck bounces her a bit on her swing. I could have picked her up anywhere, the branch of a Japanese maple or Douglas fir, or maybe when I was leaning into the vegetable garden to weed the arugula, which is going to seed. It's not so bad having a spider as a companion while I write. She seems to like it and I don't mind at all.

I give and take what pleasure I can on this summer day, a bowl of fresh strawberries by my elbow waiting to be eaten. Their red hearts clotted with cream are lovely, but then, so is the little yellow spider.

She hangs on tight as she swings above these words. When I'm finished writing this, I'll walk her back out into the garden and let her walk off onto a leaf or flower.

She's a late-spring spider whose name I do not know. My books on arachnids have no picture of her kind. Like many of the small creatures of my garden she remains nameless. Rather than have that, I name her now the near-sighted spider, the name springing from my own optic frailty. I'm sure her eight eyes see clearly enough.

By autumn she'll be much bigger and less likely to want to go for rides. For now, she seems happy enough bouncing at the end of her slim filament of web. Like a child, she trusts me to take her wherever it is she wants to go.

PLANTS

Asian fairy bells – *Disporopsis perneyi*
Alstroemeria – *Alstroemeria* spp.
Bachelor's buttons – *Centaurea cyanus*
Balsamroot – *Balsamorhiza*
Butter and eggs – *Linaria vulgaris*
Chicory – *Cichorium*
Common touch-me-not – *Impatiens noli-tangere*
Crimson columbine – *Aquilegia formosa*
False acacia – *Robinia pseudoacacia "Frisa"*
Feverfew – *Tanacetum parthenium*
Godetia – *Godetia* spp.
Hardy fuchsia – *Fuchsia magellanica*
Iris – *Iridaceae* spp. (Bearded, Beardless, Bulbous, Xiphium, Juno, Reticulata, Japanese, etc.)
Oxeye daisy – *Leucanthemum vulgare*
Pacific bleeding heart – *Clerodendrum*
Queen Anne's lace – *Daucus carota*
Sage – *Salvia*
Saskatoon serviceberry – *Amelanchier alnifolia*
Skunk cabbage – *Lysichiton americanum*
Umbrella pine – *Pinus pinea*
Vanilla-leaf – *Achlys triphylla*

Water hyacinth – *Eichhornia crassipes*
Weeping willow – *Salix babylonica*
Wisteria – *Wisteria* × *formosa*

ANIMALS, BIRDS, AND INSECTS

Bewick's wren – *Thryomanes bewickii*
Black ant – *Monomorium minimum*
Blue grouse – *Dendragapus obscurus*
Codling moth – *Carpocapsa pomonella*
Giant crane fly – *Tipula* spp.
Painted turtle – *Chrysemys picta*
Rufous hummingbird – *Selasphorus rufu*
Thirteen-spotted ladybug – *Hippodamia tredecimpunctata*
Thread-waisted wasp – *Ammophila* spp.
Willow grouse (sharp-tailed grouse) – *Pedioecetes phasianellus*

7.

Creatures of the day, what is a man? What is he not? Mankind is a dream of a shadow. But when a god-given brightness comes, a radiant light rests on men, and a gentle life.
— Pindar, "Pythian Odes," Book 8

On the breeze is a zither drone and then a touch light upon my hand. I open my eyes and a two-spotted ladybug arches the red shells of her carapace on the back of my wrist, stretches her wings, and closes them again. She clambers through the netted forest of hairs on my skin till she reaches my middle knuckle, where she sits in beetle pleasure, around her the world of flowers.

I lean my face into a cosmos and watch as a bee works her way in a circle of sound around the plant. She stops and I can hear the crisp of her legs as she cleans the pollen hairs, dragging the golden grains down into her pollen sacks. She grooms and harvests. She is like a worker in one of the old sawmills at the end of a shift who runs his fingers through his hair and beard to clean the sawdust away. She is a woman who runs her hands up her legs to straighten out the seam in her stockings. It is the same clean move.

Below her a solitary snail slides up a rhododendron leaf. His long foot is a slip of sound, a delicate, faint slick, as he rides the smooth road he makes from himself toward a destination only he can imagine. "How little do we know that which we are!" said Lord Byron.

I search through the abandonment I feel and wonder at its power over me. I was not a child left huddled by a path in some dark forest. I am not the stuff of fairy tales. What I remember of me and my two brothers after the war was how hard we tried to be part of a family and how miserably we failed. There was something grotesque in our desire. Our short lives were a looping tape we played over and over in exaggerated storytelling that verged on the hysterical. The three of us were bizarre actors in a play whose only audience was our mother and father.

There were days when we would try to outdo each other in the terrible game we called "Remember." We would end up howling with laughter as we recounted our boyish adventures before our father came home from the war. It was as if we wanted to say we existed, that we had a life before. *Look at us,* we cried. *There are wonders in us beyond your imagining,* we said, but no matter how often we played out the drama it was not enough. Our audience was not moved. They listened, amused by our antics, and then went on with their lives. We didn't. We stayed in the story, each week and month adding new anecdotes to the complex play we were writing. The myth we created became the foundation of our abandonment. We were three little boys already living in a past that was barely a decade old, but to us it seemed eternity and perhaps it was. *Remember,* we would say, *remember.*

The garden breathes. There is a susurration of sound in this early morning in July. An apple above me blushes faintly red. I lift a leaf and see its outline printed on apple flesh. I breathe with the garden. My lungs open and close without thought, open and close like the bellows I saw as a child in the blacksmith shop by the rodeo grounds in that far mountain valley where I grew up. Fire leaped to the heavy, steady breathing of the bellows as the blacksmith pushed air into the burning forge. The cells of my body too are on fire.

That old blacksmith made a knife for me, beating it into shape on his anvil as he folded and refolded a shard of spring-leaf from an abandoned Ford. When it was done he fitted the blade into the polished stub of a fir branch, bound it with copper wire, and gave it to me. The knife was a beauty I kept to myself for several years before I lost it while I was climbing some volcanic cliffs. How absorbing it was to watch him shoeing horses. There were horses and buggies back then, just as there were still a few hitching rails along a block or two of Main Street in Vernon.

The forge and the bellows and the bright flare of the charcoal as he pushed a horseshoe into the flames was a glory to see.

I open my eyes and the garden transforms like the blacksmith's iron. Shapes and textures, emptiness and fullness, distance and closeness hold me in their arrangements. Levels give way to levels, the day lilies and crocosmia lift to the Japanese maple. Bracken, sword, and lady ferns circle the fir's brown trunk, hostas below them. The trunk of the fir is a curved pillar at Delphi. It gives way to a weeping birch, demure in the corner of the fence. The grass and moss arrange my eyes. The root of the fir where it lifts from the earth behind the azalea and the Okame-zasa bamboo is unconscious art. Behind me the stone mill wheel on the cherry stump sits like a monolithic altar, its iron lantern a rusted brown awaiting light.

Today I am trying to know the garden when it is without me.

Last night I was imagining light, I stood under the studded moon and thought of Lorna's poem, "In Moonlight."

> Something moves
> just beyond the mind's
> clumsy fingers.
>
> It has to do with seeds.
> The earth's insomnia.
> The garden going on
> without us
>
> needing no one
> to watch it
>
> not even the moon.

I needed her poem. It pointed the way to my sobriety. That it took years to find this path makes me no less thankful. It is she who speaks my standing in the garden where I begin again this slow renewal. Saint Augustine of Hippo in his "Confessions" says, "Too late came I to love thee, O thou Beauty both so ancient and so fresh, yea too late came I to love thee. And behold, thou wert within me, and I out of myself, where I made search for thee." Yes, and so I search this morning in the quiet of the garden for the beauty that is both "ancient and fresh," within and without me.

There is strength in my hands that hasn't been there in years. It isn't only muscle and bone. Strength is grace and sureness. I trust my fingers under the earth, trust them among the leaves of oregano and thyme. They feel their own way to the knot where the rhododendron flower connects to its stem and where the new summer growth has already begun. They feel among the growing tips and snap off the old flower twig. They know the way.

In the distance a siren suddenly blares from the fire hall and I hear the trucks as they careen toward some conflagration. The sound catches me up in its extremity and I'm lifted back to the north and that trailer on the mountainside above Avola where I used to sit and count the sawmill whistles. One was the startup whistle and two was to shut the mill down. The whistles went on through three to summon the millwright and four for the boss all the way to six whistles, which was the call for the first-aid man. The mill was more important than a man.

I would sit in the prow of my trailer up on the mountainside and stare down at the mill with its beehive burner belching out bright flames and gouts of molten ash. The chains of the mill clanked through the night. Belts and saws, gears and cants, dust and noise. The mill ran three shifts a day. The night shift was my last watching, though I slept fitfully till morning. My ears were attuned to every clank and groan, every sequence of whistles. The moment after five whistles was less than half a second but lasted in my mind as long as a wound. The sixth whistle meant I had to get down to the mill because someone was injured.

The mill broke every safety rule in the book. If a man was injured it was not reported to the Workmen's Compensation Board. An injury cost the mill money. Production was the only measure. I was the only first-aid man they had. My training was a six-week course. I learned to stitch up wounds and to set simple fractures. If the whistles called me it was because the injured worker couldn't walk off the mill floor and I had to go. I lived in dread of a hand being cut off or a back being broken.

We were five hours from the nearest hospital. The road was a narrow one-lane trail along the canyons and through the desert to Kamloops. The CNR main line ran through the village, but the trains stopped only at prescribed hours. If a train was in when the accident happened I could send him out in the caboose. There were times I had to drive a man out when I couldn't fix him in the first-aid room. Workers hated to be taken out. It meant they'd lose days of work. Women refused to leave. Who was going to watch their children while they were gone? They suffered their illness and injuries in private. I was the only man other than their husbands to see them. I had nothing but aspirin and words of comfort and compassion for them. I had no sulfa or penicillin, no morphine, nothing to relieve pain or cure infection beyond an alcohol wash and soap. I delivered a child in that north. It was the first time I'd gazed upon a woman's open cleft.

Fear of failure walked in my boots. The thought I couldn't help or, worse, make a mistake and cause further injury or death rode me like a hag. My stomach grew ulcers and my shit was studded with black clots. I drank cheap Calona Ruby Red wine at two dollars a gallon when I couldn't get whiskey. The liquor train came in every Friday. By Wednesday the village was dry. Men had the shakes as they detoxed on the job. Thursday was the day for accidents.

If a man was injured or shaking so bad he couldn't come to work, then my boss and I, along with a few strong workers, would wait for the night freight train to stop. We'd walk along the tracks by the gondola cars and sledge-hammer the rusted steel walls. Drunks and itinerant wanderers would peer bewildered from the cars and my boss would point at this or that one. The men with us would climb the car and haul the chosen men off. When the boss had enough workers to replace the sick or injured he'd lead them to the cook-house where they would get coffee and a meal. No one fought back, no one complained. They were too frightened. A quiet talk with the boss would leave them shaking in the bunks I took them to. I passed out blankets and they lay down. The next morning they would be stacking lumber on the green chain or stumbling beside the log pond as they tried to push a log toward the chains. The impressed laborers never complained. The sight of the boss with a ball-peen hammer in his hand was enough to keep them quiet. They usually worked a week before escaping on another train or simply walking down the road south. Many left without their pay.

A man came to the door of my trailer one Thursday night at suppertime. I was exhausted from nine hours of adding log scale on a hand-crank adding machine. The man at the door said he'd hurt himself a bit and could I fix him up. He was respectful. I was like a doctor in that little village. I told him to wait outside until I'd finished my meal. He looked all right and he'd walked to the trailer. I thought it was something minor. I was tired and angry, miserable in my life, and I took it out on the injured man. After dinner I washed up and went out to him and we began to walk to his pickup truck. He walked stiffly, his left leg not bending at the knee. When we got the truck he asked me to drive. He said he had a bad sliver.

At the first-aid room he sat and I undid his boot. It was full of blood. When I got his pants off I could see a broken end of wood sticking from the meat of his lower calf. The other end of the wood came out in a spear-tip at his hip. The splinter was almost three feet long. The stub end was an inch across. He asked me to remove it and I did. The spear hadn't touched an artery and the veins he'd severed were minor ones. The spear sucked out of his leg with a licking *smack*. I wanted him to go out to the hospital, but he refused. He couldn't afford to go. He had been working for a little over a month and it was the first money his family had seen in almost a year. He owed six months' food charges to the store. He couldn't afford to leave. I begged him to go out, but he shook his head, asked me to stitch him up, and so I did. Why he didn't die of infection I'll never know. He was back at work the next night, stiff-legged, limping badly, and saying he was OK to anyone who asked.

Six whistles.

I dream of them sometimes. I still hear the cries of the woman whose child I delivered, the man I drove out to Kamloops, his mangled hand in an ice-cream bucket between us packed in cracked ice from the river. I worked my days, slept my fitful sleeps, got drunk with my wife every Friday and Saturday night, played with my children as I could, and in the rare moments of dark while my family slept I sat at the kitchen table, drank Seagram's 83 I'd stolen from the boss's stock, and wrote the poems that began my life as a writer. I can still hear the dull screams of the chains and my dreams still echo with the count of whistles. There were months when my wife and children were gone to Vernon to stay with her mother. I buried myself in poems and whiskey, records of Sarah Vaughn, Ella Fitzgerald, and Duke Ellington, and tried not to think of my family.

Those were desperate times, yet I accepted them, for what else was I to do? Looking at them now I wonder at the struggle, the deprivation, and the desolation of those years. I thought then that what my family and I went through was normal. We were leading what I thought was an ordinary life. Even as I wrote my first poems, I had no notion that it would lead to a life's work. Poetry allowed me an escape. It let me enter an imagined world with its ordered reality a thing I could control.

The day-to-day survival of trying to provide my family with food and shelter and some modicum of illusory happiness was what everyone struggled to provide in that little northern village far from the world. When President Kennedy was assassinated, our village didn't hear about it for three days. There was no television, no radio, and the only telephone was in the mill office. No one from the outside world bothered to let us know.

We were a tiny fragment of the whole, separate from the world, autonomous but for the trains that passed through. I used to stand by the tracks and look at the people in the transcontinental passenger trains that sometimes pulled onto the siding to make way for a long freight heading east to Edmonton or west to Vancouver. People in their suits and bright dresses sat in the dining car or sleeping rooms and stared out at me. I must have seemed some strange inhabitant of an unknown world to them. I could read their incredulity in their faces. To them I was less interesting than a moose or a bear they might have glimpsed from behind the safety of their glass windows.

❧

"It has to do with seeds," says Lorna, and she is right. The early-spring flowers that bloomed in March through May have begun to create next year's garden. The bees, butterflies, wasps, hummingbirds, ants, and winds have done their early work. A pollen grain taken by a bee from the anther at the tip of one plant's stamen has been left on the sticky stigma of another. The grain has found the pistil and slipped down the long throat of the style and entered the flower's ovary. My seed too has traveled such a path. Five times it has made the journey to an ovum and five times I've seen my seed grow to man and woman, and from them to another generation.

The magenta blossoms of the foxglove are color, scent, and form designed to bring the pollinators to them. Flowers flaunt their trembling desire. No one who has gazed upon a woman's cleft could mistake the crimson lily's flesh. Bees fall on the lip of a foxglove flower, stare past the pale white to the flare of weighted rose deep in the throat. Delirious, they struggle up the dangle of flower tube, finding footing with the help of a climbing stair of jutting hair points. At the end of the tube is the nectary gland that secretes the sweetness the bee craves. The smell of this nectar has ridden the faint wind.

The seedpods of the foxglove have been growing, each in succession, as flowers have bloomed one after another up the long stalk. The lowest seedpod is already mature. A gentle touch ticks the mariachi sound of tiny seeds rattling inside. When the pod splits, the seeds fall into the warm crevices of earth. It is the same for all the flowers of spring now that summer is here. The day lilies blossom and fade in their twenty-four hours of grace, the feverfew sends out its last flare in a thousand white blossoms, the cosmos swings its many shades of cream through deep magenta, and pillars of yellow ligularia blossom in the modest dark of the shade garden.

I begin to understand that when things fall apart it doesn't mean they're broken, it means they are forming themselves into other things. The intense confusion of the past eight months has left me feeling that nothing would ever be the same again and, of course, why should it be? Things change and I am changed because I am a thing. I sound childlike to myself, but I think that's what I've been for many years. I have stayed a child when what I wanted to be was a man. How hard I've tried not to grow up, to keep to myself the childish matters of this world.

There have been moments of great beauty in my life. I remember staring into the forest outside my trailer on the North Thompson. It was early evening and I had gone out into the night to breathe after a long day at the mill. A man had ripped open his hand on a jagged edge of fir and I had put in seven stitches and wrapped it so he could return to work. A great gray owl's cry had drawn me into the night.

An owl's flight is one of the perfect silences, like the sound of snow falling. I tried to reach through the shadows to her and caught another sound, the brush of paw against a leaf. A cougar had come to the creek pool to drink. His head was low to the water and his shoulders arched above him as he drank. His long tail twitched. The cougar knew I was there, but to him I didn't matter. He was willing to share the night with me. He lifted his head after lapping and looked into my eyes. I could see the water drops on his whiskers.

The deep forest had come to see me. Satiated, the cougar raised himself up, then turned and moved back into the shadows. The muscles under his golden hide were long and lean and hard. I got up from the stump I was sitting on and walked over to the creek. There in the sand were the splayed tracks of his front paws. I reached down and placed my palm inside one of the paw prints. It was far larger than my hand. I thought of my brother in Vancouver among poets and writers and at that moment the far cities meant nothing. There among the trees I was myself. It was there in the north where my poems had to be made. I swore I would never betray them.

The owl called again high up the mountain. The echoes receded, then died, and I lifted my hand out of the cougar's mark. I stared at my trailer and where I had been sitting only a few moments before and I saw myself as I had been seen.

It took a long time for me to be human again.

Such moments of beauty have always been allowed me though I missed many of them in my blackouts and selfishness.

Lorna is away at her annual retreat at the monastery in Saskatchewan. This is a fearful time for me and this first morning I stare at a whirl of flies and think the mad thoughts of an alcoholic. The absence of others has always meant excess to me. Bottles of vodka clink in my mind like wind chimes. I know my sickness will abate, the sickness of drinking will slip away, but I pray to the garden that I live this one day sober.

I cleaned the filter box at the pond. The fish are feeding heavily. Sometimes, gazing deep into the pond I see a surge, an echo of color among the water ferns and water lettuce. The pond is bordered with large stones on three sides and smaller ones where the path meets the water. Right now the large pink hydrangea beside the pond has started to bloom over the bamboo spout. Its blossoms make me think of the many-headed hydra of Greek mythology.

There is nothing more welcome, nothing more soothing than the sound of water. The most ancient gardens of the Near and Far East were defined by water. The Hanging Gardens of desert Babylon were drenched with water brought from the Tigris and the Euphrates, a gift given by a king to a wife who missed her mountain home. All the great gardens of the world have water at their heart. Water in a garden brings life to space and time.

Fish circle and play under the falling turbulence and bubbles float out among the lily pads. They are small domes of sound. They plink and blink as they pop. As I watch, a small koi raises her head inside a large bubble, amazed at a sky made entirely of rainbows. When the dome of water disappears the fish is held in the shock of another element. On a hot day, Lorna and I sit under the shade of the Seiryu maple tree and read to the sound of plashing water. If we are still we can watch as juncos come to bathe. They rest on a lily pad and when the pad sinks under them, water floods in and they flip their tiny wings in pure pleasure. The chickadees perch on the spout and sip from the water as it pours out in a thin stream. It is as if I have made it only for them and perhaps I have. The living things of this world are never far from water.

A garden pond is a special room of retreat. Mine is almost hidden from sight and only the invitation of paths and splashing water indicate its presence. They draw the visitor down to the bottom of the garden, a quiet turn between the bamboo and the maple and there are two cedar chairs side by side and the pond just beyond them. Darning needles stitch the air above the lily pads in their quest for tiny flies. A green salamander rests like a jewel upon a moonstone. A tree frog hangs from the shelter of an overhanging hydrangea leaf. There are three spiderwebs in the bamboo, and the single new stalk of the chusquea bamboo sways in the slight breeze. Everything leans toward water. The thought of that leaning takes me back to the water of the Selkirk Mountains and a girl I knew there the summer I drove Cat just north of Craigellachie on the new Rogers Pass Highway. I had been married for just five months. I was nineteen.

What I remember most was the steady *clank clank clank* across the grade, pounding stones and earth to powder. The Rogers Pass Highway was a torn artery that ran ahead of me toward the Rockies. Blasting echoed through the crags and narrow valleys, and thick sheaves of rock slid into creeks and rivers. I watched black bears lift their huge heads into the sound and clamber away in search of wilderness. I spent my days dragging a pack-roller up and down the new grade, beating the fill down while trucks worked ahead of me, dumping their loads on the approach to the new bridge over the river. Two miles behind us was the spot where they drove the last spike on the Canadian Pacific Railway. I squatted once on the cinders where they drove the golden spike. When the dignitaries left, they took the spike with them.

I worked on the highway for five months back in the late 1950s. It was mindless work. My mind was numb most of the time. I squinted through a fog of blue exhaust and slathered weak repellent onto my face and neck and arms. It would keep the mosquitoes off for a while, but there were always some that would ignore the slick poison and bite off bits of skin. Horseflies settled on my skin so softly I didn't know they were there until I felt their bite and slapped at the place where they had been. Deer flies were worse. They came in swarms, their wedged bodies landing on any piece of bare skin they could find. There were tiny scabs on every piece of my exposed flesh. I tried to think of my wife at home in Vernon. She would be having the baby in another few weeks. Her face would surface for a moment and then slip away. My mind was a void. There was only the *clank clank clank* of the treads grinding on stone.

Day after day after day I drove up and down the same stretch of highway. The same mountain stared down at me, the same meadows and swamps, the same flies and mosquitoes.

At lunch, the dump-truck drivers would stop their trucks and get out. I'd pull the Cat up to the end of the grade, put it in neutral, and climb down to where the men were sitting with their belly buckets and Thermoses. Someone would have started a kerosene smudge in a twenty-gallon pail. I'd climb into the smoke with them, open my bucket, pour myself a hot coffee, and light a cigarette.

The truckers mostly ignored me. I was too young to know anything. In the hierarchy of men and machines, I was at the bottom. The only thing lower than me was a flagman or someone who operated an idiot stick or a pick. A packer Cat driver was nobody. Above the truck drivers were the mechanics, the foremen, the bosses, and the grader and drag-line operators. I was just a kid to them, a greenhorn. To them I'd barely lost my baby teeth. I didn't care. The talk would go on around me. The new highway, the money rolling in, the unions and how they were trying to break the outfits from the States who'd come up to build the road through the mountains.

On this day, their conversation seemed to have little to do with me. I ate my lunch and thought of the Indian kid at the camp. The boy's mother worked in the cookhouse as a dishwasher during the day and a whore at night. Half the men sitting had used her at one time or another.

The Indian boy had sat in the sun with me a month earlier. I'd been carving elephants out of chunks of brown soap from the wash-house to pass the time away. The boy had asked me for one of them and I'd given the carving to him. I told him about the elephant graveyards and how the huge animals, when they knew they were sick, would go off to a special cave in the mountains to die. I told him there were piles of bones and ivory, if only you could find the place. The Indian boy had listened quietly as I spun the story I'd learned from Edgar Rice Burroughs's books. When I'd finished, the boy told me of his people's graveyard. When I'd asked him where it was, he'd said it was gone now, buried under the grade of the new highway. Later that day the boy had shown me where it had been.

The truckers and I were sitting on the edge of the graveyard now. Under us were the graves of the Indians. I looked up from my sandwich at the men around me. They'd settled into silence, their lunches finished, their cigarettes out, and their coffees steaming in their hands. Some of them had their eyes closed, waiting out the hour until they had to go back to the trucks and Cats. I thought I would tell the men about the graveyard they had buried under the grade, but I knew that would make me more of a stranger than I already was. They'd just shake their heads.

I brushed deer flies off my sandwich and took a last bite. In another four hours I'd pass the Cat on to the next shift. I'd hop into the truck and go back to camp where I'd grab my bathing suit and towel and go down to the railway trestle across the slow river where it pooled before falling into the canyon almost four miles away.

She'd be there, the Indian boy's sister. She waited for me there every afternoon. We'd change into our bathing suits and then climb up the railway bed to the trestle. Up in the grid of rusting iron we'd wait for a moment and then leap into the slow brown water. When we were glutted on the cold and I was clean of smoke and diesel and grease, we'd drag ourselves up the bank to the meadow and lie there. She'd rub mosquito repellent into my skin and then she'd roll onto her belly and I would rub the repellent into her shoulders and then down the blades of her back. Her black hair was long and thick. I would always hesitate for a moment, almost afraid, and then I would flick up the small zipper of her bathing suit with my finger and slowly pull it down to the small of her back.

The last afternoon of light would slip away in our hands.

I knew there was betrayal in what I did with her. There was my new wife, my child to come. Sometimes I'd look up at the trestle and see the girl's brother watching as his sister moved under my white hands. The boy was supposed to look out for anyone who might happen along, but mostly he watched us.

She would always say that I looked so white. *You're a ghost,* she'd say.

When I asked her once what she meant by that, she said that her mother called white men ghosts. When I laughed, she just stared at me. It was a flat look as if she were seeing me from a long way off.

You're my first ghost. When she said that I stared past her at the river and the trees. In the distance I could hear the sullen roar of the machines as they pushed the highway through the wilderness. The sun had gone down behind the mountains and the valley was in shadow. Behind me the river flowed.

I think perhaps I was a ghost back in those days.

Confucius said, "A wise man delights in water," and though I am not yet wise, I take what I can from the never-changing peace of the pond. Walking down to it from the deck seems a great journey. Worries and cares slip from me like the clothing I shed when I go to my lover. I arrive naked at the many-shaded waters.

A koi rises among lily pads and for a brief second I see a cutthroat trout rise in the murky water of the Nicola River behind the trailer park where I lived in Merritt in 1960. The river was the repository of broken bottles, truck and car tires, and everything else that people didn't want. I would stand there listening to babies cry and drunken men and women curse in the heat of that deadly sawmill town in the mountains. The nights were the worst. In the day the men were gone to the mills or into the hills for logs or down to the bars to drink and fight.

There was a summer day I leaned against the narrow windowsill of the trailer and looked out. My woman was away in Vernon. Two neighbor women sat on the stoop of our joyshack, that cheap plywood room that trailer people tacked on to gain a few more square feet of space, room for a washing machine and a box of tools. The women cradled cups of bitter midmorning coffee. In front of them in the dust and gravel their children played with plastic cars and trucks building bush roads in the dirt. As the children scraped new roads leading nowhere, the wind came behind them and filled in their faint scratches. Sand and dust sifted into the tracks. My son stood away from the other children, naked except for a cloth diaper that sagged under his round belly. His diaper was wet and smeared with mud from him sitting in the dirt where the public hose leaked.

I had changed his diaper only ten minutes ago. The women sat barefoot. They wore blue cotton dresses that the wind flattened against their legs. I sat at the table outside and listened to them talk about Marge, the woman who lived three trailers down the row. They hadn't seen her for a week. Both women had knocked on her door, but Marge wouldn't open it. They knew she was inside because they'd seen a light go on at night. Something was wrong, but they didn't know what. It wasn't like Marge to hide herself away, they said. They knew Marge's husband left her a week ago. They knew just like I did, because Marge told them he had taken off after they fought the same fight they fought every night.

Marge's face had been bruised from her husband punching her. A week ago she had stood at our door with her baby in the crook of her arm. It had looked sickly to me. It was asleep, its mouth sagging to one side, a frown on its thin face. Marge had rocked the baby a bit, but that was all. It was the last time my wife talked to her. After that Marge had stayed holed up in her tiny trailer with the three-month-old baby. As the women talked about her I looked down the row at Marge's trailer. Its yellow curtains were pulled.

The women had talked to me and the other men from the mill, but we had told them to leave it alone. There was nothing we could do. A neighbor said Marge's husband would be back after he cooled off in Kamloops where he was celebrating his freedom.

I put down my coffee cup and walked over to my son. He was crying. I swooped him up, laid him on the wooden step, and changed him while his brother watched from his tricycle. I didn't want to go over to Marge's trailer. I knew there was something wrong, just like the women knew, but I didn't want it to be me who found out what the trouble was. I argued with myself and tried to rationalize that it was probably OK, that Marge was just a little crazy right now because her man had beaten her up again and then left her and the kid behind to fend for themselves. What was I supposed to do about that? What could anyone do? It wasn't against the law for him to take off and it wasn't right that he knocked his wife around. I knew that. Everyone knew that. In Merritt, people didn't interfere in other people's lives. I felt it was up to her. If she didn't like it she could've left or kicked the guy out.

I said it all, but it didn't make any difference. I knew that everything I said was an excuse. I didn't want to go over there because something was wrong and I didn't want to deal with it. Whatever it was, it was bad. That night I finally got mad at myself. I rummaged around in the back of the joyshack for a crowbar, my neighbor Charlie standing beside me muttering about women. There was nothing I could say to him.

I pushed junk aside and dragged a torn cardboard carton out from behind the washing machine. I took out the chainsaw and the box of wrenches, the hammer, the handsaws, nails, and everything else. I found the crowbar tangled in a chain at the bottom of the box, pulled at it, and cut the back of my hand on a loose saber-saw blade.

I wrenched at the bar and it jerked from the carton, spilling a can of screws and bolts on the floor. I stepped down into the night. I knew my neighbor was right behind me and I knew his wife and the other women were at their windows watching us both as we walked across the gravel and down the row to Marge's trailer.

They had been married a year. She was sixteen and he was nineteen, just a little younger than me. A shotgun marriage, just like my own two years earlier. He had started beating her up a few months after they were married. She had told my wife about it and one night I had been walking past their trailer to go down to the creek to cool off and heard them fighting. I could hear him swearing and the sound of blows coming through the thin aluminum walls of their trailer. She was screaming at him to stop, screaming at him not to hurt the baby.

Then there were the bruises, soft green turning to yellow on her cheeks, and the way she'd turn away from me so I wouldn't see, the high collars and the long-sleeved blouses. There were the days she didn't appear at all, but not a whole week.

Gravel crunched under our feet. The night had just begun to cool and there was a breeze off the creek. It washed over my face and chest. We knew she was in there. A light was on in the small room at the front.

I knocked and then banged on the door with my fist, but there was no response. I stepped back, wedged the flat tip of the crowbar in the door jamb, and leaned my body into it. The door sprang open, the lock splintering, the aluminum siding bent out from the pressure. I kept the bar in my hand and poked my head inside. I called out her name and her face appeared.

I asked her what was going on and she said she was fine. Her hair was combed. It hung long and brown over her shoulders. It was her face that was wrong. There was nothing in it, nothing at all.

I stepped up into the trailer. I didn't ask what the smell was. I didn't want to know. Then I asked the question I didn't want to ask. She said that the baby was fine too.

I dropped the crowbar and took a step past the tiny stove to the door where the bedroom had to be. I opened it and the smell bellied out. I didn't have to look. I'd smelled that smell before. I pulled the door shut and told my neighbor to call the police.

When he left I sat down across from her at the table. I asked her what had happened and all she said to me was the one word, *Nothing*. Her voice was querulous, the kind a child has when she is very tired and is just about to fall asleep. I took her hand and told her to come with me. I had to get her out of there. When she asked me about the baby, I told her it was OK and that we'd be right back.

The police came and took her and the dead baby away. I never found out what she'd done to it. It had been dead for five days. Her husband had been gone for a week.

It was the time of the Cold War. Nuclear circulars had been distributed in our little mill town. We'd been told we had to shelter fifty thousand refugees from Vancouver whenever the Russians dropped their bomb there. It all seems somehow amusing now, but it was terrible at the time. I had a case of Campbell's tomato soup under our bed. That was our survival kit. It was supposed to feed the four of us until the radiation went away. We were told to stay in our trailer for a week after the bomb dropped and we'd be OK. Merritt was a place of sad Indians from the Nicola Reserve, feral dog packs, and drunken millworkers and their wives. It was a little sawmill town where the law was never called to solve anything but murder. Whenever I remember that dead baby my mind freezes a little. None of us did anything.

We drank, that was one thing we could do. Every weekend I got as drunk as I could along with everyone else, anything to escape the misery of that life. I didn't know I was an alcoholic back then. Everyone drank, my friends, the men in the mills and the bush, our wives. Friday and Saturday nights were oblivion. There was always a party at somebody's trailer or just at the bar, the Coldwater Hotel. There were fights and affairs, pathetic fumblings behind trailers or down by the river or in the alley behind the bar. I thought I drank to escape, to have a little fun. Drinking was my life. I couldn't imagine anyone visiting our trailer and leaving sober. They brought liquor with them or I had liquor there. What I didn't know then was that I *had* to drink.

It was 1960, the year I began writing poetry. I began because it gave me something I didn't have in my life. I had always wanted to be an artist, a painter, but there was no money for oil paints or acrylics. Writing was cheap. I had a tiny portable typewriter, a worn black ribbon, and a sheaf of canary-yellow paper. I had a number two pencil and a pink eraser. Where the typewriter came from I don't remember. Late at night after my wife and children were asleep I would sit at the tiny kitchen table in the front of our trailer and try to turn words into poems.

Never in my life had I tried to do anything so difficult. I knew what a good poem was. I'd read the poets, but I couldn't do what they could do. I couldn't write about daffodils and skylarks or about Massachusetts, Black Mountain, or San Francisco. They weren't what I knew, their words were not from where I had been made. Without advice or help from anyone I wrote about what happened around me. A dead baby in a trailer, a woman who died when she tried to abort herself with a coat hanger, the sound of the rivers that coursed down the mountains I walked. A bear rummaging in my burning barrel in Avola was the subject of the first successful poem I wrote. That was in 1961. I knew it was good, but why it was good I couldn't have told you. It sounded right, that's all. It caught the night in the mouth of the north. I sent it and some others off to the *Canadian Forum* magazine in Toronto and they published three of them.

My first publication and I was bitten and bitten hard. From the moment when I saw my poems in print for the first time I never looked back. After that I never stopped writing, no matter what happened. I disappeared inside words. I don't think my wife and family ever found me again. I knew what I had to do with my life. The early death of my brother Dick was three years away. My father's murder was seven years away and so was my divorce. Things were going to happen to me that would change my life forever, but the writing stayed. I had no teachers, no mentors, no education beyond high school, but I had what all artists need and that was an obsessive and total commitment to the voice I heard inside me. I think back to that time, the mills and first aid, the poverty and struggle, the joy and bitterness, and I know the only thing that kept me going, the only thing that kept me alive, was poetry.

When we bought this house, this bit of land was the bones of a garden. I studied it for a year before I began to plant. The day we moved in I squatted on the paved driveway below the kitchen window and looked out on a neglected garden. There was an old vegetable garden lying under tall firs, but what flower beds there were had gone back to weeds. Trees had been planted that were cute when they were small saplings, firs and cedars, a redwood, and, worst, eight Lombardy poplars along two fence lines, trees that were better served on the plains of France or Alberta where the eye can see for miles. They were not trees for this small half-acre bounded on all sides by roads and houses. In my mind I eliminated the trees I didn't want and stared instead at the earth itself. The ground sloped away from the house toward the eastern fence. That day I began to formulate the garden I wanted to end up with ten years later.

I did not try to impose myself too much upon this space. I didn't want an architectural rigidity. I wanted a natural flow. I didn't make changes to the land other than to raise a bed, lay a stone path, and here and there plant a small tree or generous shrub to make a visitor move to shade or sun, pond, or flower, shrub or bamboo. For me, the art of the garden is to assist a natural order. I wanted the forgotten gods to return to this place.

Done well, a garden is a poem, and the old lesson of gardening is the same in poetry: what is *not* there is just as important as what is. This autumn I will move the myrtle bush and cut the forsythia back. If it still seems crowded I'll take the forsythia out altogether. Eyes that wander the garden should be able to rest occasionally. There are no empty spaces in a garden. You also see what isn't there.

It's an early July morning, just after the sun has risen, and I am standing naked in deep color. The light has not bleached the Peruvian lilies nor seared the dense mauve of the purple coneflowers. The black-eyed Susans and shasta daisies glow with light, their yellows and whites dazzling. My robe lies on the grass and I walk as Adam walked in the garden. It is just after five on a Sunday morning and my neighbors are sleeping the good sleep after a week of work.

I am turning in a silly, primitive dance, utterly in love with the morning. It's impossible for anyone to see me here unless they can fly or unless they have climbed the fence and are hiding in the ferns. Were they here they'd see a sixty-two-year-old man, slightly paunchy, bald, his arms outspread and balanced upon one leg like some goofy, guru-mummer greeting the sun. I turn and counterturn in the morning's blessed hour. Like Blake was in far-off England, I am one with my garden. The cats ignore me. My dance on the lawn is just another odd thing that their human does, no different than their prance across the moss in joy at the sun's first shining.

Pleased with myself I don my robe and take a seat by the pond to drink my coffee. Other than watering there's little to do in the garden. Some deadheading and some staking, turning the compost bin, mowing the lawn, and throwing a bit of dried chicken manure on the vegetable plot. I planted more lettuces yesterday to replace the ones I've pulled.

Other than that, it is a day to admire my flowering Hebes with their sprightly white and mauve flowers or clip a few tired blooms from the lavender plant in the ochre container by the witch hazel. I moved my sage plants last year to a new bed just behind a fir tree and they've responded by doubling in size. Their leaves have the feel of soft, foamy leather and are thick with oils. I reach down into their soft leaves, parting the branches and there on the dirt is a full mickey of vodka covered in dust and the dried trails of slugs. It is like some strange artifact, some Wallace Stevens's jar left on a hill in Tennessee that changes everything around it into a human need.

I pick up the vodka bottle and take it into the house and empty it into the sink. The alcohol pours out like thick nectar, crying as it vanishes into the drain. Every bottle I find seems to be a clue to a mystery I'm living, but somehow I seem to have the story backward. I know who the murderer is, it's the victim I don't know. I think about that as I go to the front of house.

I pulled out of the driveway this morning. I was off to find an anniversary present for Lorna. We've been together twenty-two years, good and bad. Always we have abided in each other. *Abide* and *abode*, two words from one root. We have made a home in each other.

She will be back from Saskatchewan in a few days. She goes every summer and every summer I miss her, even more so now I'm sober. My own retreat here is made too consciously alone by the physical break from her. I think of how hard it must be for someone to live alone forever, and doubt I would live long if she were to leave me or to die.

Morbid thoughts, perhaps, but sometimes they occur, even on sunny summer mornings after finding a liquor bottle. Breakfast lay ahead and the thought that I might find the perfect gift for her picked my spirit up. I drove down to the highway and stopped at the light. As I waited I noticed an orb spider riding on the edge of my partly opened window. She was half the size of a dime, big for a July spider. She was easily the largest I've seen and I wondered, stupidly for a moment, why she was there. But, of course, she had built her night web on my truck and when I opened the door to get in I had broken the web's filaments. The remains of it fluttered against the pane. I knew that if I pulled out onto the busy highway she would blow off in the wind and be lost among the cars and trucks heading north to the ferries. I reached out to pull her in, but she dropped away and I quickly pulled my hand back in. A brief moment later she crawled back up and sat once again on the blade of clear glass.

She was soft brown and gold with russet-spotted legs. The small hairs on her back and sides were like a mist at dawn. I backed up in the line and the man behind me honked his horn. I waved at him and he backed up a little bit, but was obviously unhappy by this idiot driver. Once there was room I made a U-turn to the sound of horns and drove home slowly, the spider fluttering on the glass, holding on as best she could. Once back in my driveway I dipped my finger into her broken web and carried her to the star magnolia at the edge of the drive. I draped the web across the slender leaves and watched the orb spider climb quickly up and hide under one of them. I got back into the truck and drove back the way I came, happy she had returned to my garden. Sometime in the early evening when the breeze arises she will hang from a long filament and let herself be carried until she anchors on a far branch and then she will pull her webbing tight and build another dream-catcher, beginning again the business of making insect catafalques, building up her strength for her egg-time this autumn.

There's not much I want this early morning in the first heat of a summer day. At least, not much beyond this new sobriety I am only beginning to understand. Honors, prizes, and awards are of little importance to me now. I've won enough of such things in the past, a time when I wanted them if only to have the world prove to me its love and respect for my endeavors. Yet a life can turn into quietness, and peace and the affairs of the world, the place where such benefices occur, can seem far away and less important than the day. So it is this quiet morning as I sit under the apple tree with a cup of hot coffee and watch a hairy woodpecker on the branch above me working away at the bark.

It takes time to know what beauty is. It is not given us and must be worked for. It is in the private eye and is not innate in the thing seen. The little woodpecker is quite content to be himself and my finding him beautiful is as much to do with a lifetime of observing birds as anything. To find beauty I must first find it in myself. Does the bird think me beautiful? I wonder. Every few seconds he tilts an eye at me to make sure I am still there and quiet. If I stare directly at him he gets nervous, so I stare just to the right or left of him and he relaxes. Nobody likes to be stared at, animals and birds as much as humans. A bear hates to be looked at. He takes it as a challenge, and woe betide the wanderer who tries to stare down a bear. When you meet one look to the side as if uninterested. And pray a bit if you can.

Prayer is speaking to what knows you. The names of the gods are silent and to speak them is to risk much, in the Christian faith or any other. The gods are not to be trifled with. For years I used God's name in extremity. Some pain I might have felt, some struggle, would have me calling out for God to damn the hammer that had just struck my thumb or the cupboard door that banged my head.

Today I speak to the gods daily, in the quiet of an ordinary moment.

This morning I am full of prayer though I do not utter it. I pray all goes well this fine morning. Lorna is back from her retreat. I've just seen her at the kitchen door in her red robe. She is letting the cats out and once they're on the deck she calls my name as if it were a question and I answer and say, *I'm here, here in the garden.* She comes to me then with two cups of coffee and as she walks across the moss I see what beauty is and am undone by it. I say to her, *You are beautiful,* and she smiles as she comes to me barefoot, her feet wet with dew.

Pray God, there be many more days, I whisper.

PLANTS

Black-eyed Susan — *Rudbeckia hirta*
Ligularia — *Ligularia przewalskii*
Peruvian lily — *Alstroemeria*

Pond lettuce – *Pistia stratiotes*
Purple coneflower – *Echinacea purpurea*
Shasta daisy – *Chrysanthemum* × *superbum*
Water fern – *Azolla caroliniana*

ANIMALS, BIRDS, AND INSECTS

Great gray owl – *Strix nebulosa*
Two-spotted ladybug – *Adalia bipunctata*
Yellow Douglas fir borer – *Centrodera spurca*

8.

What I have done is yours; what I have to do is yours; being part of all I have, devoted yours.
— WILLIAM SHAKESPEARE, "THE RAPE OF LUCRECE"

WHAT IS LOVE that I should fear it? What is it in the heart that breaks me, what in the spirit I cannot find to praise? I can love a wood mouse, a ponderosa pine, a thrush on a cactus singing his fierce song, a tree frog in the shade of a day lily waiting out the silence of the sun. I can be wrenched by my love of things. I can pick up a stone from a beach and feel myself wholly alive among the tallow striations in a bit of agate, the blood in a polished shard of jasper. I can love these things of earth and spirit and speak of it aloud and no one would question me. Yet love of another, man or woman, raises fear, and silence reigns when I should speak.

"Those have most power to hurt us that we love." So said John Fletcher in 1610 and nothing has changed since then. I can ask myself when I was first afraid of love and go back to my childhood and find there stories enough to illustrate my fear.

I remember the heat of the Okanagan in summer, its weight on my head and shoulders. Yellow-pine chipmunks who had chirred their angry cries at me when I stepped from the car vanished among broken limbs below the poplar in the ditch. Beyond me lay a field of ripening alfalfa, the heads swollen with green. Everything was still.

I leaned over the hood of my father's car.

My father had ordered me to strip naked and I had. The hood of the car burned my hands as my father raised the green limb he had torn from the poplar tree. I could hear the whip of the branch in the air and then the blow struck me across the small of my back. It fell on me again and again until I slid to my knees on the gravel. My father raked the branch across my shoulders and told me to stand up and I did. I bent over the burning metal of the car hood and braced myself as the beating started again.

At some point the pain left me and what I felt was a thickness as if what I was made of was leather and lard, a thing without blood or bones. The blows came down on me and I felt not pain but the swelling of my flesh. After a dozen blows I stopped counting and instead of quailing in anticipation of the next I waited for it, wanted it to come, almost begged that what was happening would never stop, but go on and on forever, my father's hands on me.

I fell a second time. My father struck me twice more, then threw the branch away and told me to get dressed and get back in the car. I didn't cry and I didn't cry out, I just pulled my jeans on and struggled my T-shirt over my head. As it slid down my back I felt nothing, only the sensation of the edge of the shirt riding over the thick welts. Blood seeped into the cotton on my back.

My father was beside himself with me. I had started a fire, burned a pile of fifty cedar fence posts and a five-acre field of ripe wheat. I had not done it out of malice, just to start a small fire on a hot afternoon. But it had gotten away from me. My father had to pay for the damage I had done. I think he would have liked to kill me. Instead, he had driven me out into the country and beat me half to death.

What I remember, beyond the beating itself, was the love I had for him as we drove home. I thought my punishment was a kind of forgiveness, that in my father's mind the breaking of a son was love. I perched on the edge of the car seat, my back and buttocks and thighs burning now, and deep under the skin, the heavy pain of my muscles and bones. When we got home I was sent to my room. After an hour my mother came in and wiped salve on my wounds. She said nothing to me beyond the single admonition that was a question, *Why do you anger your father so?*

That was the last time he beat me. The only other time he raised a hand was to punch me in the face hard enough to drive me backward down the hall and through the open basement door. I fell down the basement stairs and landed in a heap like a pile of discarded clothing. I had sworn at my sister for taking so long in the only bathroom. My father had come around the corner as I yelled at her and punched me, hard. I was then fourteen. He never said a word to me, but continued on into the kitchen where he finished his cup of coffee and then headed out the back door to the car and so to work.

I thought I deserved what I received, that the rare violence in him was no worse than his silence. He was who he was. The world he came out of was one of violence, from the raw acreage of Pincher Creek, with his father a hard man, to the years in the mines and the war.

He was more than just the man who punished me. I remember well the night he walked two blocks down our street to where a crowd of drunken men and women were stoning a house. The men had driven up the hill from the bars downtown and thrown wood and boxes on the front lawn of a little bungalow and set them on fire. The crowd stood in the street and jeered and cursed the people inside. They were a young Japanese man and his white wife. They had been married that day. It was eight years after the war with Japan had finished. My father knew them both.

I followed him down the street. He turned once and told me to go back home, but I simply stayed back in the shadows of the young trees. I had heard him put down the phone and when my mother had asked what was wrong, he'd simply cursed and headed out the door. I paced him step for step down the street and watched from a house away as he pushed through the crowd of men and women and walked around the fire and up the steps to the front door. He turned then, arms folded on his thick chest, and told the crowd to go home. He said, *This is over.*

I stared at him standing above the flames. There were a few more shouts, a woman crying out to someone to throw another stone, and then silence. My father told the crowd again to go home and they backed away from the fire and got in their cars and trucks and drove away. When they were gone, my father kicked the fire down so the boards and boxes lay in a great, smoldering circle.

The Japanese man came out and my father told him that it would be all right and that he should go back into the house with his wife. He told him it was over and that they would not come again. I came out from behind a lilac bush and met my father as he stepped down onto the sidewalk and began to pick up empty beer bottles and stack them on the edge of the Japanese man's front yard. I helped him clean up the street and then I walked home with him. He never said anything and neither did I, but my pride and love for him was as great as the stars that surrounded us.

Such was the town I grew up in, and such was my father. My worship of him that night was of another order entirely. The great distance he stood from me in those years was a gulf I couldn't bridge. He was what I had been meted out and I took what I was given and was thankful for it, whether it was a beating that left me half-dead or an act that made me proud of his strength and authority. He had stared down a crowd of drunks who were close to burning out a man and his wife because of race, miscegenation, and a war that had not yet left their minds. The police had been called but had stayed away.

No matter how I try to understand that time of my life all I remember in the end are my fears of abandonment, though I would not have been able to express it that way then. I know I lived in a family of words where nothing was said. Like scars, the old fears feel nothing now, yet I touch them over and over. Memory begets injury, love insists on pain. Both bring sorrow, whether it is a beating or an act of heroism. I can sit in front of the fire I have made of my life and feed another faggot to the blaze, saying this mother or that father, this wife, this lover, this boy or man, this child, this friend, this self, has crippled me. I can watch my life burn and, never satisfied, like a phoenix rise to burn it again. I feed the fire alone. No one helps me.

I have learned that the fire cannot be extinguished even when my life's intent is love. It is hard to walk away and let it burn without me.

I have lived with and loved my woman for twenty-two years. We have never married, and I wonder at my fear of ritual. I can pay lip service to mythologies, folk tales, sagas, and poems. I can find in them metaphors for love, but in my life I'm less sure. We have talked of marriage many times and each time we've had a hundred reasons why we shouldn't. We've never had children so there has been no need to legitimatize an offspring. My marriages, the disasters they represent in my life, and the idea that somehow a new marriage would be a loss of my freedom are only two of my reasons. The vow to "love, honor, and obey" has always rankled both of us. The Judeo-Christian ritual with all its old trappings of institutionalized religion has seemed archaic to me.

I'm a child of the postwar years, and part of my rebellion has been against rituals I've seen as traps rather than freedoms. Feminism has argued against marriage and I have agreed with its argument even as I used it to my own ends. Women traditionally have taken on a subservient role in marriage. Why would I subject my woman to that?

I sit here by the pond and wonder what it is in me that refuses marriage. There seem to be a thousand reasons and none. The very word *reason* disturbs me. It smacks of logic and thought and I know they have nothing to do with love. The truth is I'm afraid. I'm afraid of love because love has always hurt me. It sounds pathetic when I say that. I'm sixty-two years old. Surely I'm past such a childlike explanation?

I scour my mind even though I know my mind has nothing to do with my fear. I remember ten years ago at a family reunion for my mother's seventy-fifth birthday when I drunkenly jumped off a twenty-foot cliff into a shallow river, shattering my ankle into cornflakes and fracturing five vertebrae in my back. I know now it was only another attempt at drug-crazed suicide. It's only recently I can walk near a cliff edge or the balcony of a high-rise apartment or office tower without my ankle exploding with pain and my back going into spasms. My bones remember their injury. And so does the heart.

I also ask myself why the idea of marriage has returned to me. Why now? I don't want to marry Lorna out of some kind of misguided guilt over my alcoholism. It would be like marrying because I am in remission from cancer. So what is it then?

For hours I listen to the committee of voices in my mind talking to me about the should and the shouldn't, the why and the why not. Finally I banish the voices. They are a cacophony of dissidence and doubt and allowing them to spin their complicated arguments is just the way I have of avoiding any kind of decision.

I think I'm almost healthy for the first time in more than forty years and I also think I'm seeing with a clarity I've never had before. Marriage to me has always equaled psychic, emotional, and spiritual pain. But that doesn't mean another marriage equals them. Why wouldn't I ask her to marry me? Why not now?

That said I feel as giddy and foolish as a young man buying a ten-dollar, gold-plated, zircon ring at a street market. Suddenly it occurs to me she might say no and what will I do then? I begin to laugh in my chair under the golden bamboo. Both cats jump and then look at me curiously. And so they should. I am becoming a curiosity the longer I sit here and argue with myself. If I base my decision on my heart instead of my head then the answer is yes. I will buy her a beautiful engagement gift and I will take her to our favorite restaurant and after dinner I will get down on my knee and ask her to marry me.

Three days later I get up, make my coffee, and before going outside to sit in the early dawn I stand at the end of our bed and look at my woman as she sleeps. The night was warm and all that covers her now is a cotton sheet. Her form, the bend of her leg and the curve of her hip, are beautiful. Her bare shoulders are beautiful. I watch her breathing and I am undone by my love for her. I glance at the bureau and see my gift to her, an antique jade necklace, lying where she left it after we came home from the restaurant last night. We will marry in three weeks. I touch her hair lightly and then go out to the garden. I feel as if I have passed through a veil.

A moment ago I heard the steady thump of bass notes from the boom box of dazed teenage boys as they raced their slung wreck of a car down the street in front of our house, their libidos so alive their bodies were wrenched by its song. They think girls will willingly climb into their car, tear off their clothes, and be only and forever with them. *Boom! Boom! Boom!* Hormones have drenched them with lust.

The garden quells under their attack.

Peace is the hardest thing to find, a place away from the clutter of human noise. What I call silence is not the absence of sound but the presence of the garden when it is not weighed down by traffic noise and talk. Silence has weight and density. It is the world going on without us.

Perhaps quietude is only a man in his sixties who desires peace after long years of lust and rage. Didn't I race down similar streets with a girl by my side while Little Richard, Fats Domino, and Elvis Presley sang of love and love lost? Or perhaps my search for quiet is part of my healing. "Whatever it is that a wound remembers / After the healing ends," said Weldon Kees. My healing is not at an end and may never be. Forty-five years of drinking and drugs have left scars. It's as if I've spent my life dragging knives and razors across my skin. My body still feels the injury of drinking when I pass a liquor store or whenever I pass a dealer's house or apartment building. Old wounds, old injuries. In telling stories of the past I find the wounds I've used to keep myself alive. But this is the last time I will tell them.

There is a heaviness in the air today, a thickness in the garden that lends itself to gloomy thoughts. I pull the darkness out of myself and discard it like a shadow torn from my heels.

August is a month of sated fullness. The brace of early summer has been replaced with a mood of stolid grace, a turgid weight like that of the wool blankets my mother used to cover me with when I was ill as a child. Even the day lilies in their bloom seem weighted down. The sun insinuates itself everywhere in this drought-ridden land. The heat is a dull weight that buries and burns everything in its path.

Snails have sealed themselves in and slugs have crawled into the coolness under leaves and bits of broken bark and shingle. Flies stare out from under the hanging, deeply cut leaves of the bear's breech. Only the golden jewel beetles seem content. Several scuttle on the bark of the fir tree above the pond, their wings like fractured emeralds. They love the sun.

The stillness of August is more than waiting, more than patience. What blooms now holds knowledge of the fall to come. The surfeit of nectar and pollen is not quite done, but in spite of midsummer flowers there is less each day. The sunflowers are finishing. The golden circles of pollen are becoming smaller and smaller and by the end of the month their petals will have withered and chickadees will pluck their black seeds.

But not quite yet. The garden is nearing its last full flush of bloom. The cosmos and daisies are still in tempestuous bloom. Most day lilies are on their last blossoms, but the later varieties are only now growing their long pale buds. They will bloom sequentially all month. Nasturtiums are sprawling through the vegetable garden. The lettuces, chard, and spinach have bolted and the nasturtiums twine among them with their huge, circular leaves and their flowers in shades of pale yellow through to blackened orange. I should curb their excesses, but I won't. They will bloom later into the autumn and their peppery flowers will decorate my salads for weeks to come.

The heliopsis and rudbeckia have huge buds just beginning to open. Two large penstemon drape their tubular red flowers along the path at the edge of the pond shade garden. One is a bright lipstick red and the other a deep maroon. I've deadheaded the earliest bloom and new suckers are pushing out from the interstices of the lower leaves. A second bloom will come with fewer, smaller flowers. The astilbes are raging among the ferns and the clump of false thistles beside the deck will bloom soon. The bees love to climb around their purple spheres. The pink phlox has begun to flower and the white phlox will follow it in a week.

There are empty places in the beds where earlier flowers, the bachelor's buttons, bulb lilies, and irises, have died back. I could search for the pitcher plants that bloomed in late spring, but I know that their dark leaves are gone. There is no trace now of their long, deep cups that fed on the bodies of unwary wasps and flies. Deadheading goes on steadily as I encourage the daisies and feverfew to bloom a second time.

The pond has greened up with a midsummer algae bloom. The water lilies have been better this year than any other I can remember. I diligently clipped the dead and dying lily pads and flower buds and the plants have responded. They grow new buds every few days. This summer has seen dozens of blooms.

The water-lily pads regularly sport ants who have wandered out onto the pond. The ants seem to know what they're doing though what they search for out there is anyone's guess. Bumblebees and wasps come regularly to drink. They are like cats and lions as they lean to the water. The fish ignore them though they'll rise to a fly in a second. I'm sure they can read the danger signs in the yellow and black striations on the bodies of the insects.

I've seen only the rare mosquito this year, thanks to the fish feeding on their larvae. Red and orange salamanders have appeared here and there and so have a couple of grass snakes, but I think the cats have killed the snakes. I lament their going as the snakes are slug predators, but there's little I can do about it. The cats love the garden and they have it in their nature to kill snakes. They don't seem to bother the salamanders or frogs. The salamanders sit as still as stone on stone and it may be the quick movement of the snakes to escape a predator that attracts the cats' attention. The tiny frogs blend so perfectly with whatever they rest upon it's hard to see them. The cats pass them by even though the frog may have been croaking only seconds before. Finding a tree frog is like finding a jewel from Opar. They shine with wet light, their tiny bodies green reflectors of the leaves they've chosen. A green frog does not sit on a red geranium unless he's gone a little mad.

Oregano, thyme, mint, and sage are all blooming now. The bees go mad for the oregano and mint blossoms and at times weigh down the flowering stems. I've seen five bees drawl like lovers upon one frothy blossom cluster. If I bruise oregano or thyme leaves lightly in my fingers I can smell a hundred scented meals, the rich perfumes like spilled Greek honey.

Of all the herbs there are none so rich or wonderful as basil. As I smell it I think of thick slices of ripe tomatoes drenched in cold-pressed virgin olive oil, lemon juice, or balsamic vinegar, and topped with fine goat cheese from Saltspring Island. Fresh basil leaves, a bit of ground pepper, a dash of sea salt, and there is no summer salad that can come close to its aroma and taste.

Watching Lorna cup her hand to her face to savor the basil's scent is enough to make me want to carry her off to bed. I dream of her breasts and thighs covered in rich basil leaves. What an exotic herb, what sensual pleasure there is in picking its rich leaves for a salad or sauce. Fresh basil and fresh oregano bring to a meal a level of mystery no one can plumb. I can't brush up against the plants without carrying the scent on my clothes for hours.

The day eases away.

❧

An hour ago I saw a trailer being hauled past the house. It brought back the time I had a forty-foot trailer moved north from Merritt to

Avola back in the early 1960s. When it left, we followed it on the dirt road north in our 1947 Dodge coupe. I was on my way to my job with Merritt-Diamond Mills.

Avola was an industrial village surrounding a sawmill. The mill sat on the edge of the North Thompson River six miles below Blue River Canyon. Just south of the mill it fell into rapids and the beginning of a canyon near where Mad River joined it, but at Avola it seemed a peaceful river until you got close to it and saw the huge current swollen with mud and dirt scraped from the sides of the mountains. In the spring, hundred-foot fir trees were torn from the banks by the swollen river. They swirled in the deep brown waters as they tried to ride the current south to Kamloops. They never arrived. They hung up on rocks or in narrow defiles until they were broken by the weight and power of the river. The smashed skeletons of trees were left on sandbars and gravel reaches where they turned to bone. Stumps became carved monoliths, huge sculptures of white wood that were perches for belted kingfishers, herring gulls, and bald eagles.

Below them the river rolled in its stone bed, a living thing, huge and implacable as it forced its way toward the Fraser River. It was a surge of brown foam and heaving waves. Boulders thundered on the river bottom in spring, a drum roll under the runoff surge.

Ahead of us the trailer ground its way north and our ancient car bounced behind it over the ruts and rocks. The tires were old retreads and the springs were shot. My young son was sitting on the seat between my wife and me. She was holding the baby in the crook of her arm. This would be the first time she would see Avola.

Avola had maybe a hundred or so people, mostly men living in bunkhouses. The foremen, millwrights, and sawyers had cabins or shacks or small houses and had brought their wives and children with them. They were the privileged men whose skills were important and so they were pampered with their own dwellings. There were only fifteen women living in the village. There were no police, no mayor, and no village council. Claude, the boss of the town, was the boss of the mill. His word was the law and he ran Avola like a petty dictator. There was a small store that served as a post office as well as a repository for wilted vegetables, canned everything, and fly-specked meat. The man who ran it owned what part of people's lives the mill didn't want. He had made indentured slaves of half the village.

The mill had reopened after a two-year shutdown. The families that had stayed during that time were deeply in debt to the store. They had been charging groceries and gas for a long time. Each month they had signed over their petty welfare checks. To me they seemed like peasants from another century. I had read Tolstoy. Avola could have been in Russia in the nineteenth century.

I had been promised there would be a school the next year, one teacher for eight grades. Most of the children up there had never seen a teacher, never been to school. They couldn't read or write. They knew nothing but that tiny village perched on the edge of a river between two mountains. If they were lucky they might have made it out to Kamloops, but most of them weren't lucky. The station for the Canada National Railway main line that ran down the side of the river had room for an agent and his wife and kids, to live upstairs, and there was a cluster of railway houses and shacks where the men who worked the rails lived. They were the section gang, mostly indentured Portuguese who had to work for the CNR for years to pay off their immigration debt. None of them spoke English. Somewhere in Ottawa a fat bureaucrat counted the money he was paid by the railway for assured laborers who would never dare complain.

High up the hill by the dump above the village were two shacks where the Sikhs lived. Fifteen men crammed into two small cabins. They worked the green-chain at the mill. The Sikhs weren't allowed to live in the main bunkhouses with the white men. They were sequestered, locked in the prison of their culture and skin, just as the Portuguese were. The Sikhs had left their families in India and they sent money home and as well gave plenty each payday to the man they owed for their passage. At the end of the month they had only enough money for a weekend drunk. No one in the village spoke to them. I was the only white man allowed into their shacks because I was the first-aid man and was treated as if I were a doctor.

I sat in the car and pretended we were happy. I would work out of the office, laboriously adding log scale on a hand-pull adding machine. At least it was work. I was Claude's man in the office, as much a wage slave as anyone else there. Whatever he said to do I did.

I ran the cookhouse, the bunkhouses, the office, and I made up the checks for the men who were running three shifts a day, six days a week, pumping spaghetti lumber out the back end of the mill for export to the United States.

I thought that I would spend a few years there and then maybe get the chance to move to the head office in Lumby just outside Vernon. I was going to start taking an industrial accounting course. I would do anything to get out of doing what I had been doing. There were the three years of scraping by in Kamloops and Merritt; the three years of poverty and pinching nickels in the hope they'd turn into dimes. At the end of every month I'd looked in my wallet only to find a handful of hardship.

As we passed through the deep shadow of the canyon my wife stared out the window at the river that rolled and boiled twenty feet from her elbow. The road had descended down the canyon walls and now we were driving along six feet above the river. A bald eagle sluiced down the canyon and over us. Ahead, the ragged tail of the trailer swung out over the river, the scratched blue aluminum flashing briefly in the sun before our wretched home crawled around a tight corner. I stopped the car at a passing spot and we got out and walked to the riverbank.

I held my son and my wife held the baby. The four of us stared at the turmoil at our feet. The noise of the water filled our minds. Water splashed onto our shoes. We'd met no one that day. It was Sunday and the bush was shut down, all the loggers gone home. No one traveled that road unless they had business there. There were no such things as tourists. Everything came to Avola by train. Food, clothing, liquor, medicine, whatever, it all came in by freight once a week from Woodward's in Vancouver.

We had a trailer and a car, I had a job, and we all had a place to live. Everything was in order. I pretended to be optimistic but little of it rubbed off on my wife. My unhappiness was also hers. We loved our children, but that love wasn't enough. The mountains loomed above us, two huge green walls that blocked the sun. Between them there was a narrow ribbon of sky. It seemed no wider than the road we were on.

I told her not to worry, that the river valley was wider at Avola and that we would get the sun by ten o'clock there. I tried hard to make it all seem good, even as I knew that where we were going would likely be a dead end, in spite of my dreams of getting to head office. My wife nodded as the child squirmed in my arms. He wanted to get down and play. I carried him back to the car and closed the door. I stared over the hood at my wife's slender back as she gazed down into the mud of the heaving water.

The day was beautiful, the air clear and warm. We drove on to a new life that was no better than the last. There were just long days and nights of work with the only reward a drunken party at someone's shack, a dance at the community hall where there was one woman for every twenty men. There were fights and beatings, suicides, and every other misery a small, isolated town could give us. In an unmarked grave by the village dump we buried an old alcoholic who died with dead flies stuck to the lemon extract on his lips. It was the middle of winter. We carried his body up to the dump in the backhoe bucket, dug a trench with the same bucket three feet deep, and rolled him in. The boss stood over the grave and said, *Ashes to ashes, dust to dust,* stopped a moment and said, *That's it, that's all I know.* After we tamped the grave down we went back to work.

Sometimes the only surcease I could find was to walk into the bush with a bottle of whiskey and drink myself senseless under the band of stars that riddled the narrow sky between the mountains. I wonder at the young man I was back then, the family I had, the poems I typed on cheap canary-yellow paper as I stared through drying diapers at the river far below, the sound of the saws and chains from the mill eating into my bones. A drink, another drink, and then passing out in bed beside a silent wife who pretended she was asleep.

The Sikhs, lonely and ostracized, fought each other on weekends with fists and knives, the white men in the bunkhouses raped Indian girls they'd had shipped up from Kamloops, the seventy-year-old Chinese cook sat drunk in his room drawing pictures of his child-bride back in China, the white husbands locked their wives in closets and bathrooms to keep them quiet, people drank and traded a wife or daughter for a bottle of whiskey. Drunks, passed out, never saw their wife or husband abuse a child or sleep with a best friend. I writhe with the memory of those bitter, unhappy times. I roll over, get out of bed, and walk into the garden.

Today my mother appeared again. I was sitting by the pond and saw the flash of her red babushka among the sword ferns and bracken under the fir tree. She was on her hands and knees digging the dry earth with a broken trowel. Wisps of wet hair lay flat against her forehead. Her hand on the trowel was clenched so hard the white of her knuckles glowed while her other hand held hard to a heaved root of the fir tree. She was trying to dig something up and I could see the frustration on her face, the obsession in the lines of her cheeks and mouth. As I watched she picked at fallen needles and dry cones and then crawled deeper into the bracken. Strangely, she wore an apron with bright cherries splayed across her belly. The ties at her waist were knotted, but the loose ends caught at the dead cones as she moved away. I put my head in my hands and closed my eyes.

Now I look up at the night. Sirius is high in the eastern sky. My mother's latest visit has left me depressed. I don't know why her spirit can't find rest. Since she was here I have driven myself back into the past and now don't seem to be able to find my way out of it. It's a labyrinth and there is no one to guide me. I've been staring into the bull's head of alcohol, that beast at the center of the maze. I feel at times I am a stone swung at the end of a string that keeps getting shorter. Each time around the circle is smaller, tighter, and I spin faster.

Last night I dreamed of a bottle of vodka crusted with ice in a freezer. I woke crying and went out into the night. I curled up on the lawn under the apple tree in my robe, holding my knees to my chin. I left my body, vacated it, ran from it, and found myself looking down at a man in a red robe, shaking. He is what death is, I thought. He is what they describe and what I've never known before. I have left my body and now am afraid to go back.

Is despair all that my memory contains? Weren't there moments when I was simply happy? Yes, but it was a desperate happiness. Once in the winter of 1959 in North Kamloops I filled a glass milk bottle with heating oil and spilled some down the side of the cheap stove. It caught fire from the burner and the flames lapped at the walls, a blue shimmer everywhere. My hands were burning but it didn't hurt. Then my sweet young wife got out of bed where she was huddling from the cold and, seeing me covered in blue fire, laughed. She laughed as she threw a blanket on me to staunch the flames, the two of us sitting there in each other's smoky arms, happy with the craziness of it all. Later, we walked along the bank of the North Thompson River just where it met the Thompson in Kamloops, the two of us strolling among the driftwood, my first son just a baby, and my wife and I holding hands and me swearing inside that I would be this happy forever with this beautiful girl, this child, this someone who was more than anything in my life. I felt I was happy at Skiddam Flats with my two brothers and their wives. Dick's wife, Elaine, quiet as she always was, sitting a little aside in the loneliness of her life as she spooned food into her daughter's laughing mouth. Johnny's wife, Nita, with their bright daughter staggering around, the child so sweet, so fair, the first grandchild, and dead in a few more years of cancer. My wife, so beautiful, so delicate, I thought the world stopped when they made her. All the wives on the blankets and the babies around them like fat bumblebees, and I so happy to be with my brothers, the three of us leaping across creeks, wrestling, throwing javelins made from aspen branches, doing the hop, step, and, jump, the broad jump, the shot put with a river boulder, a Lane Olympics. We argued about each miss, each goal, until we, boy-men, fell down laughing beside those girl-women and ate warm potato salad and roasted wieners on store-bought buns, and drank tepid Kool-Aid, and were so happy our hearts were breaking.

And another time, the afternoon growing late and me lying more dead than alive in the vague shadow of a Saskatoon bush, sleeping off the days of work, Dick gone fishing up a tiny stream, Johnny sitting alone gazing into the light around us, so much alone even I was afraid of him, Nita clucking at her daughter, her belly full of another child, Elaine following her daughter across the desiccated grass, Elaine's eyes sharp, and me gazing at a stone I've found and my wife beside me, and we both think it will always be like this. Then Elaine starts clearing up and the kids are tired and Dick's not back and Johnny's mad, and I don't care.

And there were times playing twenty questions or cards late into the night with my brothers that I thought the world began and ended with us. I thought there was no one in the world as happy as the six of us, nowhere in the world as pretty a place as Skiddam Flats in the summer of 1959, nothing as lovely as walking with my wife, the two of us looking at the Milky Way, talking quietly of a play, a poem, a song, a child, a friend, a brother. It was a time when the sun rose and set and we were young, full of yearning and delight, the day as sweet as any day in all my life.

An hour later I rose from the cool, night lawn, walked back into the house and sat in my chair in the living room, still afraid, but knowing I had escaped a drink if only for this night. I woke in the morning in our bed and told Lorna of my dream. She held me while I lay there talking, and it was good to be held, good to be in a place where I could cry out and there was someone to hear me. We are getting married in a week.

The dream has not returned, but I know that whatever the thing is inside me, this disease I have, it is alive in my flesh. At times I think the past itself is a disease. I am still afraid, but I am sober.

❦

Today I squat in the vegetable garden. It feels good to have my hands back in the earth. The soil is rich and fluffy. The composting and manures I've plied it with over the years have made it a feather bed for vegetables. I turned the earth again a week ago, burying nasturtium, lettuce, and foxglove, and other seeds that happened to fall within the plot. I'll see their progeny next spring.

This afternoon I planted kale, spinach, arugula, radicchio, romaine, oakleaf, and parsley seedlings and some red-spinach seeds a friend gave me earlier this summer. It should grow well even now. It's important to get plants and seeds in late in August; too early and they'll bolt. The slanting sun, cool days and cooler nights, and the early autumn rain will suit them fine. I've left a row of chard. It's still producing rich green leaves for steaming and serving with lemon juice, butter, sea salt, and pepper.

Mid-August and a rain has come at last. For four months I've hand-watered the garden. I've collected water from the rain-gutter downspout and stored it in large plastic garbage cans. I've caught gray water from the bathtub and sink and poured it on beds and shrubs. The toilet is never flushed just for a quick piss.

The last three days the rains have fallen heavily and while I know it doesn't mean I can be profligate with water, at least the drought has eased a bit. The rains will replenish the top few inches of parched soil, but won't reach the tree and shrub roots. Some of the leaves on the plum trees have turned brown and fallen a month early, and the conifers have dropped a lot of needles.

This will be a day to go for a Sunday drive with Lorna. I have dough cooking in the bread-maker. It will be a Zuni bread rich with cornmeal and molasses just right for wild sockeye salmon sandwiches spiced with dill. The salmon was jarred by a friend. We'll pack up a lunch and walk north along the beach to the point where we will find a teredo-riddled log thrown up by last winter's tides to lean against. We'll eat and watch the gulls swing in white arabesques above the sea and herons standing in their elegant patience. Mute swans and black brants will pass and pintail ducks and lesser scaup will dip in the waves. If we're lucky we'll see a common loon or two, their backs low in the water as they hunt for the fish that swim beneath them. You have to come down at dawn or at sunset to hear their cello cry. The cormorants will stand on the low-tide rocks and dry their feathers with outstretched wings. They are mute birds and do not sing.

Two days ago Lorna and I were married. We both feel shy with each other, tentative. It's as if we're afraid to touch each other's skin, afraid to look fully in each other's eyes. We both feel vulnerable.

At midnight on our wedding day, our friends sent us away to the Empress Hotel where they had reserved for us the honeymoon suite in a tower overlooking the harbor. Earlier, poets read their celebratory poems in honor of our marriage and a justice of the peace blessed us in the garden. We exchanged gold rings. They carry a carved raven, the ancient symbol of the Pacific Coast peoples, the one who opened the clam shell and let humans out into the world. That night we lay in the erotic solemnity of our first round bed and held our rings up to the light. The light reflected back on our faces and then we moved into each other's arms and there was night.

"'Tis visible silence, still as the hour-glass." Dante Gabriel Rossetti said that, and I finally feel the stillness I've searched for in the past two or three months. I think it is because of our marriage and the vows we made. The stillness came as it always does, when I was least expecting it. This early morning, I stopped just past the lilies where the stone path begins. The Bible in Kings speaks of God not being in the earthquake or the wind, but being instead, "a still small voice." That is what I heard this morning.

I was stopped by a glimpse of an opal drop of water on a bamboo leaf. A moth lifted from among the saber leaves of a lily. It was only a tiny moth, and it lifted from under a green spear where it had rested from the rain and flew in silence. It circled my head, its wings the palest gray shot with a dust of blue, and landed on my forearm and rested there, its small wings folded back.

Then it drifted away into the bracken and was gone. I stepped onto the next stone and followed the path to the pond and the cedar chair. I sat and looked upon the many hundreds of stones Lorna and I have brought home from various beaches and stream banks and mountains.

There were moonstones with their circles of white quartz that Lorna carried from Sombrio Beach and from the South Saskatchewan River, green jades from the Coquihalla River I found with my friend Brian, the stone like an ostrich egg brought to Lorna from Haida Gwaii, which still bears stripes of salt from seaweeds that dried on it in the tidal sun. A black bit of lead-riddled rock from the mouth of the Kootenay Bell mine where my father worked in the 1930s. Hand stones and pebble stones, eye stones, and ear stones, stones you can stare into and find the man you are.

Above me, clouds drifted east across Georgia Strait to the Coast Mountains and the wind I could see but could not hear went its way to the far valley I grew up in. Bright water flowed from the bamboo spout and purled upon the sandstone before falling in the pond among the lily pads and their oily blossoms of white and yellow and red. A golden koi broke the pond's surface and then slid back into the shadowed water. Basho appeared from under a budding rhododendron and Roxy stood on a stepping-stone and cleaned her white paws in the sun. My new wife called to me and I answered her and she came down and sat beside me in the stillness of an ordinary Sunday morning.

I sipped my coffee and spoke to my new wife about the night and the long sleep I'd had beside her, and she told me of the dream that woke her in the night and it was a good dream. She was a child in her dream, a child playing among the tall trunks of prairie lilacs where no one could find her. And I listened and was happy for her.

I told her of my dream where my dead brother spoke to me and I heard his true voice for the first time in almost forty years. We were young and we sat by our secret pool above the scar of the Rogers Pass Highway and Dick talked about his daughter and son and his poetry. I told Lorna it was my first brother-dream in many years, and that I thought it was because I was happy and that my brother must know that, so he came from spirit to bless me. And my wife said she thought her lilac dream was a good dream, for at the end of the dream she had stepped out of her hiding place for the first time and entered the world.

A rufous hummingbird tipped a hanging fuchsia flower with his needle beak, drank, and then he suddenly left, a blur of iridescent green over the cedar fence and we looked up at a sound and saw a small falcon come to rest on a fir bough above our heads. The falcon looked at us, then dropped his curved beak and settled the feathers on his wings. The blue highlights on his shoulder feathers shivered as he worried the feathers on his breast. The water in the pond below held the falcon's reflection and it was morning and it was Sunday and I was a married man and in love with my wife and I left the garden and came up to my office and wrote about these presences so that they would not be lost.

PLANTS

Allium – *Allium giganteum*
Bear's breeches – *Acanthus mollis*
Crocosmia – *Crocosmia masonorum "Lucifer"*
False thistle – *Echinops banaticus*
Fuchsia – *Onagraceae* spp.
Heliopsis – *Heliopsis "Ballet Dancer"*
Penstemon – *Penstemon*
Pink phlox – *Phlox paniculata*
Pitcher plant – *Nepenthes* × *hookeriana*

ANIMALS, BIRDS, AND INSECTS

Belted kingfisher – *Aceryle alcyon*
Black brant – *Branta nigricans*

Common loon — *Gavia immer*
Double-crested cormorant — *Phalacrocorax auritus*
Golden jewel beetles — *Buprestis aurulenta*
Herring gull — *Larus argentatus*
Lesser scaup — *Aythya affinis*
Mute swan — *Cygnus olor*
Northern pintail duck — *Anas acuta*
Pygmy nuthatch — *Sitta pygmaea*
Sparrow hawk — *Falco sparverius*
Yellow-pine chipmunk — *Tamias amoenus*

9

The day becomes more solemn and serene
When noon is past – there is a harmony
In autumn, and a lustre in its sky,
Which through the summer is not heard or seen,
As if it could not be, as if it had not been!
    — PERCY BYSSHE SHELLEY,
        "HYMN TO INTELLECTUAL BEAUTY"

"SEPTEMBER BLOW SOFT till the fruit's in the loft." So goes the old sixteenth-century proverb and so begins this season that follows our marriage. September is perhaps the most beautiful month of the year. It has an edge of wistfulness to it, a gentle regret as if what has passed will not be seen again. There are those who would argue that spring is best, but their argument is always made when the first bulbs grin like fat buddhas in their beds.

September is thought of as the beginning of the end of the year's flamboyant beauty, but it is not. It is a time of fat and flesh, the fullness of ripening. Seedpods hang swollen from the memory of their petals. The orchards and fields lie bloated in their excess. Pumpkins and squash, cucumbers and zucchini, rise among their slow leaves and show their thick backs to the thinning sun.

The summer's new bamboo stalks, etched with fine green leaves, sway with innocent provocation above the sullen ferns and fallen fir cones. Hydrangea dry their heads above the pond, their petals slowly turning from melted blue and pink to thin gold. Spiders fatten on the blundering victims of fall. Small flies dance on their wings in this season's penultimate ballet.

When I was a boy I loved to help my mother when she was canning. Every year she would put up hundreds of jars of fruit for the long winter ahead. The canning began in early July when the first cherries and apricots were ripe and continued through to autumn and the pear season. Apples were crushed and made into apple sauce. Hours were spent shelling peas and cutting green beans for bottling. The woodstove threw its heat into the summer while my mother moved through the haze and steam, the canner boiling, rubber rings and metal lids warming in a pot at the back of the stove.

My brothers usually vanished during canning season and my sister, Linda, wandered off with her friends. My young brother, Mike, was still a small child and played in the yard or got underfoot inside. The riches of the fruit, my father bringing yet another box full of cherries or peaches into the house, was wonderful. My mother would shake her head at his Depression-inspired largesse and begin the long labor of putting up the extra fruit. Peaches had to be scalded, skinned, and pitted. Empty jars had to be brought up from the basement and sterilized. The fruit had to be placed in the jars, syrup poured, and lids had to be turned down hard before the jars could be cooked in the canning vat on the stove.

The heat outside on an August day might be ninety-five degrees Fahrenheit, but in the kitchen it was one hundred and twenty or more. Sweat poured down my mother's arms and face. Her cotton dress clung to her like wet newspaper. A hundred jars done and hundreds more to do. My father was now carrying sacks of potatoes and carrots and crates of cabbages and onions down to the root cellar. Wasps seethed over overripe tomatoes set out on the back porch. Squash the size of basketballs were taken in the wheelbarrow down to the root cellar.

I would stand at the sink and slip the skins from scalded peaches. My mother would take the fruit and split them to remove the pit before packing them into jars. I loved the vast treasure the food represented. My favorite job was to take the cooled jars down to the basement and stack them on the shelves I had made. The different fruits and vegetables each had their own shelf, and in the pale light of the sixty-watt bulb, the fruit shone with the rich glow of winter meals to come.

Once the cold winds of late autumn came I would go to the basement two or three times a day to fill the furnace hopper. It burned only sawdust and one end of the basement was full of dried sawdust delivered from one of the mills. Like any boy I was often late to do it or would forget altogether, but one of my secret joys was to walk to the back of the basement and stare at the many jars of food. I never forgot the labor it took to put the food up, but also never forgot the safety and security it represented.

Eight years later I was married and poor. The plentiful days after my father's arrival in the middle-class vanished from my life. I had very little money and often by the end of the month there wasn't much to eat beyond the most basic foods—macaroni, potatoes, carrots, and canned meat. The thought of baloney or Spam to this day makes me ill. The poverty of those years combined with the poverty of my childhood forever brushed me with want.

Even today I find it hard to resist a bargain for food and will come home with bags of rice or potatoes that will take weeks for the two of us to eat. Often the food goes bad, but I find it hard to escape those early lessons. Like father, like son. I had learned to take advantage of largesse, for who knew what the next day would bring. I still have dreams of those shelves of fruits and vegetables my mother put up when I was a boy.

Hard times are never forgotten. Poverty is a fault in my life and it still trembles in my writing and in my behavior. Years ago I watched well-off matrons picking through sweet red peppers or T-bone steaks and their disdain at a spot on a pepper, a streak of yellow gristle on a steak would anger me. What I must learn to do is to forgive myself for the times I couldn't feed my family.

❧

The death of children is, I think, the hardest death. Dylan Thomas had it right. Johnny's first daughter, Julie, the first grandchild of my parents, died of cancer when she was five. My brother lost his daughter and I lost him for twenty years. He disappeared into himself and was never the same again. The pretty little girl who died went to the grave in a white coffin so small Johnny could have carried it under his arm.

Dick's death from a cerebral hemorrhage followed hard on Julie's. I remember trying to imagine his freckled hands among the ashes and bits of bone. His face in my mind was what snow would look like if it didn't fall. They dug a small hole in the ground beside Julie and placed his ashes there. The same people stood at the graveside with the same faces, the same grief. Nothing had changed. Death just repeated itself.

Dick was dead and in my youth and confusion I had nowhere to put my grief. Mike moved around the house, utterly lost. He was twelve years old and no one talked to him, this kid, this afterthought, my mother's last child and a brother too young for me to understand. Linda stood by my mother at the kitchen door greeting people. I don't remember seeing my father. He was somewhere, but I can't find him in my memory. My mother and father's firstborn, their favorite son, was dead, but I didn't see my father at the funeral, didn't see him at the wake. He was there, I know, but he was invisible. My father had only four more years to live.

I last saw Dick on the side of the dusty highway outside Merritt, hitchhiking to Vancouver. I'd kicked him out of my house after two months of his living with us. My wife had said she couldn't take having him around any more, and I understood though I was torn apart by having to ask him to go. I would do anything to keep peace in my family, yet I loved having my brother close to me. I had spent the two months worried about his dark moods and gloom.

Kicking my brother out was the hardest thing I'd ever had to do. I knew he had nowhere to go. I will never forget his face when I told him. He said he understood. I left him on the side of the highway hitchhiking west to Spences Bridge and then down the Fraser Canyon to Vancouver.

Now he was dead and I was lying on my mother and father's bed crying like a small child. I didn't know how to get out of my fear and grief. My mother stood by the bed. She told me to stop crying. *How dare you,* she said. She was very angry. *There are people out there,* she said. *They'll hear you.* She was dry-eyed and fierce and because I was afraid of her wrath I got up and went back into the living room. I remember nothing after that.

There are no images, no memories.

There are her angry words, *You stop crying,* and I remember them because I remember my eyes sealing over. That moment my brother suddenly appeared inside me, his face inside my face, his laugh, his snicker, his loneliness, his despair. I could hear him talking to me as I went around the room filling people's drinks. He was inside me and I accepted his presence. It didn't seem strange at the time to be inhabited by him. I was already living in another place.

I moved through the room and I remembered him on the roadside in Merritt asking me to look after his kids if anything happened to him. I promised I would, but I didn't look after them at all, not even my own children.

But that afternoon and for five years after he lived inside me, homunculus, spirit sitting inside the cave of my chest, sleeping inside my bones.

I'd come home to bury him and had found there was no home. Home is lost when a childhood is lost. I lost mine that day. From then on everything was crazy, everything a madness. In the next four years I would destroy everyone and everything around me, pulling the warped strings and lighting the fires in the wreckage of my family and friends.

Sometimes in the night I hear a child whimper his way to his parent's bed and struggle down between the bodies that made him. Sometimes it is one of my children. Nietzsche said, "We burn something into the mind so that it will remain in the memory; only what still hurts will be retained." There are moments in my life I find impossible to write about. It's not that they are secrets too terrible to tell, but rather they contain such pain I can't bring myself to let them live again. My night sweats now are no longer soaked in alcohol, but rise from the forgotten come alive in the illusory safety of sleep.

When I was a child I loved early fall. With my friends, I coursed the fields and gardens, stealing apples and pears, packing huge pumpkins down alleys where we broke them against trees and fences. Autumn nights, we went anywhere but home. The wealth of the season was ours to take and waste. The illicit plunder of our neighbors' gardens became tokens of our wild ways, the gourds and fruit metaphors of our desire.

The poverty that kept our mothers and fathers sleepless in the night kept us immortal. Yet somehow there was always food on the table and blankets on our cots. In our world, Captain Marvel, Superman, the Green Hornet, and Plastic Man danced their loony tunes. Bugs Bunny, a kind of horrible dream hidden behind the closet door, had the trickster's noose around the neck of Elmer Fudd. At the Empress Theatre at the end of Main Street, the Saturday serials went on forever, and every child who walked out into the dazzle of summer light hung from a cliff or lay tied to railway tracks. Lash and Rocky, Tom and Hoppie, rode like one man west into the blue hills, always womanless, a feral dog following them in the dust.

In childhood everything is flesh. Last night I watched a boy and girl walk under the boulevard trees with their arms around each other's waist. Her black hair swung against his shoulder and his narrow hip brushed against her skirt. There was no other love like theirs. What clouds there were studded the western sky like opals under water. The young in each other's arms move like no others.

One Boxing Day back in the 1950s I visited a girl. I was fifteen, and for three years I had come to her home on the same day. It was the only time we saw each other privately. Her room was in the basement and we lay on her bed as we had done each year and talked about friends and school and our dreams. As I lay beside her she sat up as she had done each year and slowly removed her blouse and brassiere. Then she lay back down. I have never felt such desire as I did on those three days. Yet I did nothing. I felt utterly helpless. I simply lay there with my hands crossed on my belly and continued talking while she lay there on her back waiting for me to touch her. She was beautiful. We lay there for hours. I remember the way her breasts lifted slightly with each breath she took, her soft nipples. How she wanted me to do something and how much I wanted to. Such terrible, sweet innocence. Such fear. Every few years I dream of her tumbled beauty.

In these September nights next year's May and June babies are being made in rumpled beds. These will be the spring infants, the ones who will have the summer to grow fat on their mother's sweet milk.

Last night their mothers and fathers were all hands and thighs and wanting among the sheets and crumpled pillows, the blankets thrown back and the stubs of white candles burning on the bedside tables. They smelled the other, the rich musk of their thighs and sex, and they were lost entirely to want.

A girl runs across a lawn somewhere, in her hands two apples stolen from a Spartan tree. A boy waits among slanted shadows to share the plunder with her. On the breeze are the scents of pearly everlasting, beautyberry, bell heather, goldenrod, silver lace vine, and freesia. The boy and girl are feasting in the glow from the corner streetlight. The long lawns beckon and the children run off with screams. Parents shake their heads, a little afraid of what goes on in the long, unending nights.

✺

"I want death to find me planting my cabbages, but caring little for it, and even less about the imperfections of my garden," said Montaigne, and today I feel the same way even though I do not plant cabbages. September 11 and the terror of towers falling in New York is now a few days behind me, and only now do I feel I can return to words. I don't want death to find me, not now, and never in a plane crashing through a wall of steel and glass. The good earth shudders and goes on. The seeds bear down. Late flowers bloom.

Like Montaigne, I don't want to take this garden of mine so seriously it banishes the pleasure I take in the planting, the harvest, and most of all the joy in being a part of it. Like all gardens, mine is full of imperfections. Purity is illusion. I find harmony as best I can and though I rarely achieve it by imposing myself on things, I find it everywhere in the accidents things make for themselves.

Sunday morning, the fifth day after the disasters in New York and Washington. Like everyone else, Lorna and I watched the twin towers crumble. Today, I walked along Wallace Drive beside the daffodil and tulip fields. They were in the long wait for next spring, but beside them red and green cabbages shouldered each other. Some of the fields had been reworked and sown with nitrogen-fixing grains, and the new young growth had sprouted green. There is war on the wind and young men and women who are now digging through the rubble of Manhattan are a step away from putting down the chunks of concrete and steel and taking up arms as their country prepares to retaliate against someone, anyone. A grief-crazed America will start its killing now. Their president is already sharpening his knives. Their revenge is their resentment. It feeds obsession, it licks its way to the addiction of war.

Today I feel every day of my sixty-two years. I was born just six months before the start of the Second World War and twenty-odd years after the first. There have been wars ever since, just as there were wars everywhere before. I spent the years of my teenage marriage waiting for atom bombs to fall on me and my family. I don't remember a time of peace among nations. I am still on my knees counting cans of Campbell's tomato soup and the bullets for my Lee-Enfield. I remember the nights when friends and workers in Merritt met in secret vigilante squads, ready to kill refugees streaming out of atom-bombed Vancouver. One of the foremen found out I knew about dynamite and I was told my job would be to blow up the approach bridges on the highway west of town. I was given no choice. If I wasn't prepared to act in defense of our town then my family would suffer. I remember sitting in front of two cases of 60 percent forcite dynamite with rolls of fuse and boxes of blasting caps.

I also remember sitting around a kitchen table in Bert Steinhoff's farm near Nakusp, British Columbia, in 1951, listening to the men talk about the new war in Korea. My father had sent me out to the farm to work for the summer. The men at the table were all veterans who had returned from Europe and Asia just six years before. They were convinced this was going to be the Third World War. I was twelve and, because I was a boy as they had once been, I was allowed to sit at the table with the men. Mrs. Steinhoff had made a huge pot of coffee and a batch of fresh bread before going out to the apple orchard with her two daughters, and the men were eating and sipping hot coffee as they talked. In those days women did not sit down when men talked of serious things. The only time I heard women speak of war was when the men were gone. I remember my mother's friends drunk and crooning on D-Day as Churchill spoke on the radio. Some of them cried. What I remember most of all is the look of fear on their faces.

It was something new to have men look at me appraisingly. They had included me. I hadn't been sent outside to play. Instead, I had a chair at the table. At one point, Mr. Steinhoff, my father's army friend, told me I might have to fight in this new war if it lasted as long as the last one. I don't remember being frightened by this sober revelation, but I was confused by the looks the men gave me. It was as if they were appraising my ability to be a soldier as they had been. I thought that if there was a war somewhere I would fight in it. I'd be a man if I did.

The Korean War didn't last long enough for me to go to Asia, but the moment stayed with me. Today, on this misty country road with the fog rolling in off the Pacific, that time fifty years ago is vivid. I am in the first generation of Lane men in hundreds of years who haven't fought in a war, and now New York and Washington are attacked, and the prime minister of my country is telling me we are with America all the way. My mind stumbles at the thought of what has happened and of what is to come. Yesterday and tomorrow have slung themselves into my mind. Regret and compassion and their companions, doubt and fear, range inside me.

I stopped walking and looked across the fields through the mist. A rabbit sat up beside the road a few yards away and looked at me. It was just a small brush rabbit doing her rabbity thing, twitching her nose, swiveling her long ears, and munching on one of the tired clover blossoms that grew out of the gravel verge. Beyond both of us the fog began to lift, but not enough to reveal the blue islands and the far peak of Mount Baker. It was a gentle, hesitant lifting like a woman hiking her long skirts as she walked into shallow water.

The fallow fields were silent. No one else was about, no one taking an early walk, and no traffic on the road. Just beyond the rabbit, Himalayan blackberry canes sprawled up out of impenetrable thickets below.

Brush rabbits rarely wander far from home. This one seemed content to sit at the edge of the road knowing there was no danger from someone as slow as me. I was just another animal, a benign one, who had decided to rest a moment. I looked at the rabbit and the rabbit looked at me. It occurred to me that she was looking at an entirely different scene out of her other eye. Like most people I assume how I see is how everything else sees. But my eyes are side by side in my head and the rabbit's are opposite each other on the sides of her head. For a moment the god Janus came to mind and

I was reminded how the Romans would place their statue of Janus in the door of the Senate when there was war. Janus too looked two ways. I wondered what it would be like to see the world through a rabbit's eyes.

How is it for you today? I asked her.

Above us a hundred muttering starlings quieted on the wires as if pondering my question. Wisps of fog slipped through their gleaming feathers as they watched and listened. It seemed an important question.

The rabbit stopped chewing and her left ear swiveled toward me. Her nose followed her ear and I could see it twitch. She resumed chewing momentarily and then, when I didn't repeat my question, leaned down and ate another clover head.

It doesn't go all that well for me or for my kind, I said as if to explain.

It didn't seem strange for me to be talking to a brush rabbit. I've spent my life talking to animals, insects, and birds and they have talked to me in their way.

The rabbit chewed for a moment, then scratched at her ear with the stubby nails of her hind paw. She seemed to be thinking and reached up and scratched her other ear as if unsure of what she had heard me say or, at least, what to make of it. Her scratched ears flicked up and turned toward me again, so I repeated what I had said. She hopped a pace toward me, sat up so her front paws rested on her bluff chest, and turned both her ears to me as if listening was the same as speech. I thought about that a moment and then, because she seemed to want me to listen with her, I did.

I heard the starlings above me suddenly whirl away. I heard the slow water in the ditch behind me. I heard a frog croak as if with a throat sore from a night of singing long love songs. I heard the wind in the blackberry canes and the tight wheeze in the clenched seed heads of the Queen Anne's lace. I heard the far sound of the wind above the wind, the one that rides the fog and I heard the creak of the sun breaking through the gray mist. I heard my old lungs breathing and my feet shift slightly in the gravel, and I thought of how sound has something to tell us beyond speech if we listen carefully and the sounds of the world were where I was and nowhere else.

I felt perfectly alive, a near-sighted, balding, sixty-two-year-old man, present on this island in the far west of North America. That seemed enough.

Seemingly satisfied I understood at least that, the brush rabbit turned and hopped back to her clover patch, bit off a frayed pink blossom, and then hopped down into the blackberry thicket. The sun broke through the fog then and the fields glowed with early light and I continued my walk beside the fallow fields at peace in the moment, happy that a small rabbit had taken the time to teach me something I knew but had momentarily forgotten. The sun shone fully at last and in the distance a flock of Canada geese rose from the glittering ocean and slowly made their way across the tips of the far fir trees and passed above me. I heard their steady wing beat and the single, admonishing voice of the old goose who was their leader in this training flight for their long journey south. This way, she seemed to be saying and I, because there was no other way to go, followed her advice into the beauty of the ordinary day.

The fires burned in New York and great towers fell and I have gone into the garden, for where else is there to go? Not the television and not the radio with their endless images looping and relooping like Möbius strips until they burn the mind with their repetitions. In times of grief and struggle I seek what peace I can. A golden-crowned sparrow sings in my apple tree. He is brother to the song sparrow in a tree on Brooklyn Heights who sings above the great bridges that lead to the ashes and twisted steel.

An orb weaver spider's web covered in dew among fronds of fern is enough to remind me of the simple world. This dream-catcher of a web is a metaphor for what transcendence there is in my life, but it is also the spider's basket that holds its daily bread. I must remember that, just as I must remember the spiraling intensity of yellows in the marmalade rudbeckia is a yellow hole of light that draws the bee into the flower. The spider in her circles follows the same path the flower makes. Color and light, nectar and pollen, smell and sight, are all motives for transcendence. My daily round is the circuit of the sun.

I have slipped unconscious into the slow drift of early autumn. The sunny, warm days and cool, misty nights create a sleep in me and I have to struggle against the complacency of fall. I have a *Clematis tangutica* to plant against the fence behind the witch hazel.

It will bloom through next summer into fall. Its flowers are small yellow lanterns that turn to silver seed heads after the petals fall. Now it sits in its pot and stares at me each morning. There are two digitalis to plant as well. They are perennial, unlike their biennial cousins that prosper everywhere. The blossoms are a pale, creamy yellow and the plants grow about thirty inches high. I have just the spot for them in the bed I will be digging up next week. They will lend a color variation to the anemone and Oregon grape.

At the nurseries bulbs have arrived in all their variations. As always, I am tempted by any and all of them, but I have steeled myself this year and will stick with whatever is already out there in the many nooks and crannies of the garden. We are only four months away from the first snowdrops and crocuses, but I don't want to think of that. I'll leave thinking of bulbs for another day. I know I'll weaken if I go near a nursery.

Bulbs are by and large extremely hardy and can take a fair amount of disturbance without ill effect. Many of the bulbs in the bed by the pond have been here for years and have to be split up. As I find them, I break the clusters apart and end up with two or three double handfuls of extra bulbs and now I have to find a place to put them. The bed I am digging is a bulb cornucopia. Some of them will have to find new homes in other beds or in friends' gardens. I might start some in pots as well. There's nothing more pleasant in late November than an early show of narcissus or species daffodils.

An hour ago my mother stood under the fir tree by the pond. She was wearing her gardening clothes just as she always does when she visits here. As I stared at her I thought I must have somehow fixed her in my mind in some past moment for she is always the same, with her red babushka knotted tight around her head. She seemed puzzled by something for she kept raising her fingers to her mouth as if there was a word or sentence there that could be pulled out and left to speak on its own. When I made a motion toward her she knelt behind the rosemary bush and was gone. I went to where she was standing and I touched the ground where her feet had been.

It is me who brings her back. She does not come because she wants to. I call her from the dead and she rises from the earth and comes to me. Where did I lose her that now I want her found? I go back to that little child who blazoned on her skin his tattooed vision. What image did I draw there? Like the words I buried under stone the picture is lost. Only the furious intent of that child remains.

My mother touched her mouth like some maddened thing. I would like to undo her babushka and let her gray hair fall as it fell upon her pillow in that last bed of hers. She combed it every day until her hands no longer moved. The heavy shades of brown had gone to gray, just wisps, thin strands that floated in the air above her pillow. I listened to her breathing there, that withered chest rising and falling in such shallow breaths I had to touch her lips with my hand to feel the air.

I put the hose sprinkler down by the *Pieris japonica* and it sprang to life as I let go the kink in the hose. Water splashed my face. I wiped my eyes and looked, but she was gone. She worries about something, something in the garden. *Tell me a story.* That is what I wanted to say to her. *Tell me the story that brought you here.*

As I stare at the spot where she stood I suddenly remember that she never once told me I had done good in my life. No poem, no book, no prize, no award, ever elicited anything from her. My life as an artist didn't seem a disappointment to her, rather my life seemed irrelevant, my art of no import whatsoever. Praise was not something she could give.

Is that why I call her back? Am I so much a child I still need praise from her?

❦

This morning I got up and had my coffee by the pond. I made my prayer and, after a half hour of staring at the murky water, I thought it's time to clean the pond filters and lament a bit the untrappable raccoon's depredations.

I put on my old clothes. The raccoon has chomped on the water hyacinths and left them a mess. He drags them out of the pond and leaves them strewn about. He simply won't be caught. Someone has live-trapped him before, so I think I'll have him for a long time. He digs holes in the lawn and mosses in search of earthworms and beetles and there's nothing I can do to dissuade him short of sitting up all night with a gun and I gave my rifles away years ago. The nights of my shooting raccoons—or shooting anything else for that matter—are long over.

The latest raccoon and I will have to share this garden space. He upends water containers, digs holes everywhere, but it's the pond he loves. I must learn to live with him. If he eats water hyacinths, then I won't bother putting any in. If he wants to tear the water-lily leaves, then I will move the plants to the center of the pond where he can't reach them. Tolerance is something I've come late to in this world. Twenty years ago I would have shot him with my 22/410 over-and-under. It was my father's brush gun and I prized it for many years, but gave it away when I realized I'd never use it again. Besides, I'd sucked the barrel of that gun. Having the rifle around would be a constant reminder of my alcoholism and the depressions it caused that almost led me to death. The raccoon can stay. There's room for his chaos here.

Now I've washed the pond filters and snipped off the dying water-lily pads I notice the fish aren't rising like they usually do. Something's frightened them, and I hope it's the raccoon and not some visiting heron. Or the fish may simply be slowing down. I've stopped feeding them and they may have decided it's time to begin their winter estivation.

I stopped in at a local nursery. They had their last ornamental fish on sale at 50 percent off. Unable to resist I bought two smallish koi, one a burnished, heavy brown with shots of gold staggering among its scales, and another, also gold, but a light yellow the color of the noonday sun. They're both butterfly kawarigoi; they have large, fanlike fins. I don't need two more fish, but I could not resist their beauty.

I have struggled these last few days with the memories that have surfaced this year. I keep asking myself why these particular memories. What do they mean? I have thought long about my father's life, his marrying my mother and having three children before the war and then his leaving for almost five years. Then, after his return, his new relationship with my mother and the birth of two more children. A second family. This morning I sat in the garden and saw that I had done the same as my father. I married, had three children and then after nine years of marriage, the same length of time my father had with us before the war, I left my marriage. I wandered for five years and then began a new relationship with my second wife, had two more children and then left again. It was as if I had fulfilled some prophecy, kept some promise I had made.

I have lived my father's life. I sat there under the apple tree, staring out at the garden, and wondered if there is any escape from the patterns we find in our lives. I wondered if there were any choices made that weren't preordained. Or did I do the same as my father in order to find the father I never had, the one I never was? I saw my own children as I saw myself as a child, and I knew what their abandoned lives have been because I have that life. I remembered how hard my daughter tried to make a father out of me when she was in her late teens and early twenties and how crazy it had been for both of us.

She was six years old when my second marriage ended. I never really saw her again until she was thirteen. The lost years could not be found by either of us. Whenever we tried to understand our love for each other we foundered, the wreck fueled by drugs and alcohol. Our conversations collapsed under bizarre behavior, anger, and recrimination. And now I know she felt like I have felt much of my life. The pattern I lived I visited on her. Her feeling of loss is mine.

I used to drive all over Vancouver with her as I printed books and distributed them. I remember her sitting beside me in the car, her bright laughter and her joy at being with me. I felt the same joy and shared the laughter. I wasn't working at a regular job those last two years before I divorced. I wrote, published, gave readings, left my family, and returned to my family half a dozen times.

Guilt is the emotion that wastes a life, I know that. I know there is no going back even as I return in my memories. My father had an expression that seems to fit what I seem to be doing. He would say about some man who kept returning to the same hell he had left, that the man was like a dog returning to his own vomit. It's a visceral expression, but one that aptly describes my own condition. Memory is a terrible mental swamp. I visit the past or the past visits me. Either way I am undone by the repetitions. I am also undone by stories. There are times I no longer know if what I have told is a truth or is a lie, a fiction. There are times I think I have gone mad.

At such moments I turn to praise and its companion, prayer, and in surrender find what peace I can. It was surrender that got me to these moments in the garden, this acceptance of what I have and what I am. It was surrender that led to almost a year without a drink or a drug in my body. I am overwhelmed at times by what I have done in this life and to whom I have done it. But now I know that the past is mine to take with me or to leave behind. The stories I tell are only stories, no more than that. Were another person who was witness to the same life to tell them, he would tell them differently, people them with other characters and events, a plot and a tone that I would not recognize. Was the blanket on my mother's bed red with a black stripe? How many rainbows did I catch at Aberdeen Lake?

These last few days I've been cleaning the pond, clipping off the old lily leaves, and reseating some of the large stones that form its perimeter. They loosen every year and I'm always concerned someone will step on a tippy stone and end up among the fish.

The garden is in early autumn. The hostas are turning yellow, as are many of the other plants. Trees are just turning color, the edges of their leaves becoming brittle. In another month the maples will be in full glory.

Apple picking starts tomorrow. Early autumn is over and though it was one of the most beautiful times of the year it was clouded by the tragedy of New York. As I think of that a tree frog sings his autumn song in the low arms of a red cedar. Birds play out the end of their family life around the bird feeder, their babies full-grown and the adults refusing to pay them any attention, no matter how they beg. The fish have begun to spend more time in the deeps. The hostas sprawl like spilled gold at the feet of the firs and cedars. The monkshood have put out their last lateral blooms. They nod in the breeze like tired men in a chilly cloister.

Birds are everywhere. A red-shafted flicker perches on an apple branch and carves white slivers from an apple with his beak. He reminds me of last winter. Yesterday a pileated woodpecker hammered at the old maple in the front yard. He tore off chunks of rotted bark in search of beetles and larvae. He was as long as my forearm and his yellow eye stared down at me briefly then paid me no attention at all. The hawks have wandered south to the tip of the island. They ride the updrafts higher and higher along Juan de Fuca

Strait before soaring out on the winds to Washington's Olympic Mountains in the distance. I will miss their beauty.

A couple of yellowthroats wandered through briefly this morning. They are rare here. They were far from their Texas home and looked like their only thoughts were of returning. I saw a pygmy owl in one of the fir trees last week. It is such a tiny little hunter, a bit bigger than my fist, no more. He slept out the day on an inner branch of the fir. I would have missed him had I not casually looked up. His black streaked sides and soft brown back and tail help him blend perfectly with the fir's rough bark. He too looked like he might head south for winter.

Autumn and visitations, eleven months since I stopped drinking. Last year I was dying. Now I am alive. I sit in my chair by the window drinking Chinese tea. Lorna sits across from me reading Charles Simic's latest poems, Roxy is curled on her lap and her hand with its gold ring rests on the cat. The raven crest on her wedding band flashes in the evening light.

PLANTS

Anemone de Caen (the Bride) – *Coronaria*
Beautyberry – *Callicarpa bodinieri*
Bell heather – *Calluna vulgaris*
Camas lily – *Camassia leichtlinii "Alba"*
Clematis – *Clematis tangutica*
Eastern redbud (Judas tree) – *Cercis canadensis*
Freesia – *Freesia*
Fritillaria – *meleagris, pyrenaica, cirrhosa, pontica, michailovsky, pallidiflora, uva-vulpis*
Ginkgo (maidenhair tree) – *Ginkgo biloba*
Gladiolus – *Gladiola byzantius*
Goldenrod – *Solidago*
Himalayan blackberry – *Rubus discolor*
Iris – *Iris tenax*
Japanese maple – *Acer japonicum*
Lily of the valley – *Convallaria majalis*
Mahonia – *Mahonia acanthifolia*
Marmalade rudbeckia – *Rudbeckia hirta*

Narcissus – *Narcissus nain*
Narcissus golden bells – *Narcissus*
Oregon grape (mountain grape holly) – *Mahonia aquifolium*
Ornamental onion – *Allium oreophilum (A. ostrowskianum)*
Pearly everlasting – *Anaphalis*
Silver lace vine – *Polygonum aubertii*
Tulip – *Tulipa linifolia* and *Tulipa clusiana*
Yellow foxglove – *Digitalis lutea*

ANIMALS, BIRDS, AND INSECTS

Brush rabbit – *Sylvilagus bachmani*
Common yellowthroat – *Geothlypis trichas*
Golden-crowned sparrow – *Zonotrichia albicollis*
Pileated woodpecker – *Dryocopus pileatus*
Pygmy owl – *Glaucidium gnoma*

10.

Summer pleasures they are gone like to visions every one
And the cloudy days of autumn and of winter cometh on.
I tried to call them back but unbidden they are gone
Far away from heart and eye and for ever far away.
    —JOHN CLARE, "REMEMBRANCES"

THE WELCOME OCTOBER RAINS have come to veil the garden. The leaves on the trees have the feel of leather, a thickness
that presages their fall to earth. They are like forgotten gloves left
too long in the weather. They've lost their oils and supple resiliency,
worn out by months of sun and drought, wind and insects. Their
edges are brittle and carry the first, hesitant crisp of yellow and red,
as the sap from the high branches starts to sink back down into the
roots and the tree's long sleep comes on.

Of all senses, smell is the deepest, and the fall air is musty and
thick. It may be that the falling rain shakes the earth and throws up
spores from the disturbed mycelia of dormant mushrooms; the air
carries that clotted fullness to the nose and the back of the throat.

I smelled a bird's desiccated body yesterday. The little corpse lay
under the crocosmia. The cat had his go at the small pine siskin and
then the beetles, slugs, and ants had their way until all that was left
were feathers, bone, and a few leathery tendons still holding the
feathered corpse together. It lay splayed out like the impression in

stone the first bird left, a fossil from some field in nether China. But the smell was of the soil and like no other. That is what the autumn rains bring to the garden, the freighted earth smell of October. It is a dour beginning to the autumn. I feel at times like a beetle scuttling for shelter from a sky that's changed from sun to perpetual cloud.

On the wires of a telephone line above the street out front a crow calls out in what could be as easily misery as glee. Of all birds, crows have the greatest argument with the rain. Perhaps it is the smell of the earth that rouses them to speak out. But is the crow vocalizing his misery at the clouds? Perhaps for him they are a relief from the summer sun.

I carry with me like a second skin the folktales, ancient poems, and old stories that tell me the crow is a harbinger of death. These black mockers clean the earth of fallen birds, rats, mice, beetles, and every other creature whose death comes through age or misadventure. *Bring out your dead,* they cry and the season complies with furred and feathered corpses. As Lorna once said, I must learn the crow's black joy.

Knowing that, I circle my father's death for a means to get close. I remember my Uncle Jack pushing my head into my father's coffin. The taste of lipstick and powder will stay on my lips forever. *Kiss him,* he cried, *Kiss your father goodbye.*

I cannot find my father. Strangely, I feel closer to the man who killed him. I have imagined him many times. I can see him sitting in the Allison Hotel, nursing one of his many beers as he goes over and over the ground of his resentment, the misery and failure of his life. I can see him lifting his beer and putting it down on the circles of sweat left by his cold glass. His cigarette burns down in an ashtray, the ash a long gray worm.

The man knows his Winchester 30/30 is safe outside, resting on the rack behind his truck seat. He knows it is loaded. He has stripped it many times of shells, cleaned it, and cleaned it again with gun oil, and then reloaded it, the gray bullets polished to a leaden sheen.

He has been sitting on the men's side in the beer parlor since the bar opened at ten o'clock. No one has sat with him. The other patrons have heard his monotonous story a hundred times, how the company cheated him out of his equipment, how he had tried to make the payments, but so many things had gone wrong. There were the summer closures due to fires and then the falling lumber prices in the early fall, and the sawmill strikes in November that shut down work in the bush. It wasn't his fault the company had foreclosed on him and seized his Cat and skidder and his logging truck to pay the debt.

He is sure of the great wrong done to him. I can see him stepping out into the bright February sun and standing there in the cold, blinking until his eyes adjust. Then he crosses the street and walks across the trampled snow in the Cenotaph Park to where his pickup is parked. He sits on its torn vinyl seat and pulls out from the curb. This battered pickup is all he has left. He has no wife now, no children. They left him weeks ago after he emptied his rifle into the kitchen wall above the sink.

The truck drifts out into rolling farmland and then wanders beyond it to the dirt road that leads up Silver Star Mountain. He stops when he reaches the end, lifts his rifle from the rack, and steps out onto the frozen gravel. Fir trees lean toward him. He looks out over the valley spread below him. There are the lakes, the town, and the Coldstream Valley drifting off to the east and to the west, range after range of hills and mountains stretching into a paler and paler blue to become one with the frozen sky. Everything is winter.

He lights a cigarette and takes a deep drag, holding the smoke in his lungs, and then he expels it in a cloud. He raises the rifle to his shoulder and points it at the town. Somewhere in the heart of what he sees is the company that took his life away. He peers down the barrel with his blue eye and sights the spot. He lines up his barrel carefully and then, as if he were sighting on a moose in an autumn meadow or a bear rummaging in the garbage behind his shack, he gently squeezes the trigger and feels the blow in his shoulder as the rifle recoils. The sharp crack catches at the walls of rock around him and echoes back the rifle's song in diminuendos of complaint.

He does not lower the rifle but keeps his eye true to the two sights. Through the wedge of metal he sees the wisp of oily smoke whisper out of the barrel. He levers down, ejects the spent shell and jacks another into the chamber. He shoots again and then again. As he shoots he imagines the bullets arcing through the bright mountain air until they hit the building he aims at six miles away. He lowers the rifle then and spits out the butt of his cigarette. Around his feet the shell casings have fallen in a circle. They are the splayed casts of ancient butterflies. He reaches in his pocket, takes out a handful of shells and reloads his rifle.

When it is done he walks back to the truck and rides slowly down the mountain back into town and parks across the street from the company. It is almost five o'clock. He looks through the frost-scarred windows and sees the men and women moving around as they wrap up the business of the day. In one office he sees an over-weight man with red hair. He and another man are both laughing at some joke. He thinks about the day two months earlier when the red-headed man told him the company was taking its equipment back. He had begged him not to do it, to give him more time, that he would get the money somewhere, but the man had told him he had no choice. He said he was sorry. That afternoon the trucks had come in and hauled his life away. The two men behind the glass laugh again at something and then they stand up and reach for their coats.

It is cold outside. The man in the truck lowers his window and lifts his rifle from the rack behind him, puts the barrel out the window and aims it at an office window. It is not the office where the man was laughing. It is an empty office. He aims his rifle carefully, high, so that the bullet will shatter the glass and frighten the people inside the building. He doesn't want to kill anyone, not really, he just wants to frighten them. He wants them to know that their lives can be destroyed too, just as his has been. He wants them to know the helplessness and fear he has felt this past month and for the months and years before that. He wants them to know how he feels. He squeezes the trigger gently and the rifle cracks and the bullet streams through the thin winter air and through the window glass and through the empty office and through a thin plywood partition into a larger room. The bullet is high now, near the ceiling, and it buries itself in a light fixture. The light explodes and sparks shower down on the stacks and shelves.

The people in the building hear only a far-off backfire, perhaps a recalcitrant truck trying to start. All they know is that a light has exploded. My father goes into the parts department and tells every-one to stay away and then he climbs up the shelves stacked with parts until he gets up by the ceiling. He is a boy walking away from a farm with a dollar in his pocket, the MacLeod Kid riding a bronco in the Calgary Stampede, a dam builder, a hard-rock miner. He is Sergeant Major Lane and he is Red Lane, the sales manager, a boss, a man who knows what to do.

At the top shelf he pulls himself up and lies down on his back. Someone has turned the power off. A small fire has begun in the fixture. The other men stand and look up at my father as he begins to put out the fire. He is Red Lane. He is in charge.

The man in the truck outside has waited, but there is no response from the people inside. Why haven't they rushed from the building? Why don't they know he is there? Why haven't they come? He levers the spent shell from the chamber and jacks in another, braces his arm against the metal of the door, and aims carefully at a spot a two feet to the right of the last one. He fires again.

The bullet leaves the shell, spins in the swirl of the Winchester's barrel, explodes from the end with a sharp crack, and swims with immense slowness through the thin winter air. The bullet travels slowly through the space where the glass window used to be, crosses the empty room, pierces the partition, races across the high still air of the parts department, and it stops.

Everything then is absolutely still, everything is frozen, and there is nothing anyone can do. The bullet noses the white cotton of my father's shirt. It is as if it is waiting for some order, some particular and crucial command, from somewhere so it can continue on with its life, and I say aloud, *Finish this, let me have an end to this,* and it does, and the whole world begins again, it begins with the fury and intensity that a bullet is when it has found its target, and the bullet, happy at last with a life it understands, enters my father's chest and finds his heart and stops there in an explosion of bright blood. The blood floods out over the white cotton shirt my mother ironed that morning. My father's hands stop. He stares at what he has done and he takes a single breath and then it is over. It is over and done with and finished and complete and forever and exquisitely over and done with, and he is dead. My father is dead.

The telephone rings.

I went mad then. Within a year I had divorced. I had fallen out of a second-story window onto my head and walked away with a headache that lasted three years. I had placed the first muzzle of a rifle into my mouth, crashed three cars, and swam out into the stinking drain of industrial False Creek trying to drown myself. I was impotent for a year. I remember only a distorted collage of highways, strange cities, and stranger people. I was crazy then.

❧

George Herbert, that old English poet, wrote down how I feel this autumn when he said:

> And now in age I bud again,
> After so many deaths I live and write;
> I once more smell the dew and rain,
> And relish versing.

A year ago I lay on the floor in the front hall having a seizure, my stomach heaving, my muscles in spasms, blood in the back of my throat. I had been drinking forty or fifty ounces of vodka a day for months. I feel I've been walking on brittle bones this October. My feet find their way gingerly as if they were finding their way in a darkened, unfamiliar room. My addiction sleeps with its claws in my mind.

Today I picked the last fruit in the garden. My hands remember apples. They feel their own way to the hidden fruit in the leaves, take the plump weight and twist or bend it so the stem breaks away. If the apple does not come away easily, then my thumb slips up and presses the nail against the stem's stump and cracks it off. The twig the fruit hangs from can easily be broken off and if it does there will be no blossom there come spring.

It was my mother who started me on the way to this garden here on the Island. I remember watching her crawl among the perennial beds in her own garden on her hands and knees until she disappeared entirely into the canopy of green. The only sign of her would be the occasional glimpse of her red babushka among the stems and leaves.

Now she creeps on her hands and knees in mine. There are the days her spirit wanders the ferns. When I see her there I quietly tell her to go back to spirit. There's something she's left undone that I'm a part of and I wish she'd tell me so I could help her. She is a benign

218

though sometimes angry and resentful presence. When she comes I ignore her threat, feeling only an uneasy anxiety as she fusses awhile with some plant or stone that will not do as she intends.

A week ago I returned to Vernon and stood at my mother's and father's graves, I wanted to lay down the burdens I had carried with me most of my life. I felt only a slow sadness. What I understood when I stood before their gravestones was that much of my young life had been happy in spite of all the grief I held onto. There was a weariness and a terrible yearning for love but who was I to ask for more than they could offer? They had given to me all they had. They gave me life, and I am thankful for it. I looked up from their graves to the far hills of the Bluebush country that lies west of the valley and what I found there was enough to sustain me. There is beauty if you want to see it. The hush of blue as those hills turned to clouds was beautiful. The rain, the rain, the desert hills seemed to cry.

May my little father and little mother, side by side, rest easy in the old earth.

May my family find what peace they can.

I left the graveyard but there was still something that needed to be understood. What I learned as a boy is not so easily lost. My body carries the memory of a thousand motions: picking apples, hammering a nail, stacking wood, piling stones. The body, like the garden, goes on without me.

❦

A small, thin spider peers over the lip of a Mexican orange bush leaf. He wants to pluck the dream-catcher's strings. Below him is a cluster of fragrant white blossoms. Their scent is citrus, a slice of orange perfume that cuts the air. Attached to one of the petals is a single strand of webbing. It is tied to the leaf by six tiny anchors of thread. The main filament stretches over a gap, an opening the light breeze moves through. The small spider's long legs touch the leaf's glossy surface for a moment and then he pulls himself up out of his hiding and crosses the leaf to the flower and places the tip of one of his long legs on the string of web.

He is a male orb-weaver spider and across from him in space is the dream-catcher of a female. She is huge, her body swollen from months of steady feeding. She has moved her web around the front garden, sometimes among the bright, thorned leaves of the holly, sometimes in the lilac or the ivy that shoots out from the walls of the house, its berries slowly turning purple in the fall sun, anywhere insects gather to feed or dance in the bright air. For the last week, her web has floated here, anchored by the Mexican orange, the laurel, and the holly. It hangs at just the right height to catch the last bees, flies, and other tiny flying things of the season. She rebuilds her web once a day, usually in early evening after the sun has set, but sometimes in the morning if some passing creature has torn it in the night. It takes her an hour.

Each web has been a little larger as she has grown larger, and now it is almost twenty inches in diameter. It is a spiral nebula, a swirl that is a massive killing ground. In its lower left quadrant hang the rolled up carapaces of a wasp and a crane fly. She injected a killing poison into them earlier in the day and it has turned their internal organs to liquid. She will drink them dry when she gets hungry again. Right now she hangs in the center of the web from her two back legs. Deep in her abdomen lie hundreds of unfertilized eggs. The female and her unborn offspring are waiting for male sperm to bring them to life. Her front legs rest on walking strings, the long filaments of web that radiate from the center. Only the circling strands are sticky. The straight support strings are what she walks and runs on when prey crashes into her aerial trap.

Her huge abdomen is beautiful with shades of gray and brown and there are two pale stripes that arch up from her head and over the high curve of her back. They are shocks of light, a pale yellow-white against the deeper browns and tans. She has survived the wind, the drought, and the rare rains. She has also survived the birds of spring who eat young spiders. No bird would touch her now. She is too large, too formidable. Her eyes are bright with a cold, steady patience. I have stared into them and tried to see into her arachnid mind but what stared back at me was nothing I knew or understood.

The male spider's body is small, one-tenth the size of the female's. His legs are much longer than his abdomen and they move in front of him, constantly testing the surfaces and textures that confront him. As I watch, he places one of his two longest legs on the thin strand of web and, bracing himself, plucks the string. The bit of webbing vibrates and he plucks it again like a guitar or violin that has one pure note.

The vibrations travel up the anchor string to the web and when they reach her the female tenses. She comes fully alive in a startled vigilance. She turns quickly to face the direction his message comes from. It *is* a message. It is unlike the thrashing struggle of an insect caught in her web. She knows this song. It is one buried deep inside her, passed on to her by her mother and all the mothers before her.

The male plucks intermittently for a full five minutes or more and then, not feeling a response, climbs out on the anchor string and slowly, carefully begins to walk along it toward the far dream-catcher. As he gets closer to the perimeter the female rushes to where the anchor string leaves the last circle and stops. The male, feeling her dash, backs away down the anchor and stops as well. He turns to face the female and then plucks the string again. She races toward him and he drops on his own filament and hangs below.

He has carried his escape webbing in a gathered ball beneath him. As she came toward him he stuck it to her anchor and dropped. He swings now below her. She stares down and then retreats to the edge of her web where she waits for five minutes before walking back to its center. She hangs there upside down but she is tense for a long time. Finally she relaxes and the male spider climbs up his rope to the anchor string, his escape web gathered in a frizzy ball under his body.

He walks slowly up the strand and almost touches the outer perimeter when she attacks. The male drops down again, this time only a hand's breadth from the edge. She squats above him. This time she stays longer. Below her the male swings like a living pendulum in the warm, autumn air. She rises up and moves her body about as if uncomfortable, as if the muscles in her legs are stiff. Then, turning, she makes her way back to her perch.

Again, the male climbs back up and walks the anchor to the perimeter. Once there he reaches out with his long leg and plucks the string again. The vibrations are stronger now and it only takes two or three plucks for the female to return. Once again he drops away.

This goes on for almost an hour. Each time the male returns he advances a little farther down the gossamer string, and now he is inside the dream-catcher. Each time she rushes at him she moves more slowly and now he doesn't drop away but only retreats to the outside edge until she has returned to her perch.

Inside the female are her eggs and inside the male is a small package of sperm. His job, his life's purpose, is to deposit the sperm package into a vent on the side of her abdomen and so fertilize her eggs. It is a difficult and dangerous procedure for she sees him as the source of two things, food and sperm. His job is to get her to sit absolutely still so he can deposit his sperm and then escape. This is not so simple as it sounds. She will poison him in a millisecond once the sperm is delivered. He knows that. It's why he's been so careful, but he is implacable. He knows what he has to do.

He sits very close to her now and begins his music in earnest. He plays her a tune, his longest legs alternating on two strings. The whole of this long courtship has been like an opera, a complex and beautiful ballet. This last musical interlude takes place just before his last advance. She has become quieter where she hangs. Her legs have relaxed. Perhaps she is entranced by his playing.

Now I understand why his legs are so long. He comes up to her and touches her legs. They tense and then, under his repeated, alternating, drumming and stroking, they relax again. His legs are long in order to allow him to escape if she attacks. The male continues touching her until he can reach past her legs and head to her abdomen. He strokes her flanks, her huge, distended belly. His legs caress her. He is close now, close enough for her to kill him but she is stilled by his stroking, stilled by his gentle touch, his long caresses. She has fallen into a reverie, some place of quiet beauty all her own. Her many eyes stare into his with perfect stillness.

His penis is at the end of his longest leg and as he strokes her he comes closer and closer to her vent. He strokes and strokes and then, deftly, quickly, he slips the tip of his penis-leg into her.

Instantly, he withdraws all of his legs. He is going to drop down his escape line. As he pulls back, she transforms from the benign and sleepy female into a killer. Both things happen at once. She is suddenly pure energy, swift and sure. She grabs hold of one of his long legs. He twists and falls away beneath her, leaving his leg behind in her jaws. As he falls she stares down at him, then she drops the leg.

The male has only seven legs instead of eight, but he has successfully placed his sperm in her and has done so without becoming a meal. He swings a moment or two longer, then strings out more filament from his spinners and drops down to a laurel berry. There he sits as if exhausted from the long ordeal he has just gone through. It has taken almost two hours. His dance is done and he has his life. Above him the female sits in her web. She too is tired. He waits a moment and then, just before moving away from the huge dream-catcher above him, he plucks the filament of web that still attaches him to the female above. He plucks it three times, but there is no response. This last plucking seems a kind of farewell song. He cuts himself away from his falling string and climbs off the laurel berry onto a glossy green leaf and then under it.

I peer under the leaf and see him hanging there in the shade.

Then I peer in close at the huge female. Her eyes stare out from above her slowly moving jaws. Soon, she will attach her fertilized egg sac to a nearby leaf. Perhaps a dozen or so of the hundreds of their spiderlings will survive next year to grow as formidable as their mother, as wily and quick as their father. I will watch for them and if I catch a fly or moth I will toss it living into one of their webs. It will be my gift to one of the great mothers of the garden.

My garden cleanup started a week ago. Next month is the hard month for leaves and cuttings, but I find that if I start now then the rest of the fall is easier. By the end of the month it will be time to cut the stems of the last perennials. I planted four clumps of young chives this spring and on the first dry day I will go out and split them. The pond too is ready for its autumn cleaning. The resident raccoon is doing his best to eat the last of the water hyacinths. Yesterday I found a half dozen spread on the lawn. It is time to clear them and the water lettuce off the pond. Time to lift the water lilies and trim the stems of the leaves and the few sagging flowers that I couldn't reach. They'll winter in the deep water.

The witch hazel I planted this past spring has grown mightily and its leaves have turned a striated red-gold. It startles me each time I look at the branches splayed against the wall of the cedar fence. They are a perfect counterpoint to the dull gold of the boards. In the sun the conjunction of color is lovely. The same with the redbud tree. It has already lost its pale, yellow-green leaves, except for the largest ones at the ends of the branches. Many of the fallen leaves float in the birdbath like small boats. I try to clear them out each day so they don't rot in the water.

At the side of the house in the new shade garden I walk through drifts of huge maple leaves that reach to my midcalf. I haven't raked them up yet as I am waiting for a good wind to bring the last ones down. There's something childlike about walking through leaves. Even in the rain they crackle underfoot. I lift some up and the earth is littered with sow bugs, slugs, beetles, and the red whips of worms that have risen from the wet earth. They are all feasting on the leaves that have already begun to soften under the cover of the newer, drier arrivals.

Through the still, black branches of the fir, the moon's light reaches in white fingers. Lorna sleeps with Roxy close beside her. Their breathing becomes one in the night, their chests rising and falling in unison. I glance in through the door, listen a moment, then step out onto the deck and down into the yard. Moonlight flickers across my shoulders. It seems made of fragments, a reflected light, the sun slanting to my world in broken beams.

I love the night. I sit in the darkness and remember how I was last year and the years before. D. H. Lawrence tells me I have to build my ship of death. He says that I will need it for my journey toward oblivion. Autumn is the season of real and imagined death. I understood that seven years ago when I built my mother's coffin from black walnut. A little ship of death for my mother to embark on. On top of the coffin I glued a soapstone sculpture of a woman's head with medusalike coils. The head was carved by my brother Mike. Inside the lid I glued a fire opal to light her journey in the darkness. It eased my grief to make it. I sanded the dark wood, oiled and polished it, and when it was placed in the earth beside my father's grave I thought I had found completion.

The cats come to the night deck and brush against me before setting off again to prowl for rats or other cats who have dared to enter their territory. Above me a little brown bat flutters through the evening sky. In a matter of days I won't see him again till spring. It is late for this or any other bat. They crawl under loose shingles or shakes, in attics, under wooden siding, anywhere it is warm and fairly humid. The heat from the house will keep them warm through the cold, damp nights of winter.

"Blessed are the dead that the rain rains on." So goes the proverb. I think of those words as I think of my mother and father in their graves overlooking the mountain valley where I grew up. May the rains that fall here, fall there tomorrow and bless them where they lie.

Hugh Latimer, in his "Second Sermon to the King," said to his monarch, "The drop of rain maketh a hole in the stone, not by violence, but by oft falling." Latimer's gentle reminder is a teaching I take to my garden every day. Patience and endurance are two virtues I have tried to learn this year. Last year I watched a slender wisteria vine flail in the breezes coming out of the south. The tendril slapped against the high, flat wall at the front of the house. Each day it grew and each day it reached a little farther until, finally, it found a thin crevice in a shingle. The tip of the wisteria tendril curled into the thin slit and took purchase there.

A year later, I watched the same wisteria vine send out new tendrils from its anchored spot, each one seeking another point in the closely shingled wall. They too found purchase and now hang there, their leaves yellow. Next spring the process will begin again. There is a tenacious beauty in this garden.

There are times I seem to stumble about, unsure of what to do. My father seemed to know. My mother too. Yet I wade into my garden at times and flail about, insisting that the plants do what I want even though I know it is against their nature. I feel like the monarch Latimer was trying to teach. I feel like the carpenter with a chisel who ends up with a pile of shavings and no beam left to hold up the roof. I feel like a mason standing among rock chips with no stones left to build the wall with. I approach my garden at times with the same kind of violent insistence Latimer warned against.

I carry my sobriety into a new year. I remember getting up that early morning a year ago and drinking thirteen ounces of vodka, then searching for more, my hands stumbling through the bookcase. Did I hide a bottle behind the books on myth, or was it behind the poetry books? All I know is that the bottle I drank was not enough, never enough. I'd already drunk two bottles in the night and there I was with another while my hand slipped along the thin spines of poetry books in search of more. Then the morning, the spasms, the wretched collapse of a body gone so far past life it was a thing and nothing more. Tears, but not *for* anyone. I licked them in hopes they were tears of alcohol. I licked my skin for the sweat of alcohol.

A year ago. I keep saying that as if the words will give me a feeling of triumph over adversity, nobility of purpose, grace, or anything resembling what it is I am supposed to feel. So what do I feel? I feel immensely tired. I feel as if my body and my spirit have been pulled through a pinhole in the night. I feel imagined here in the moon's light. I have gone a year without a drink or a drug in my body. I have gone a year with every cell remembering those drinks, those drugs, remembering and then letting go.

I am standing under a tree that is maybe forty-five years old, as old as my drinking. I place my hand on the trunk and feel the rough bark under my palm. I would cry if it was a time for crying, but it's not. It is not time at all. I am a man of blood and bones, and tonight is a night like all the nights of the year. I lift my hand and it doesn't shake, it doesn't tremble. I stare into the southern sky where the old warrior, Orion, cartwheels in his slow circuit around the pole.

The Mongols called the sky the world-tent. The stars were light shining through the tiny holes that sparks from their fires burned in the skin walls. Beyond the sky was only light. It is such a tent I stand beneath. An old Japanese lantern sits on the millstone a few yards away. It is rough with rust. In it are the remains of a candle.

> When I sleep the birds come to the garden
> with their gifts of seeds. Out of ice
>
> last year's leaves of grass lift into night.
> All my songs have been one song.
>
> The palm of my hand and the sole of my foot
> remember everything I have forgotten.
>
> The old lantern by the pond has always been there.
> Now is the time to light it.

I walk over to the millstone, open the tiny door of the lantern, and light the stub of candle. I close the door and sit on the stone bench I built for Lorna.

The light of the garden is as small as this.

PLANTS

Cherry laurel – *Prunus laurocerasus*
Mexican orange bush – *Choisya ternata*

ANIMALS, BIRDS, AND INSECTS

Little brown bat – *Myotis lucifugus*

11.

Rain, rain, and sun! A rainbow in the sky!
A young man will be wiser by and by;
An old man's wit may wander ere he die.
   — ALFRED LORD TENNYSON, "IDYLLS OF THE KING"

MY BODY IS HERE and my wit wanders. The drenched garden glows like the womb must to an unborn child. When I was
young I used to hold the glass of a flashlight in my mouth and stare
into the mirror in the dark of my room. The pathways of my body
shone, the rich blood flowing. Every child stares in some way at their
blood, often shining a light through the palm of her hand. I had to
shine it into the place where words come from. The leaves of the
seiryu maple are that same rich color as my cheeks were and staring
at its flare of crimson I am taken back to the image of myself, my
blood moving in its many rivers beneath my childish skin. The boy
I keep inside me stood transfixed in the shadowed outline of his
flesh. The light shone through my face, my blood singing.

There are reds so vital I imagine, seeing them, that nothing dies.
The maple lives though it loses its leaves in wind and rain. The garden this evening is like the hours of fasting when the body cleanses
itself. It has the same urgent simplicity. The leaves I raked this
morning from among the plants and off the gravel path are not the
carmine leaves of the seiryu maple. It still holds its leaves, a heart

beating in front of the fir's green limbs. The huge leaves I raked were from the old bigleaf maple at the end of the shade garden.

The old tree puts out new limbs just below its pruned top. This punk hairdo of new branches produces leaves the size of turkey platters. The bigleaf always promises glory in autumn, only to fail. It begins to turn to yellow and gold and then suddenly goes to brown and the leaves fall, curled up like the fingers of old men in their last beds. My rake flipped a stone from the pile of leaves. An hour later I found it on another path. Tomorrow the stone will have seemed there forever.

The autumn garden is full of fleshy fungi. They push up like urgent penises from the lawn and garden beds. They shove their blunt heads through the fallen apples like skulls rising from the earth.

I ate my first boletus in the autumn pine forests of southern British Columbia back in the 1950s, frying them up with breasts of blue grouse, sharp-tailed grouse, or spruce grouse, all of which I hunted when I was a boy and a young man. Mushrooms like the giant agaric gave the wild meat an earthy taste. I couldn't hunt the birds now, but back in the early years I killed, plucked, gutted, and cooked many a grouse. I could no more kill them now than I could any bird.

My father taught me how to shoot. He didn't sit me down and talk to me about respect for the wild world, though I know he cared greatly for it. He didn't spend any time with me at all after I turned eight or nine. Perhaps he expected more of me than I was, a boy with a gun and ranging the hills without guidance. I think to him the desert hills, a few blocks from our home, were there to be used and nothing more. It's not that he was crass, cruel, or neglectful, but that he had grown up in the early century when wild animals were part of a family's diet and thought his childhood was mine when it wasn't. It is the mistake most generations make.

I see California quail every morning on my walk. They are delicate as they forage among the blackberry canes in the thickets that huddle in the road margins and ditches. The little birds never stray far from the wild cover. I love the black, bobbing feather on their heads and the quick, scurrying nervousness of their scavenging. They chatter to each other, holding extensive, lively conversations with relatives and friends just to let each other know where they are. The spring chicks are all grown now but they still stay close to their parents. This morning I saw a flock of more than twenty of them worrying the fallen leaves, the detritus of bark, sticks, pebbles, and weeds in their search for fallen seeds and insect eggs and pupae.

I wandered as a boy through sagebrush and spare grasses and watched coyote hunt rabbits and mice or saw an occasional rattlesnake sunning herself on an outcrop of stone. Snakes were gods to me then. I loved them all: garter snakes, blacksnakes, and the prince of them all, the rattlesnake. The western rattlesnake of my childhood, now much threatened, is a pit viper. The paired pits lie between the snake's eyes and are sensitive to infrared radiation. The snake can follow the track of its prey by the heat-tracks a mouse or mole leaves behind.

The biggest snake I ever saw was when I was a boy. It was longer than I was tall. It had been killed by some proud and foolish man in the hills near Kalamalka Lake. Even then I knew a wrong had been done and though I admired the huge snake I quietly cursed the man who had killed it. The shovel he used to hack the snake to death was still smeared with the reptile's blood. He held the shovel up like some ancient instrument of war, a stained blade against the sky.

I watch the geese flying south in their great wedges over my moonlit garden. Each time I hear them it is the world's last night. They seem to me then like cuneiform cut into the sky, a language written in air whose only meaning is absence. What a voyage it must be for the hatchlings, as they carve the air with their steady wings in their first migration. Far away are the marshes of Texas, Baja, California, and Louisiana. The bayous will be their winter home. Their young wings ride the updrafts lifted by the older birds in front. At the head of the V is an old grandmother. Wise old bird, she is the one who knows the way to the other summer. She is the one who remembers. Below her the map unfolds in the intricate pattern of rivers and lakes, mountains and sea. She has made the journey before down the long cordillera. She leads and the others follow where she wills.

Last night I heard them. Three flocks passed over high up against the scattered clouds. They cried out and the wind answered them. *South, go south. Winter is upon us,* the wind said, and the geese called

231

back their farewell. The far reaches of Alaska and the Bering Sea lay behind them. Winter rides the tundra, and the land their goslings were hatched on is sere and frozen.

Their leaving is different from their arrival. Last night's cries were a farewell, and while I know the geese were flying in the glory of their great southern migration, the loss rides deep in my bones. I remember as a very small child the women at the train station saying goodbye to their men as they went off to the war. After the men had boarded the train I would stand at the corner of the station and watch the women reaching up to touch the outstretched hands of their men.

The way the men reached was different. The men's touch was of forgetting and farewell. The women's seemed to be saying *remember*. I know I may be imagining what I felt back then. It may have been nothing like that at all. Yet their reaching and touching remains inside me. I did not understand it then, but I was seeing for the first time what loss was. It resonated in the tears of the women staying behind and the laughter and grins of the men as they embarked on their great adventure to the killing fields of Europe.

When the train was gone the women took the hands of their young children or the hands of another woman, a sister or friend, perhaps, or a mother, and walked slowly away as if afraid to arrive at the homes they had left. What walls did those women stare at while their children slept in the night, what did they see on the empty, desolate streets as they gazed from their night windows?

Stillness. I remember that. It was clear and fierce and full of such loneliness the air was thick with it. That is what leaving means. That is what I learned back then. The dream of return that is always in the heart. But what does a small boy know? A boy who stands in the shadows of a train station in a war, his mother in a dilapidated yellow house high up a mountain's side, waiting for her husband to return?

"An anything, a nothing . . . troubles me in prayer," said John Donne, and that is what I felt in the dark last night. Then Basho came up the steps and swirled around my ankles and Roxy lifted her black head and peered at me from behind a chrysanthemum. A frog peeped from the dying feverfew and the wind drifted down to a breeze. Rain began to fall and I opened the kitchen door. The cats followed me in and I locked the door behind me, put down some food for them, took off my robe and slippers, and climbed back into bed and the warmth of my woman. She woke briefly to ask in a sleepy mumble where I had been and was everything all right. I said yes to the last question and nothing to the first for where I had been was far away in another time and place. I pulled the covers up and just before I closed my eyes I gazed into the darkness. I thought of those great birds breaking across the rocky southern shore of the island and heading out over Juan de Fuca Strait, the white mountains of the Olympic Peninsula beckoning, far Mexico a dream under their wings.

This is the season of tranquillity. The garden is mostly at rest after the furor of spring and summer. The maples wear their finest colors. Their golds, oranges, and bright reds are a reminder of how beautiful this world of ours once was. It still can be. K'ung Fu-Tzu spoke of the man of wisdom and humanity. He said that we must find the balance offered by water and mountains, action and tranquillity, happiness and a long life. He said that twenty-five hundred years ago and I try to live that way now as best I can. To be calm and quiet sometimes requires I be motionless and so I stop by the pond or under an apple tree and meditate. Yet there are also times when action is required, for action too can bring tranquillity. Some of my most tranquil moments have arrived during hard physical labor. An eight-hour day on a green chain in a sawmill pulling two-by-fours was tranquil. So are the present hours spent digging up an overgrown garden bed, lifting the weeds, and placing the old plants back in the replenished earth.

Picking up fallen apples or cutting down the dead stalks of summer's flowers is peaceful, and I have much to learn as I do it. Mostly I learn what I already know, but that learning is a reenacting of the old ways I have practiced through the years. The movement of the body as it bends and plucks apples from the lawn is peace for me.

It is a pleasure to find an apple the birds have fed upon. The carvings a woodpecker has made in an apple are the beginnings of writing. We all make our mark on the things we touch, and the curves and arabesques of the woodpecker's beak are signature to his or her hunger. Poems are like that. They are the food I carve my name upon.

Lorna cuts the stems of the monkshood, maidenhair ferns, hostas, day lilies, astilbe, ligularia, phlox, and all the other perennials that have withered in the autumn air. She moves from bed to bed with her pruning shears and scissors and fills the wheelbarrow over and over with faded plants. Kneeling on the slate path near the pond she pulls late weeds from among the ferns and penstemon. The penstemon have flowered in a last bright blossoming.

I glance at her a moment and then go back to digging up the foxgloves that filled the new bed by the deck this year. I remember dropping some canes there early last fall. When I dug the new bed I dug in the fallen seeds of the old plants. This year the plants came back in a prodigious growing. They have been crowding the new day lilies I put in this spring and will be in fierce competition with them unless I rid the bed of most of them. So, wheelbarrow load after wheelbarrow load, I carry them around to plant at the back of the shade garden. This year they established their roots, next year they will blossom.

I start thinking the garden is at rest as it waits for the first bulbs, then I notice that the first buds of the Fatsia japonica are just opening up. The flower stalk is a pale green and the buds are like great marbles. The flowers will be a dusty white, sparking stars that look like the progeny of a scientific experiment with electricity. Their great flat leaves with their deep incisions rest like fans on the air. Their leaves funnel the rain, and the water runs down one leaf, falls to the next and the next, miniature waterfalls in a stream until the last and outer leaf drops the water where the feeder roots drink.

Each time I turn around another shrub surprises me. There is no resting season here on the coast. The mahonia near the pond surprised me this morning. It's put out its long spikes of flowers. They're not open yet but when they do in another week or so the bright yellow flowers will be fragrant with perfume. The rosemary too has begun to blossom. They are tiny blue flowers close to the stems.

While some plants rest, many are active in early winter. The berry bushes are redolent with fruit. Cotoneasters and hollies are bright signals to the birds. Wild rosehips dangle above the ditches and on the road margins. The Mexican orange bush by the front window is in full bud and its white flowers will soon make the front garden bed a citrus dream. A coastal garden is always alive with growth. One group of plants falls back only to allow another group to flower.

It is so different than the prairie gardens I once designed and nurtured. There are times I envy the prairie winters and then I remember the cold and the snow. I loved my prairie garden in winter. Under a foot or two of snow the stones I placed and the various shrubs I planted took on ghostly shapes in the garden. It was another landscape, so unlike its spring and summer shape. Dostoyevsky said, "Beauty is mysterious as well as terrible." That is what a prairie winter was to me. The great cold was part of its beauty.

There is a flash of gold under the ferns and for a moment I think a spare sunbeam has caught on a hosta leaf, but no, it's Basho slipping like trembling silk under the bracken. He reappears by the pond where he sits on a large piece of jade and preens in the momentary sunlight between clouds. Roxy watches us both stoically from the deck. I turn and look back and she's gone, disappeared as all cats are when you look for them.

Last night, Lorna and I went down to the ocean. I lay on my back beside Georgia Strait and watched the ocean of the sky move. The Leonid meteor shower had made its long circuit around the sun and its wings were passing through the fringe of our atmosphere. I was covered with a sleeping bag but I still froze in the wind coming in off the sea. Then a huge meteor burned its way toward the south. As it died it left a twisted tail of smoke to mark its passing. A great dragon had flown across the sky. The smoke swirled in the upraised arm and shoulders of Orion in the south as if it could force the hunter into the darkness beyond the stars. Around and through the smoky curls, smaller meteors flashed. I lay under the dragon's flight and for a few moments I was no longer cold. I stared at the tracks of a dragon.

> When I rain down the rain of Dharma,
> Then all this world is well refreshed . . .
> And then, refreshed, just like the plants,
> The world will burst forth into blossoms.

The Lotus Sutra slips inside me as I stand in the rain under the canopy of the cedar in the shade garden. I don't know why I confuse myself in the world when all I need do is spend a few moments in this gentle space. Light streams down through the bare branches of the bigleaf maple. The bones of the tree are the fretwork of this quiet life. Its branches are violin strings that wait for the wind to play a tune upon them. Light rides the rain down the long shafts of the ferns.

The simple structures of this small garden have begun to show, now many of the perennials have died back. The hostas are still here, though their plump leaves have grown thin and they bend to the earth. Light shines through their flesh turned diaphanous and yellow by the season. I know if I clear away the fallen cedar leaves I will find the swell of next year's hostas. Like hard nipples, they thrust upward just at the surface of the earth. I've covered them lightly with a scruff of compost and steer manure and the nutrients will wash into the soil.

The rain has thinned. Small drops carve cursives in the air. In the spring I named the rain, but now in this darkening season I can find no words to describe its falling. Not here, not now. I have walked through the rain on four continents. I've woken to dark clouds brooding through the Andes above the cut stones of Machu Picchu. In the jungles by the Urabamba, I have slept below orchids whose flowering is a white song under the rain. I've sat with a tiny nun and stared through a veil of rain at the raked sand and mossy stones of Ryoan-ji. I've seen waterfalls as small as my tears pool in forests of thin lichens.

In the Cotswolds I've watched the English rain leach down through grass to the honey stone of the hills. In Wiltshire a white chalk horse dances under that rain. I've held my lover in England's wet fields. The raindrops still pearl in the web of an orb-weaver spider beside the Great Goose temple in Xian where Li Po and Tu Fu once sat together composing poems. I stared through that opalescent filigree and imagined song from centuries ago, imagined the brocade sleeves of slender women among the gardens there, a breath of dew upon their slender shoes. If I close my eyes I can stare through the jalousie the spider made and find a woman's eyes staring back at me.

I've been woken to the rain in the jungles of Ecuador by a woman who gave me thin soup made from *gui*. She nursed me in the rain after a centipede stung me in my sleep. In my delirium I thought her an angel come brown and singing through the rain.

And the mountains, the mountains of my West. Too many rains, too many lives. Part of me sits forever in a deserted cabin on the North Thompson and speaks to the ghosts of the men and women who homesteaded there a hundred years ago and more. I have watched a mouse peer from the drawer of an ancient sewing machine in that cabin. I have read the newspapered walls. The walls of rain on the great plains crossed the cordillera to reach me in my first great loneliness. I've stepped in and out of rain on the prairie, the sheer wall of falling water a demarcation only the clouds and sun understand. And I've made love in the rain. I've made love in the rain.

Who can put a name to the rain in a dying season? The psalms call the rain "angel's food" and so it is the first manna of myth. "I am become a name," said aging Ulysses at the end of his life. No wonder he set out for the far islands with an aging crew. In such ways are we lost. I cannot put a name to the rain though I sang it in the spring. Today I would like to sit with Dick beside an unnamed mountain creek west of Eagle Pass, just as we did forty years ago. We would watch a doe drink again among shattered quartz. I would call it "Lost Brother Rain." I have drunk that rain in the far mountains. I have lain by the gravestone of my brother in the rain.

It is dark here now at six in the morning. The sun has retreated south and the winter solstice looms ahead, its arrival a signal for light to return. I am one of a northern people. If a place makes you who you are then the north has made me. This morning I rose and walked through the dark kitchen to let the cats out. I opened the door, the deck lights came on, and all three of us stopped and stared at a world changed utterly. Snow was falling, a grace come down from the sky to visit us. Basho hesitated a moment and then leapt from the doorsill and slid like a wild fur ball through the snow into the upside-down container in the corner of the deck. Roxy, careful female that she is, took a careful step forward, put down her head, smelled the snow, and backed into the warmth and comfort of the house. I called her to go out, but she ignored me. She stopped for a moment by the food bowl and took a few necessary bites, then walked through the kitchen to the living room. *Why,* she seemed to say, *would a cat go out in that?*

I watched the snow for a while then put on my boots, heavy sweater, and toque and went out into the garden. The bamboo lay prostrate, the rhododendrons' branches were bent to the point of breaking, viburnum hung to the ground in huge curves, and the magnolia, that beautiful tree with branches brittle as glass, looked like it was going to lose its limbs altogether. The last bright red apples hung under caps of frothy white. I took the handle from a broken shovel and poked, prodded, lifted, shook, and otherwise knocked the snow off the plants. Their limbs lifted partway, as if dazed by this strange substance.

It was wonderful to walk through fresh snow in the dawn light. I knew the late morning or afternoon would bring rain and soon all the snow would be gone, but for a half hour I walked in the ancient world of the Interior and felt once again at home. Lorna came out at my calling and we walked and watched Basho run around the yard like a golden wind. Sir Francis Bacon said, "There ought to be gardens for all the months of the year, in which, severally, things of beauty may then be in season." My garden is beautiful month by month. I can see its loveliness now the snow has reshaped it, bringing to my eye old forms transformed, new forms unnoticed before. Lorna and I stand under the apple trees and share a world made beautiful by this rare form of water.

The snow falls silently like a cat's paw in the night. Basho runs beneath the ferns and the sky falls on him. He emerges patched in white. I take my woman's hand. Winter is here and beyond the snow are the long rains and December.

PLANTS

Boletus – *Boletus luteus* and *Boletus granulatus*
Evening primrose – *Oenothera speciosa "Siskiyou"*
Fatsia japonica – *Fatsia japonica "Variegata"*
Giant agaric mushroom (the Prince) – *Agaricus augustus* (synonym – *Psalliota augusta*)
King Bolete mushroom – *Boletus edulis*
Kocho Nishiki (Butterfly) maple – *Acer palmatum*
Ligularia – *Ligularia dentata "Desdemona"*
Mahonia – *Mahonia* × *media "Charity"*
Oak-leaf hydrangea – *Hydrangea quercifolia*
Seiryu Japanese maple – *Acer palmatum*

Simons' cotoneaster – *Cotoneaster simonsii*
White pearl bugbane – *Cimicifuga simplex*

ANIMALS, BIRDS, AND INSECTS

California quail – *Lophortyx Californica*
Camas western pocket gopher – *Thomomys bulbivorus*
Canada goose – *Branta canadensis*
Mule deer – *Odocoileus hemionus*
Spruce grouse – *Canachites canadensis*
Gray wolf – *Canis lupus*

12.

*You learned them and where they stood in relation to each other,
and then you filled in the details working from these known marks.
General to particular. Everything had a name. To live fully in a
place all your life, you kept aiming smaller and smaller in
attention to detail.*
— CHARLES FRAZIER, *Cold Mountain*

THERE ARE TIMES I want to be in the second or third person.
Like any writer, I'd rather be a *he* than an *I*. It's simpler to be a
fiction. In a novel I can imagine things that aren't real, that don't
exist, and I can make out of them a story and a place where I might
exist free from my life. Like a fiction writer, I want to create sentences of deception, paragraphs whose history can't be verified. It's
far easier to be a figment. Yet even when I try to create the past using
a point of view not my own, it is still and always mine.

Four years after my father's death I took my mother back to
Sheep Creek. I wanted to go to the place where my brothers and I
first lived. I thought if I could find the beginning, the place, I might
understand what had happened there and so, somehow, understand
what has happened since.

It was strange to take my mother back there, the more so because
she didn't want to go. It was so close upon her husband's death. I
think, in this life, I have asked too much. I look back now at that

man I was and I wonder at him. His desire for a return to first things was a kind of madness.

I want now to sit under the huge leaves of a thimbleberry and watch my younger self search in the detritus of the years for the clues to a mystery there is no solution to. He has climbed down the bank above Sheep Creek and he is searching through the dump where half a century ago people threw their garbage. Empty bottles, tin cans, bits of broken machinery, everything glass and metal that the long winters and the dry summers could not reduce to dust, lie there under the forest floor. The tired dresses and shirts, worn socks and work pants mended over and over again that were finally thrown out with the potato peelings and carrot scrapings.

This young man can barely be seen through the leaves and splayed stalks of the thimbleberry and Oregon grape. His hand moves among the spare berries and he picks up a piece of dried fir bark and throws it behind him. Beetles scuttle for cover and red ants scatter, the sterile workers carrying the unborn larvae and eggs in their jaws. The soldier ants raise their heads and clatter their mandibles as they search for the enemy who has destroyed their nest.

The man ignores their bravado and panic. He is tearing away the mass of twigs and needles, branches, and desiccated leaves. Under the dust that chokes his throat he sees a glint of glass and he reaches deeper and pulls out a small blue bottle. A label hangs from its round sides, the words on it rotted into an indecipherable text, an unreadable code that once declared what was inside, nectar, liquor, or perfume, some substance that was prized until it was gone.

The man in the dump doesn't know why it was discarded. He holds it up like an archeologist might who has just uncovered an artifact in an ancient ruin. He feels he has found the single object that defines a time so far in his past it has been forgotten. He rubs the bottle on his shirt to clean off the crust of dirt and bends the torn label back carefully, but it begins to crack. He stops and holds the paper still. The words are there and not there.

This young man is a writer who is coming into his maturity. In a few years he will begin to write his finest poems. At this moment he thinks words are his life. He has searched among them for meanings so elusive that sometimes he doesn't know what he has found and has had to lie down and wander among the instincts he has built the edifice of his trust upon. To him his poems are simulacra, shadowed images that betray what he feels. He thinks the bit of dry paper he touches is a found poem. The script is indecipherable, the directions and descriptions printed in a type too small to survive. He places the bottle carefully on a flat stone above his shoulder on the slope and starts again to dig.

I watch him clear away the cloak of dirt that covers the rubbish below. He finds another bottle and a tin pie pan with a crumpled edge. He places them with the first bottle and then widens his search. He heaves the dirt aside. Each thing he unearths is a clue to the word *was*. He is thinking that if he can only dig deep enough and far enough he will find something that will explain his life to him.

He has forgotten his mother. He left her on the flat above him where she once lived back in the thirties. The cabin her husband built for her is nothing now, just a few rotted boards and logs, and the base of a stone chimney. The old mortar has washed away long ago and the stones that her husband had built it with are now a tumble of rocks. Only the well remains. Her husband had blown it with dynamite stolen from the mine. He was a hard-rock miner and a powder monkey. He secreted sticks of dynamite, blasting caps, and fuse in his lunch bucket, and when he had enough he blew a shaft in the mountain behind their cabin deep enough for water to gather. He had promised her that she would not have to walk the trail down to the creek for water. He had promised her anything and everything in the hope she would be happy in the canyon where the mine was. She wasn't used to cabins and wells and hard-rock miners. She wasn't used to their wives, their children, their kind of life.

She looked down into the well after her son had walked away from her and then turned away. She did not drop a pebble into it like her son had done when she showed him where it was. The tiny plash of a pebble hitting the water was not something she wanted to hear. She remembers lowering a bucket on a rope and lifting water out of the earth. How many thousands of times had she had done that? How many times had she walked the trail to the cabin and poured the water into the washtub on the stove that burned winter and summer? No, she does not want to drop a pebble in the well. She does not want to remember water.

Her third son has brought her here to this place, to Sheep Creek, where she had birthed him and his older brothers. Three sons in four years and a husband who left her each day in the darkness of morning for his shift at the mine. Winter and summer, spring and fall. She had watched his back walk away from her up the trail that threaded through the other shacks and bunkhouses as he climbed up to the mine shaft and the men who were waiting to descend into the pit. Each day she had touched the palm of her hand to the great stone outside the cabin door as if with her touch she could feel him in the tunnels under the earth. Clouds and rain, sun and snow, she had touched that stone in all weathers, and each day she had felt him there and imagined the lamp on his forehead glowing in the shafts. She imagined his hands and his laughter.

The stone is still there and she stares at it, but she doesn't touch it. Whatever is under the earth now can't be touched. He is no longer in this place, and the deep shafts and tunnels are empty. Only water is down there. It trickles and splashes among stones but there is no one to hear it. There is no one to hear the sound a falling rock makes, no eyes to watch the water's silver threads drip in the huge darkness where stalagmites and stalactites have begun to form. They are infinitesimal nipples of new stone growing from stone.

She passes by the rock at the door that no longer exists. Her son has climbed down over the edge where the land falls away to the creek. She is alone. The creek roars as it has always roared and the mist from its crashing among boulders and mine slag lifts through the trees. There were fewer trees back then. The forest had been cut down for mine timbers. These trees have grown since the year her husband came back from Nelson to tell her he had joined the army.

She had turned her back on Sheep Creek then and had never returned, not until now, not until this son of hers had made her come back. She hadn't wanted to, but he had begged and pleaded and when his entreaties fell upon her deaf ears he had demanded she go with him. He had said that only she could tell him where it began, only she could show him the way to this place, this spot in the mountains, this small piece of ground where a cabin once stood and where she had nursed him. And so she had finally agreed. She looks down at the worn flowers of a purple aster growing in a bit of sunlight. She remembers that it is named an aster because the flower looks like a star. She remembers many things she doesn't want to remember.

The flowers stop her for a moment and she stares at the violet petals, then opens her purse and takes out the plastic box that holds her rolled cigarettes, puts one in her lips and lights it. She stands there smoking. Her son is somewhere over the edge of the bank, but she doesn't go there to see what he is doing. She knows he's down there somewhere rummaging around and she doesn't care. She drags on her cigarette and pulls the last bit of smoke into her lungs, then drops the butt and stubs it out in the moss. She doesn't want to be here. The day she left here she swore she'd never come back. Now she is here and it is as if she had never lived here. All the mine buildings are gone, hauled away by the company to another mine site above Kootenay Lake. The other buildings, the bunkhouses, shacks, and cabins collapsed under the heavy snows. The years have borne them away.

She looks at the forest. What light there is comes as glances, as fragments among the heavy boughs. As she looks through the mottled light she sees steps leading up the side of an old tree, one that was here even then. There are seven steps. She clutches her purse and pushes a wisp of gray hair away from her face. She remembers those steps. She remembers the day her husband built them into the tree. They led up to the clothesline stand. The seventh step was the platform she stood upon as she hung the shirts and pants, the dresses and underwear, the sheets and towels, and the countless thousands of diapers she washed by hand on the scrubbing board in the washtub. Summer and winter she stood on that seventh step and hauled the clothes out into the sun and the rain and the snow.

She walks slowly over to the old tree and tests the first step with her foot and finding it firm she slowly climbs one step at a time until she is on the platform. She plants herself there and stares out through the trees. By her shoulder hangs the iron wheel that once held the rope. She touches the rust. The wheel is frozen and no longer turns. She stands there on the gray boards and stares out at the washing line that isn't there.

Her son hasn't thought of her since he left her there by the well. He is frantic now. He is throwing chunks of bark and stones to his right and left as he burrows into the bank. He has found three more bottles and hundreds of rusted tin cans. He digs deeper in his excitement. He knows there is something down there, something that will tell him why he is here. Then he sees a dull glint of red and he clears away some cans and sticks and reaches into the till and picks up a toy car. The red paint has mostly moldered away, but there are still streaks in the crevices where the metal was bent and folded along the fenders and windows. There are two wooden wheels still attached to the rusting wire that is the back axle. He sits and cradles the toy in his hands. He remembers it. He holds it in one hand and with the other he turns the wheels. The creak of the axle is the faintest of whispers, a tiny scream in the forest.

He stands up. He must show his mother, he thinks. She will remember it too. She will tell him the story of the toy car. He looks up and he sees his mother floating among the weave of branches, high above the ground. For a moment he thinks she has died and is now, at this moment, ascending toward some heaven only she knows. The toy is in his left hand and his right hand is shading his eyes. What he sees is his mother in the sky.

❦

It was summer when I took her back. I remember how hard she argued against going. We sat up night after night drinking as I begged her to guide me back. Then she finally told me she would go. We bickered and argued all the way there, the truck climbing up the mountains to the high passes and then down again into the desolate, isolated valleys of southern British Columbia. She sat beside me and rolled her endless cigarettes, the tiny butts sticking from the corner of her mouth long after they had gone out. Whether she was cooking or ironing, sweeping floors or making beds, the corner of her mouth always held a dead butt gone brackish from her saliva and lipstick. All the years I had lived with her as a boy it had been like that. Nothing had changed.

She was very angry with me, but I didn't care. I had wanted to make the journey for years, and for years she had refused. Now she was there in the truck and I wasn't about to stop until we got to Sheep Creek. As we passed through Nelson and began the climb up to Salmo and the road that led even higher to Sheep Creek, she became quiet. Her hand gripped the door handle the whole way as she stared out through the side window. I thought at first she had turned away from me, but it was more than that. She didn't want to see where she was going. The trees stuttering by her window must have seemed like an old film from the thirties. The only thing missing was the clatter of the projector and the white sheet stretched out against a wall where images bent and twisted around the folds of the cotton. Missing too were mothers shushing their children as Rhett turned to Scarlet and said his bitter words.

It was as I have described it. I stood up with the toy car in my hand and saw my mother floating among the trees. I didn't know how long she had been there. It could have been a minute or an hour. Time had ceased to exist as I dug down into the dump. When I saw her floating there I thought I had gone a little mad. I clambered up the bank. When she saw me she turned on the fragile platform, went down the steps, turned her back and walked away through the trees to the road and the truck. She never spoke. I heard the truck door slam. I went over to the platform and placed my hand on the gray boards. I looked at the rusted pits where the nails still held and thought of my father building it.

It was such a long time ago.

I look back at myself and wonder at finding the toy car. How important that moment was to me, how fierce I was in my desire to prove I had once been her child. I had found a remnant and I packed it carefully behind the truck seat along with the bottles I had found. Before I did I showed the toy to my mother and she looked at it for a moment and then shrugged. Her fingers began fluffing the tobacco in the Export "A" can. We hardly spoke on the long journey back.

When we got to Vernon I took her to her apartment and I left the toy car with her for safekeeping. I was going on to Vancouver and I was afraid I'd lose it. What I wanted to do was to give it to Johnny. I knew he would remember the toy car and, perhaps, take the same joy from it that I had. When I returned a week later I asked her for the old toy, but she told me she had thrown it out. *What do you want with an old thing like that?* she asked.

What I remembered for years when I thought of that journey was finding the toy. Now, ten years after her death I remember best her floating in the sky. It had frightened me for a moment until I saw she was standing on the clothesline platform. Her face and her body were perfectly still and her eyes were staring out through the trees toward the creek and the roar of the water. I don't know what she was looking at or what she was thinking. It would be easy for me to say she was lost in time and had gone back to those early years, but I don't know that. I don't know if what she felt was bitterness or joy, happiness or grief. Perhaps she felt nothing, nothing at all, yet I know that can't be true. If I have learned anything in this year in the garden, it is that everything is built upon the pediment of love. There is nothing else.

What do you do with the pieces of yourself you lose? I wrote that question in a poem back in the early 1970s just after the journey. I believe the question defines the one who asks it. Small things get lost. Little toy trucks get thrown down a slope in a mining town in 1940 and then get placed in a garbage chute in an apartment building. Sons return to their mothers and then they leave again.

I think of her standing on that platform and feel her reach through my mind to me in this garden. She floats down into the ferns. I know it is not my mother reaching for me, but me for her. I am the one who brings her back. Like her journey into the mountains at Sheep Creek, her coming here is not what she wants. It is no wonder she seems restless and angry each time I see her. She wishes to remain in spirit. I sit here by the pond and I quietly open the hands that grip her here. As I do I can feel her vanishing. The ferns tremble and then she is gone.

I have not lost her. The walnut coffin holds her ashes and the fire opal shines upon her bones. Her spirit is not there. She does not roam. I hope that she lies with the man who loved her, her husband, my father.

There is only, in the one world, water reaching for the earth. Deep in the mine where my father toiled, water falls upon stone. It falls now in my garden. I slip into the rain and find myself among ferns. What ghosts I see are only of myself and made of green memory, a flicker of life in the night. I stand in the dark and see the light of a window. It flutters softly. It is both cave and beacon, a far sanctuary I have left.

I have come out on the longest night and wait now for the sun to rise and show the way to spring. Like the heave a body makes at dawn, the whole earth will turn again to face the light coming like a god back to the world. What I thought was retreat is turned to advance. This night gleams and creatures move among the fallen bamboo leaves, a raccoon's paw grinds on a leaf, a rat's nail clicks on quartz, a winter moth, far from the blinding light that drove it into dance, searches among azalea leaves for shelter. The thin rain comes down and the moth is here, is gone. I lift a leaf to find it clinging upside down, its wings tight shut in prayer that this cold night will end and the sun return.

Each name in the garden comes to life, and what was stillness quickens. All that was dead is alive in me. My eyes ride the air like hands reading the braille shadows make. What do I do here under the fir? What has brought me here to stand in rain and watch the night's last stand against the day? Is it the coming brightness that drew me here? I have prayed for the sun as all soft creatures must.

Here I stand beneath the fir to call the sun's return. Around me fallen cones lie on the blossoming moss. Slow to release, the fir seeds wait for a squirrel's busy teeth to free them from their carapace. One seed might survive her gnaw and like an eyelash fall into a crevice in the earth where it will make life during the quiet hours.

Winter turned in the day. The year begins again. The solstice comes and goes within my knowing and on the turn the months begin their slow march to the sun. Somewhere in the south the star has turned and like a stone upon a mountain, starts its fall into the valley of the north. Here in the garden the long night drifts away. It is hard to remember the earth is what I am, an animal who turns its face away from the dark. It's not the snow that stills the heart. Darkness does. And now the dark retreats. I live again, as sure as my hands on a tree's rough bark, the silk of stone, the moss. There is a season. The sun will rise, and all the garden will be blessed.

❧

Today I realized that weeks had gone by and I hadn't once thought of drinking. What a strange moment. My whole life, my every waking and sleeping hour was once consumed by alcohol and drugs. But those years had somehow slipped through some tight lattice and I have found myself on another side. Fifty-nine weeks of sobriety. Four hundred and thirteen days and nights.

"Still falls the rain," said Dame Edith Sitwell in cloudy England back in the last century. She might well have lived here on Vancouver Island. Rain is the womb I wake in each morning. Darkness and water surround me, and while there are some mornings I pray for light, I can still find comfort in this season. A coastal December is a time for rest and reflection: as it is in the garden so in me. The biennials, perennials, shrubs, and trees are somnolent after a long year of growth, blossoming, and the making of seeds. Yet there are many that do not sleep and find these short days a perfect time for display.

Cotoneasters, holly, and wild roses are now redolent with bright red berries. A ruby-crowned kinglet danced among them yesterday. The holly's fruit looks like blood against the winter backdrop of green and brown and is even more beautiful when it snows. Water drops pearl on the tips of branches and puddles shimmer. Birds flick through the trees and search the lawn under the feeder for fallen seeds. They gather together now in flocks, sure in their companionship after the seasons of breeding and raising young. They find great joy in winter. For them this is release from the many burdens of the year.

I turn to the last task. The half-circle of earth that is the front garden must be transformed. It is time to complete what has for ten years been an imagining. Today I have begun to clear out the undergrowth beneath the redwood and the deodar cedar. The plants and shrubs, the weeds and wandering vines planted by defecating birds, must all be dug up and removed.

What I want here is a meditation garden. I want to be able to sit in the early morning with my coffee in the front of this property. What better place to put the quietest of garden retreats than where it is busiest. My long-ago impulse to build it here is the right one.

It's been three days of hard work, but I've cleared off almost everything that wasn't necessary to the new garden. At the very front by the street I've left the stag's head sumac, a laurel, the Indian plum, and two low conifers. I've crawled on my belly under the shrubs and climbed up on ladders to prune dead branches and living ones so that the shrubs will come back thicker next year. I trimmed back the understory of the two trees as well. Their branches now will just touch the bamboo fence I am building. Just behind the screen of shrubs I've dug holes and sunk timber bamboo in cement for the posts. Between them I've strung split bamboo screens and fastened them to the posts with pins and twine. There are no nails.

The redwood and deodar dominate the space, but their first branches are now twelve feet off the ground. Everything is bare earth beneath them except for two large, rather spindly rhododendrons. I pruned them back judiciously. I'm unsure of pruning these shrubs and have been tentative. Still, I've propped up some of the longer limbs and they look a bit like elegant old pensioners leaning on canes. The rest of the space is uneven and I like it that way. I've spread cloth over the whole bed to stop anything growing up from underneath. The whole space is now covered with crushed and shredded redwood and cedar bark. Around the perimeter I've placed small paving stones to form a boundary wall between the bark covering and the paved driveway and street.

As I cleared away the undergrowth and stripped the earth of years of fallen cones and needles, I found the skeleton of the squirrel. Part of her ribcage was crushed and both her back legs broken. Lying in the space under her broken ribs were the spider-thin bones of three babies who died there with her. The beetles and worms had their way with their flesh. I lifted the four of them and placed their remains on the front porch steps.

I have to bury them properly, but where? I take the wheelbarrow, shovels, rakes, and other tools and sit on the front stoop and stare at the space I've created. Now comes the moment I've looked forward to, the placing of large stones and the Crimson Queen maple I will plant just behind them. The key is in the location of the zenigata stone. It is ten inches thick and thirty inches in diameter. It's solid granite carved with four ideograms around a central, square hole that will be filled with water.

I stare at the space and then get up and roll the stone into the garden and let it fall. It comes to rest exactly where I want it. It took two minutes to place it and ten years of staring at the space to know where. A few hours later I had maneuvered large granite stones in a semicircle behind it.

There are four stones, each a miniature rocky peak of an imagined mountain range. When I was a boy I arranged stones and I am still doing it. Between two of the stones I dug a hole and planted the Crimson Queen maple. It hangs its delicate limbs over the largest stone. In spring it will put out its lacy, deep-cut leaves. Next fall the leaves will turn their signature red for two weeks and then they'll fall upon the miniature mountain and upon the Zenigata stone.

I will need a seat of some kind and a pathway, and a moss forest to surround it all. As I sit back on the stoop a nuthatch flitters down from the redwood where she has been stuffing sunflower seeds into the bark. She lands on the Zenigata stone, looks around with quizzical amusement and then hops to the water, dips her head, and takes a drink.

I take a deep breath and look down at the corner of the step where I placed the squirrel skeletons. I lift them gently and carry them into the new garden. There I lay them down on the bark and lift the Zenigata stone onto its edge. I pull the earth apart gently with my hands and in the small grave I have made I place the squirrel who was companion to me for years. With her are her dead babies. I cover her with a skim of earth and frayed bark and then settle the huge stone on top of them. It is done.

A new squirrel has been coming every few days to the bird feeder. She appeared soon after the death of the other. This morning Lorna and I laughed aloud as we watched her play at the foot of the fir tree with some fallen cones. The squirrel tumbled and flipped herself over, made mock charges at dormant foxgloves, hid under the plant's leaves, and then shot out to roll in the damp earth and needles, all the while tossing the cones in the air. What joy to have a full belly of sunflower seeds and a garden to cavort in.

It's colder now and at night the temperature hovers at a degree or two above freezing. The snow we had in November is long gone but another storm could blow in at any time. The winds rage out of the southwest every few days, breaking the brittle limbs of firs and cedars. The roads are littered with branches. Last night I lay in bed and listened to the wind off the Pacific. The seething around the house seemed as ancient as my blood. My old cells remembered the sound from a thousand years ago and I cringed a little. I curled down tighter under my blankets.

These are the first days after the winter solstice, and I wonder again with Shelley, "If Winter comes, can Spring be far behind?"

The season of birth in spring is followed at the end by death in winter, yet always there is the promise of the season to come. Persephone is already thinking of climbing the long stone tunnel out of hell. Once again she is ready to say goodbye to her dark lover. His lamentations will not draw her back. She is the green goddess and it is she who wakes the earth. The old mythologies are mine. I was born into them, an amalgam of all the winter myths that arise from peoples everywhere.

Go into the garden and try to learn the world that surrounds you. Look at how you've placed a stone. Now the trees and shrubs are bare you can more easily see how they harmonize with the garden. Imagine. Let the images in your mind be companions to your practice. Don't think of the coming year and what it will bring, rather settle into the now of this season. Rest, reflect, prepare. Listen. There is a story the earth has to tell you.

The winter roses are lovely. They're a welcome sight in this season. The snowdrops have been up now a week and one beneath the holly bush has pushed its white bud out and down. A male robin pulls a worm from the earth beside it. Above the bird, his companions pluck red berries and swallow them. The holly is rich with fruit. Winter retreats with each day. I mustn't let it run away without stopping a moment to look, smell, taste, touch, and listen.

❦

There are two fir trees at the head of the driveway in front of a house where I used to live as a boy. It's up in the Okanagan Valley on a patch of land my father bought. My father moved us to that house half a century ago, and this week I drove there to visit the trees. The house was on three acres of land and the gardens, once beautiful, have been allowed to wither away. I can see the faint curves of my mother's flower beds under rampant weeds. The original shrubs and fruit trees have grown leggy from lack of care and pruning.

To celebrate our move to the country my father drove the family up Silver Star Mountain. It's a huge ski resort now, but in those days it was just another mountain with logging roads crawling along its flanks. We went there to dig up trees for transplanting. I remember learning what to do. My father told me I had to dig up a root ball large enough so the trees might live. We took two small fir trees from the rocky soil. When they were safely tamped down in our garden, my brother Mike and I stood beside our father and looked at the two small trees. My father looked proud and so did we. We had accomplished something important.

The two fir trees are now more than fifty years old. It was good to see them prospering and to remember my helping dig the holes for their fragile roots. They grow near the maple my father planted the following year along with the now-old weeping willow by the fence. I stopped the truck and walked over to touch them. I didn't want to go to the house. Strangers live there now. I walked over to the trees and touched their trunks and branches. On the west coast they would be three times as big, but in this desert valley with its spare rains, its hot summers and cold winters, the trees have grown slowly. Still, they were there. They are as old as I am.

Maybe that's what a garden is, a memory that gives us pleasure as it grows. "You may allow me moments, not monuments," said the poet John Newlove. In my memory, the green mosses in this west coast garden still bear the outline of my lover's foot when she stepped there back in April. The green shaped itself to her white foot and that shape remains inside me.

❦

My mother's destroying of the artifacts of the past went on for years. She kept only what she said brought happy memories, her photograph albums and not much more. She never explained why she burned my great-uncle Jack's papers or why she burned all my father's letters to her from the war years. Perhaps they had been love letters, I don't know. I do know she never regretted their destruction. Many times she admonished me, saying, *You live too much in the past.* She was right, of course, but I needed the past to hold on to, to prove I had a life.

She never, in all her life, said she loved me. I wish now that she had.

Her life was her own. It did not belong to the child I was or the man I have become. She was the first woman of my life. When she stood on that clothesline stand I saw her as if she were a transcendent thing, a woman risen from the earth. It was in that narrow cut of rock between two mountains that she birthed her first three sons, all writers, all tellers of stories. She was there when her father died, a man she deeply loved despite the physical wreckage and spiritual and emotional chaos of sexual abuse. It was in Sheep Creek her husband joined the army and left us all behind. The journey to that vanished mining town was a burden she took on for me. I thank her for that.

I love her, you see.

I have always wanted to "live fully in this life," and a life is made from the smallest and most particular details, as Charles Frazier says. I simply have to remember and I can still walk the far hills of my childhood valley. I can close my eyes and follow the path near Cactus Hill where I once played. I can go from jasper and quartz to bear's paw cactus to ponderosa pine, and I can measure the distance to Coldstream Creek by the turtles and frogs that still sing there in my mind. I know that far-off place just as I know each handful of earth in every corner of this garden of ours here on Vancouver Island.

When I moved here from Saskatchewan I whiled away the hours driving through the many mountain ranges by counting the places I had lived in my life. By the time I passed through Golden in the Rockies I had counted eighty-seven places. When Lorna and I stopped in Vernon to visit my mother I told her the count and she added five more I had forgotten. Ninety-two houses, apartments, and rooms.

Mine has been a wandering life. I have roamed four continents, from the high valleys to the beaches of every ocean there is except the Arctic. I have known the touch of women and men and children from jungles and mountains, and I have grown in their many hands. But all my wandering was only a circle leading me at last to here. My quest has always been to find what I could not leave.

Every stone in my garden is a story, every tree a poem. I barely know myself in spite of the admonishments of wise men and women who tell me I must know my life in order to live it fully. What I know is that I live in this place where words are made. What we are is a garden. I believe that.

When I was a young man I struggled hard to learn *how* to make a poem. I had no education to speak of other than high school. It doesn't matter now why I wanted to write a poem. What I knew in my bones was that there was a truth hidden inside words and that I could reveal that truth if I only knew *how*. There was a hidden truth inside me I wanted to uncover. The speaking it was all.

I sat in my scruffy little trailer, my suffering wife and children long gone to bed, a full ashtray and a half-empty bottle of Seagram's 83 beside me, and I stared at the patterns my words had made on the canary-yellow paper that stuck out of my little portable typewriter. Thirty words, perhaps forty, but they would not do what I was asking them to do. I couldn't shape them into what I knew was a *real* poem. I sipped my beer, smoked my cigarette, and stared at the page. Then I tore it out and began again and then again. That was the beginning of my life's work.

A few years later I wrote my way to the middle of a poem and stopped at the word *sorrow*. I was trying to use it so that it was no more and no less important than the words, *it, the, gray,* or *stone,* and I couldn't do it. *Sorrow* kept leaping off the page and shouting its importance. I am SORROW, it seemed to be saying, *Look at how important I am.* I even looked the word up in the dictionary in the hope it might help me understand what was meant.

> **Sor-row** *n.* 1. Pain or distress of mind because of loss, injury, or misfortune, the commission of sin, or sympathy with suffering; grief. 2. An event that causes pain or distress of mind; affliction; a trial; misfortune; woe. 3. The expression of grief; lamentation; mourning.

The meanings seem so simple now, but it was complicated when I was twenty-four years old. *Pain, misfortune, loss, woe.* I didn't know how to write the word into a poem. I tried to sneak up on *sorrow* like the boy who played at war on a small hill and slip the word in the way I used to slip into a make-believe slit trench and bayonet the chosen victim of our war game.

I've never forgotten the day I chose the word. I have used that moment to illustrate lectures I've given for twenty years to writing students. *Learn how to put the word sorrow in a poem,* I've told them over and over again. I might as easily have told them to try with the word *joy.* So, why the word *sorrow?* Why did I choose it? Perhaps now I have an answer.

There are no accidents, there are no serendipitous moments. There are only fragile interludes of clarity and sometimes I don't understand them fully when they happen. There was sorrow in me as I sat by the Skeena River, but I didn't understand that. I knew that in the last seven years my six-year-old niece had died of cancer, my brother had died of a brain hemorrhage, my father had been murdered, my mother-in-law had died of a heart attack, my mother was living in a self-enforced silence of grief and alcoholism, I was divorced, and my children were somewhere in Vancouver living with my former wife and another man, their new father.

Was there sorrow in my bones, in my chest, and on the pads of my fingertips as they typed the word? Yes, there was. Did I know it? No, I didn't. I did not know what Keats meant in his "Ode on Melancholy," when he said,

> Then glut thy sorrow on a morning rose,
> Or on the rainbow of the salt, sand-wave,
> Or on the wealth of globed peonies.

I do now.

When my mother lay on what would be her deathbed I read to her from *The Old Curiosity Shop* by Charles Dickens. She was asleep in a morphine dream. I was awake in the bottom of a bottle of vodka. I was reading quietly in the hope that she might hear the words from a book she had dearly loved. Halfway through a paragraph she suddenly sat up in her bed, tubes dangling, reached out, and gripped my wrist. She couldn't have weighed ninety pounds, but her grip was hard, the bones in her hand rigid. She held my wrist and stared into my eyes and said, *At every turn there's always something lovely.* She let me go and fell back on the bed. They were her last words to me. Three days later she died.

At one point in his novel, *Under the Volcano,* Malcolm Lowry has his central character ask himself two questions: "You like this garden? Why is it yours? We evict those who destroy!" He says they are, "simple and terrible words." They are. The man who asks the questions is an alcoholic. He is wandering in his garden in Mexico looking for a hidden bottle of gin. The questions weren't real to me when I first read them. They're real to me now only because I too have wandered in my garden searching for hidden bottles.

The meditation garden I built is waiting for me. In the back of the pickup are three bags of mosses I've collected from the deep rain forest behind Port Renfrew. I go downstairs and walk out to the garden and there I begin to lay down the mosses. They are a forest that laps up against the stone mountains. I huddle the patches of moss against each other until they and the rocks look like a small island floating in a sea of cedar and redwood bark. When all the moss is laid and watered I build a narrow walkway with leftover paving stones. It leads in the shape of a crooked moon up to the Zenigata stone. I am almost finished. I reach behind me and pull from my back pocket a wooden spoon I bought in Chinatown a year ago. It was carved more than a hundred and fifty years ago. The proprietor had found it and a hundred more in an old carton in the basement of his store. He sold me one for a dollar. *They're old spoons,* he told me. *No one wants them now.*

I lean down and dip a spoonful of sweet water from the stone and sip it slowly. Refreshed, I replace the spoon on the moss then look at the cedar round I have placed to the side of a rhododendron for a seat. The ground is already a fretwork of fallen deodar cedar needles. They make a script of seemingly immense complexity, but like the characters on the stone they have no meaning beyond their presence. I sit down and quietly look upon the new garden. As I sit there a woman passes on the street, looks in, and admires what I have done. *How long did it take you to build this?* she asks. I look at her and say, *Sixty-two years.*

I began this book in the confusions of clouds and rain. I could ask the old question Job asked, "Hath the rain a father? Or who hath begotten the drops of dew?" I don't know the answer, but I have stood beside the apple tree in my garden and lifted my face into the rain and felt its many small hands on my skin. Perhaps it is enough just to know that. Perhaps it is enough to stand there with Lorna and praise the rain and our lives together. And perhaps it is enough to know I have now begun a life. There are years to come.

Spring beckons. The snowdrops are in blossom and all the other bulbs have pushed their green nipples out of the earth. They too will flower soon. There were three bees in the ivy today. Lorna and I were in the garden when we saw them. We both said, *Look, look at the bees!*

It is a cold and cloudy day. It is raining.

As I write this, a tiny spider lilts across my computer screen. It pays no attention to my cursor as it pushes its way to the end of the line:

PLANTS

Crimson Queen "Laceleaf" maple — *Acer palmatum dissectum*
Dust lichen — *Lepraria*
Fairyslipper — *Calypso bulbosa*
Frog pelt — *Peltigera neopolydactyla*
Great northern aster — *Aster modestus*
Thimbleberry — *Rubus parviflorus*
Winter rose — *Helleborus argutifolius*

ANIMALS, BIRDS, AND INSECTS

Burrowing wolf spider — *Geolycosa* spp.
Golden-crowned kinglet — *Regulus satrapa*
Marbled orb-weaver spider — *Araneus marmoreus*
Red ant — *Formica* spp.
Ruby-crowned kinglet — *Regulus calendula*

BOOKS BY PATRICK LANE

POETRY

Letters from the Savage Mind
Separations
On the Street
Hiway 401 Rhapsody
The Sun Has Begun to Eat the Mountain
Passing into Storm
Beware the Months of Fire
Unborn Things: South American Poems
Albino Pheasants
Poems: New & Selected
No Longer Two People (with Lorna Crozier)
The Measure
Old Mother
Woman in the Dust
A Linen Crow, a Caftan Magpie
Milford & Me
Winter
Mortal Remains
Too Spare, Too Fierce
Selected Poems 1977–1997

The Bare Plum of Winter Rain
Go Leaving Strange

FICTION

How Do You Spell Beautiful?

NONFICTION

Breathing Fire (with Lorna Crozier)
Addicted: Notes from the Belly of the Beast (with Lorna Crozier)
Breathing Fire II (with Lorna Crozier)